A SECOND
ANGLO-SAXON READER

HENRY SWEET

A SECOND
Anglo-Saxon Reader

ARCHAIC AND DIALECTAL

SECOND EDITION
REVISED BY
T. F. HOAD

OXFORD
AT THE CLARENDON PRESS

Oxford University Press, Walton Street, Oxford OX2 6DP

OXFORD LONDON GLASGOW
NEW YORK TORONTO MELBOURNE WELLINGTON
KUALA LUMPUR SINGAPORE JAKARTA HONG KONG TOKYO
DELHI BOMBAY CALCUTTA MADRAS KARACHI
NAIROBI DAR ES SALAAM CAPE TOWN

New Editorial material
© *Oxford University Press 1978*

First published 1978
Reprinted as paperback 1979

British Library Cataloguing in Publication Data

A second Anglo-Saxon reader, archaic and dialectal
 – 2nd ed.
 1. Anglo-Saxon literature
 I. Sweet, Henry   II. Hoad, T F
 829   PR1505   77–30207

ISBN 0–19–811170–3
ISBN 0–19–811176–2 paperback

*Printed in Great Britain
at the University Press, Oxford
by Eric Buckley
Printer to the University*

PREFACE

THIS new edition of Sweet's *Second Anglo-Saxon Reader* follows closely in both content and presentation the original book, published in 1887. As before, 'The primary object . . . is . . . to give the student—as far as the often scanty materials will allow—the means of making himself acquainted with the leading features of the non-West-Saxon dialects of Old English.'

The inscription from the Bewcastle Column has been omitted, in view of its poor state of preservation, and in its place have been added some other inscriptions (runic and non-runic; nos. II. 3, 5, and 6) which besides being of general linguistic interest provide additional memorial texts comparable with that on the Falstone Stone. The important version of *Cædmon's Hymn* in the Leningrad MS. has been included, while the duplication of the text of one of the charters (nos. 15 and 16 in the first edition, as in Sweet's *Oldest English Texts*) has been rectified. Some items from the early glossaries not printed by Sweet but at least possibly containing Old English glosses have been added; so too a smaller number of glosses from no. X (though not those which consist of one letter only), and a previously omitted passage from one of the charters.

The principal concern has been to make the various texts as accurate as possible. The recording of alterations and other peculiarities of the MS. texts is generally somewhat fuller than in the original edition (interlined letters are not normally noted, however), but for most other kinds of annotation, for grammatical discussions, and for the information which a glossary would provide the user of this book must turn to the many scholarly works now available. It should be noted that the texts of the inscriptions offered here are intended as working versions, and in some cases represent a much simplified treatment of the less

certain readings; for detailed information on the nature of the
evidence, the reader will have to consult such fuller, specialized
accounts as have been published, and ultimately the monu-
ments themselves.

In the case of the early glossaries it has been possible to add
comments on a few items (as where the Old English word
appears to have been attached to the wrong Latin lemma); and
the differences between the Latin texts of the portions of the
Lindisfarne and Rushworth Gospels represented in this book
have been indicated, if they bear significantly on the Old English glosses, in footnotes to no. IX.

The MSS. of all texts preserved in this form have been
collated, with the exception of nos. III. 1–5, VI, VIII, and
XI. 13, and of the Erfurt glossary (in no. I). A microfilm of
the last was used, while there were facsimiles available for each
of the others. The texts of the inscriptions in no. II depend
almost entirely on published editions and photographs, and
on material and advice generously provided by Mr. C. J. E.
Ball (to whom thanks are also due for help with nos. III. 2–4)
and Dr. R. I. Page (who is also to be thanked in his capacity
as Librarian of Corpus Christi College, Cambridge, for his
kindness when I needed to consult the Corpus glossary). For
permission to use Dr. Elisabeth Okasha's *Hand-List of Anglo-
Saxon Non-Runic Inscriptions* as the basis of my texts of
nos. II. 3 and 6, and in part also no. II. 4, I am indebted to the
publishers, the Cambridge University Press.

I have naturally made much use of published work which
cannot be specifically mentioned here, but to which I gladly
acknowledge a large debt, and I have furthermore received
most valuable help and advice from the following scholars, to
whom I here express my deep gratitude: Professor T. J. Brown,
who advised on the dating of some charter MSS.; the late
Professor A. Campbell, who commented on the charters as

well as giving more general advice and encouragement; Dr. Rima Handley, who gave an opinion on some difficult readings; Mr. C. A. Ladd, with whom I discussed the early glossaries; Mr. J. D. Pheifer, whom I consulted on the Épinal and Erfurt glossaries, and who kindly made available the text of his *Old English Glosses in the Épinal-Erfurt Glossary* in advance of its publication by the Clarendon Press; Mr. R. M. Pinkerton, who gave unstinted help with problems in the Latin of the early glossaries; Professor E. G. Stanley, who assisted in particular with the Lindisfarne and Rushworth Gospel glosses but who also gave less clearly definable support with characteristic generosity; and Dr. J. B. Wynn, who kindly gave permission for the use of material from his unpublished edition of the Latin–Old English items in the Corpus glossary (Oxford D.Phil. thesis). I have also benefited from notes on charters supplied by Professor D. Whitelock. I owe a special debt to Mr. R. W. Burchfield, C.B.E., who led me to undertake this revision and whose continued advice and friendly encouragement have been very much appreciated.

It remains for me to make grateful acknowledgement, for permission to examine material in their care and for help while so doing, to the Librarians, Keepers of MSS., and other staff of the Bodleian Library, the British Museum and British Library, the Cambridge University Library, and the Bibliothèque Municipale, Épinal, as also to Miss A. Oakley, archivist at the Cathedral Library, Canterbury. My thanks go to the Director of the Wissenschaftliche Allgemeinbibliothek, Erfurt, for supplying microfilm of the Erfurt glossary. A visit to France to consult the MS. containing the Épinal glossary was made possible by a generous grant from the Central Research Fund of London University.   T. F. H.

Queen Mary College, London
October 1976

CONTENTS

NOTE ON THE PRESENTATION
OF THE TEXTS

Italics are used to indicate expanded contractions, but in the
inscriptions (no. II) they represent letters imperfectly preserved but probably identifiable. Letters in the inscriptions
which have been worn or damaged less seriously are not
specially marked. For the use of italics in the text of the right
side of the Franks Casket see fn. 2 on p. 102. In the Erfurt
glossary, non-Latin glosses printed in italics are partial or
complete Germanisms by the German scribe.

Square brackets enclose letters supplied because missing
from or not legible in the MSS., and in the inscriptions they
enclose letters for which little or no evidence remains on the
monument or which are more doubtfully read than those
printed here in italics.

Erasures are marked by ':' (or mentioned in a footnote),
single points being used to indicate lost or illegible letters which
have not been supplied editorially. The approximate number
of letters erased or lost is suggested (by the number of colons
or points) only when it is small. Note that in no. X a number
of the glosses consist only of the letter or letters with which
a word or phrase begins or ends; in such cases a series of points
represents not lost letters but the part of the word not written
by the glossator. ':' in the inscriptions indicates a mark of this
form on the monument and not an erasure.

In the early glossaries, round brackets enclose corrections
and normalizations of the Latin lemmata; in many cases a
Classical Latin or alternative medieval form is indicated, as
an aid to the identification of the lemma, without implying

error in the MS. spelling. Round brackets are used similarly in no. X, where they also, however, enclose the words occasionally included from the Latin context of the words glossed to assist in the interpretation of the latter.

In the inscriptions, runic texts are represented by lower-case letters enclosed in ' ', non-runic texts by capitals. Ligatured symbols are shown as their two component letters separated by '/'.

The extract from the Lindisfarne Gospels, following the practice of Professor A. S. C. Ross and others, prints as small superscript letters those which are to be considered optional in the spelling of the words in question, and as e.g. 'e/^{i}' those which are to be considered alternative to one another. Thus 'iu^{i}h' = 'iuh *or* iuih', 'mone/^{i}ge' = 'monege *or* monige'.

The system of cross-referencing used in the texts of the early glossaries is explained on pp. 2–3.

Throughout, an asterisk indicates 'an erroneous or anomalous form, being thus equivalent to "sic"' (Sweet).

For ease of reference, Sweet's numbering of the items in the early glossaries and in no. X is retained (with additions marked as at Corpus 136a); and in the charters, the numbering from the *Oldest English Texts* is added in brackets where it differs from that used in the selection printed here.

I

OLDEST GLOSSARIES

CORPUS

*(Corpus Christi College, Cambridge MS. 144, fols. 2 ff.
8th or 9th century. Mercian.)*

Corpus[1]

Interpretatio nominum ebraicorum et grecorum

Adsida (-isa): flood.
calvariae locus: cualmstou.
coliferte (collibertus): geþofta.
clavis (-us): helma.
5 *crepidinem:* neoþoúard.
doleus (-ium): byden.
dasile (ra-?): boor.
decurat: horn naap[1].
ferula: hreod.
10 *fundus:* bodan.
foratorium: buiris.
gemellus: getuin.
gacila: snithstreo.
glebulum (cp. cribrum?):
hrider.
15 *jungula (jug-):* geocboga.

ledo: nepflod.
lancola (cp. lanx): cellae.
libitorium (-atorium): saa.
lignarium: uuidubinde.
20 *mantega (-tica):* taeg. (cp.
Cp². 1300.)
malina: fylledflood.
mappa: cneoribt.
maculosus: specfaag.
ment[h]a: minte.
25 *rastrum:* raece.
sicini (siccine): ac ðus.
scisca: eoforþrote. (cp.
Cp². 1816, 1868.)
sublatorium (suffl.): bloest-
baelg.
trilex (-ix): ðrili.

---

[1] horn naap *not certainly Old English; represents Lat.* ornat?

EPINAL-ERFURT

((*a*) *Bibliothèque Municipale, Epinal MS. 72, fols. 94 ff. 8th century. Mercian.* (*b*) *Wissenschaftliche Allgemeinbibliothek, Erfurt MS. Amplonianus f. 42, fols. 1 ff. Early 9th century. Mercian.*)

[† Indicates words wanting in Corpus². The numbers refer to Cp.²; those in ( ) to repetitions in EE itself.]

    Amites: loerge—loergae. 143¹.
    axungia: rysil—risil. 256.
    *argillus*² (*-a*): thohae—thoę. 207.
    andeda (cp. *andena*): brandrad—brondrad. 157.
5 *arula*—**anula*: fyrpannae *vel* herth—fyrponne *vel* herd. 208.
    alea: teblae—tefil. 110.
    *aleator*³: teblere *both*⁴. 111.
    *axedones*⁵: lynisas. 257.
    *aulea*⁶ (*-aea*): strel *vel curtina, ab aula*⁷. 249.
10 [*h*]*ariolatus*⁸: frictrung—**frictung. 196.
    amites: reftras *both*⁹. 150.
    albugo: flio *both*. 112.
    axis: aex *both*. 259.
    aplustra (*-e* sg.)—**apulustra*: giroedro—geroedra. 178.
15 *abilina* (*abellana*): *hrutu—hnutu. 33 (cp. 50).
    al[*l*]*ium*: garlęc—garlec. 113.
    aneta (*anas*): aenid, *a natando*—aenit. 158.
    armilausia (*-sa*): sercae *both*. 210.

---

   ¹ *first gloss in both* apodixen: fantasia.   ² i *indistinct in Ep.*
³ a . . . *Erf.*; *now covered.*   ⁴ tebl.re *Erf.*; t *now covered.*   ⁵ o
indistinct.   ⁶ *from alea, indistinct* u *above first* a.   ⁷ . . . baula
Erf.; *now partly covered.*   ⁸ *glossed as if a noun.*   ⁹ *after*
areoli (30) *in Erf.*

30 *tantalus*: aelbitu.
    va[e]: euwa.

31a *vertelium (til)*: uerua. (cp.
    Cp². 2108.)
    vomer: scaer.

Corpus²

Incipit glos[s]a secundum ordinem elimentorum alphabeti

[† Indicates words wanting in Epinal-Erfurt. The numbers refer to
Epinal-Erfurt; those in ( ) to repetitions in Cp. itself.]

Abelena (abellana): haesel-
    hnutu. 15 (cp. 243).
abies: *etspe. cp. 37.
35 *absinthium*: wermod. 66.
35a *abdicavit, negavit vel*:
    *discerede. 73.
abortus: misbyrd. 80.
ablata: binumine. 104.
†*abunde*: *genycthlice.
†*abiget*: wereth.
40 †*ab euro*: eastansudan.
†*ad euronothum*: eastsuth.
†*abditis*: gehyddum.
†*ab affrico*: suðanwestan.
†*ab borea (a borea)*: eastan-
    norþan.
45 *aconito (-a)*: þungas. 23.
†*acervus*: muha.
†*a circio*: norðanwestan.
†*actionari[i]s*: folcgeroe-
    bum.

†*acisculum*: piic. (cp. 467?)
50 †*acies, et ordo militum, et
    oculorum visus, et acumen
    ferri*: ecg *vel* scearpnis.
a[c]erabulus: mapuldur. 33.
*achalantis (acalanthis), vel
    luscinia, vel roscinia*:
    nehtegale. 26 (cp. 1746).
acrifolus(-ium): holegn. 34.
acega(acceia): holthona. 41.
55 *accearium (acia-)*: steli. 49
    (1431).
acitula (d): hromsa. 59.
acitelum (d): hromsan
    crop. 60.
accitulium (acid-): geces
    sure. 63.
acinum (-os): hindberiae.
    69.
60 *acris, fortio (-is) vel*: from.
    71.

alba spina: haeguthorn—hagudorn. 114 (cp. 956).

20 *apiastrum*: biouuyrt—buuyrt. 181.

anet[h]um: dil *both*. 159.

aesculus[1]: boecae—boeccae. 93.

aconita[2]: thungas *both*. 45.

apio: merici[3]. 182.

25 *alchior* (*alcyon*): isęrn—isaern[4]. 115.

achalantis (*acalanthis*), *vel luscinia*[5], *vel roscina*: *nctigalae—nęctęgela[6]. 52.

asilo (*-us*): briosa *both*. 225.

antiae: loccas *both*. 160.

[h]arpago: auuel *vel* clauuo *both*. 211.

30 *areoli* (*-lae*): sceabas—scebas. 197.

asses scorteas (*-eos*)[7]: lidrinae trimsas—lidrinn.[8] trynsas. 226.

*atflarat—*adflarat*: ansueop—*ansueus[9]. 235.

acerabulus—*acterabulus: mapuldur—*maefuldur. 51.

acrifolus (*-ium*): holegn *both*. 53.

35 *alnus*: alaer—aler. 116.

alneum: fulae trea—*fala treu. 117.

abies: saeppae—*sępae. cp. 34.

ascella (*axilla*): ocusta *both*. 227.

auriculum (*orichalcum*?)—*ariculum: dros *both*. 239.

40 *arpa* (*harpe*): earngeat—*aerngeup. 212.

acega—*accega* (*acceia*): holthana—*holtana. 54.

ardea, et dieperdulum: hragra *both*. 198.

aquilium (*aculeus*): anga *both*. 192.

auriculum: earuuigga—*aeruuica. 240.

45 *auriola*: stigu *both*. 242.

---

[1] ae *and part of* sc *now covered in* Erf.   [2] *torn off in* Erf.
[3] a . . . . meru Erf.; *now covered.*   [4] *last two letters indistinct.*
[5] luscina *Ep.*   [6] *Sweet* 'open a, possibly = u.'   [7] corteas Erf.
[8] *last letter now covered.*   [9] us *now covered*; *the rest largely indistinct.*

actionabatur: scirde. 86.

actuarius: wraec. 87.

accetum (*i*): gefeotodne. 105.

†*acegia*: sníte. (cp. 54.)

65 †*aceti cotilla* (*-ula*), *vas i.*: bolle.

†*acus*: netl *vel* gronuisc.

†*accidia, t*[*a*]*edium, vel anxietas i.*: sorg.

67a †*accintu* (*acanthum*): *de netle.

†*adsutae*: gesiuwide.

addictus: forscrifen. 52.

70 *adridente*: tyctende. 85.

†*aduncis*: gebegdum.

ad [*ex*]*pensas*[1]: tó nyttum. 93.

adsensore (*ss*): fultemendu*m*. 95.

adclinis: tohald, *vel incumbens*. 96.

75 *atqueve*[2]: end suelce. 98 (238).

adem[*þ*]*to*: binumini[3]. 102; cp. 100.

adsaeclum[4] (*assecula*): þegn, *minister turpitudinis*. 101.

adgrediuntur: geeodun. 76.

†*adlido*: *tonwinto.

80 *adnitentibus*: tilgendum. 78.

†*ad libidines*: wraene.

†*adtonitus*: hlysnende.(cp. 237.)

†*ad fasces*: to weorðmyndu*m*.

†*adfligit*: *gehuaeh.

85 *adrogantissime*: wlonclice. 112.

†*adplaudat*: *on hlior rouuit[5].

†*adcommodaturus*: uuoende.

†*adventio*(*adinv-*?): sarwo.

†*advocatus*: þingere.

90 †*adhibuit*: gelaðade *vel* advocavit.

†*adplicuit*: geþiudde.

†*aequatis*: efnum.

aesculus: boece. 22.

aegit (*egit*): wraec. 90.

95 *aestuaria*: fleotas. 107.

aere alieno: geabuli. 115.

†*aegesta* (*eg-*): *gors.

†*aequipensum*: ebnwege.

†*a finiculum* (*-lo*): ellende, a finibus procul.

100 *afflarat*: ansuaep. (235.)

---

[1] *from* penses, a *above second* e. by alph. order. [3] gebinumini. [5] onhliorrouuit.

[2] *originally* adqueve, *as shown* [4] *from* adsaeculu*m*, *first* u *er*.

almeta (aln.): *alterholt—alerholt. 119.

alga: uaar[1]—uar. 120.

argella (-illa): laam—lam[2]. 199.

accearium (acia-): steeli—steli. 55.

50 avellanus: *aesil—haesl. 243 (cp. 15).

[50a anconos: uncenos both[3].]

altrinsecus: an ba halbae—on ba halbe. 121.

addictus: faerscribaen—faerscrifen. 69.

argutie—argutiae (-u(i)tio?): thrauu—*trafu. 200.

asfaltum (aspalathum?): spaldr—spaldur. 228.

55 albipedius: huitfot both. 122.

alvium (-eus)—albium: meeli—*meelu[4]. 123.

alviolum (eo)—albiolum: aldot both. 124.

*alga—alg[a]e: scaldthyflas—scaldthyblas. 125.

*actula—accitula (acid-): hramsa both. 56.

60 acitelum—accitulum (acid-): hramsa crop—hromsa[5] crop. 57.

arrius (varius): faag both. 201.

*ascolonium—ascalonium: *hynnilaec—ynnilec. 229.

accitulium (acid-): geacaes surae—gecaes *sarae. 58.

ambila: laec both. 154.

65 arniglosa—armiglossa (arnoglossa): uuegbradae—uegbradae.
213.

absint[h]ium: uuermod—*uermodae. 35.

*armos—armus: boog both. 215.

anguens: breer both. 161.

acinum (-os): hindberię—*hindbergen. 59.

70 arbatae—arbate (artabae): sibaed[6] both. 216.

acris: fraam—from. 60.

---

[1] from paar, u above p.   [2] from sram, l above r.   [3] prob. not Old English; Cp. has anconos: urcenos.   [4] after alviolum (57) in Erf.   [5] from hramsa, o above curved stroke as of c between first a and m.   [6] perhaps intended to explain similae, which in the probable source occurs adjacent to artabae.

†*a fafonio* (*v*): suþan-
    westan.
affricus: westsuðwind.
    118.
affectui: megsibbe, *vel*
    dilectione. 109.
agre[*s*]*tis* (*-es*): wildę. 99.
105 †*agastrum*: aegmang. (cp.
    1435.)
†*agitatio*: unstilnis.
†*agitate*: onettad.
†*agapem*: suoesendo.
†*agmen*: weorod.
110 *alea*: tebl. 6.
aleator: teblere. 7.
albulo (*-ugo*): flio. 12.
al[*l*]*ium*: gaarleec. 16.
alba spina: heagoðorn.
    19.
115 *alcion* (*cyo*): isern. 25.
alnus: aler. 35.
alneum: fulae treo. 36.
†*alietum* (*haliáetos*): spaer-
    habuc.
alneta: alerholt. 46.
120 *alga*: waar. 47.
altrinsecus: on ba halfe.
    51.
albipedius: huitfoot. 55.
aluuium (*alveum*): meeli.
    56 (250).

alviolum (*eo*): aldaht. 57.
125 *alga*[*e*]: scaldhyflas *vel*
    sondhyllas. 58.
alternantium: staefnen-
    dra. 75.
alacris: snel. 77.
†*alacer*: suift.
alveus: streamraad. 88.
130 [*h*]*alitus*: aethm. 89.
alumnae: fostorbearn.
    108.
alapiciosa (cp. *alopecia*):
    calwa[1]. 116a.
†*alvearia*: hyfi.
†*altilia*: foedils.
135 †*alcido* (*-edo*): meau.
†*alcanus* (cp. *alta-*):
    þoden.
136a *alites* (*-ter*): challes.
    116b.
†*alveum*: edúaelle.
†*alitudo*: fothur.
†*alligeo* (*-ego*): recceo.
140 †*altor*: fostorfaeder.
†*allox*: tahae.
†*allauda* (*alauda*): lauricae.
amites: *laergae. 1.
†*amis*[*s*]*ionem*: forlor.
145 †*ammentum* (*amentum*):
    sceptog.
†*ambrones*: gredge.

---

[1] *not certainly Old English.*

aucapatione—aucupatione: setungae *both*. 244.

addicavit—abdicavit: bisceredae—bisceridae. 35a.

†*adstipulatus* (*-or*): fultemendi *both*.

75   *alternantium*: staefnẹndra—staefnendra. 126.

adgrediuntur[1]: *gihiodum—*gaeadun. 78.

alacris: snel—*blidi*. 127.

adnitentibus: tilgendum—tilgendun. 80.

anxius: soẹrgẹndi—sorgendi. 169.

80   *abortus*: misbyrd *both*. 36.

ausus: gidyrstig—*gedurstip. 245.

appetitus: gitsung *both*. 184.

astu: facni *both*. 230.

amiculo: *hraecli—*hraegl. 155.

85   *adridente*: tyctendi *both*. 70.

actionabatur[2]—*accionabatur*: scirde *both*. 61.

actuaris: uuraec—uraec. 62.

alveus: streamrad—*streumrad. 129.

adlitus—[h]alitus: æthm[3]— . . .[4]. 130.

90   *aegit* (*egit*): uuraec—uraec. 94.

avehit: an uueg aferidae[5]—an uoeg aueridae. 246.

*aquilae—*aquila*: segnas *both*. 194.

ad expensas[6]: to nyttum—to *nytum. 72.

annua: gerlicae—*gernlicae. 170.

95   *adsessore—*adsessores*: fultemendum *both*. 73.

adclinis[7]: tohald *both*. 74.

apparatione: gitiungi—*getoing[8]. 185.

adqueve—atqueve: aend suilcae—end suilce. 75.

agrestes: uuildae *both*. 104.

---

[1] ad: grediuntur *Ep.*   [2] *the ultimate source probably had*
auctionabatur.   [3] *æt apparently made from* æ *and* & *combined.*
[4] *left blank.*   [5] *from* aueridae, f *above expuncted* u.   [6] *curved*
stroke as of c *between* x *and* p *in Ep.*   [7] *from* adclinas *in Erf.,*
second i *above* a.   [8] geting, *with* o *written above* t; *read* getiong?

†*ambages*: ymbsuaepe.
†*ambrosea (-ia)*: suoetnis.
†*amens*: emod.
150 *amites*: fugultreo *vel* ref-
　　tras. 11.
†*amtes (ant-)*: oemsetinne
　　wiingeardes.
†*ambulas*: þiustra.
†*amilarius*: mearh.
　ambila: laec. 64.
155 *amiculo*: hręgli. 84.
　amentis: sceptloum. 106.
　andeda (cp. *andena*):
　　*brandrod. 4.
　aneta (anas): enid. 17.
　anet[h]um: dili. 21.
160 *antiae*: loccas. 28.
　anguens: breer. 68.
†*antefata*: forewyrde.
†*anastasis*: dilignissum.
†*antemn[a]e*: waede.
165 *antemna*: seglgęrd. 111.
†*antedoque*[1] (*antidotum*):
　　wyrtdrenc.
†*ansatae*: aetgaere.
　anten[n]a: boga.
　anxius: sorgendi. 79.
170 *annua*: gerlice. 94.
　anate (amites?): clader-
　　sticca. 116.
　anser: goos. 117.

†*anus*: ald uuif.
†*anguil[l]a*: el.
175 †*anceps*: tuigendi.
†*antulus*: caecbora.
†*aporians*[2]: anscungendi.
　aplustra (-e sg.): geroe-
　　ðro. 14.
†*aper*: eobor.
180 †*aporiamur*: biað þreade.
　apiastrum: biowyrt. 20.
　apio: merice. 24.
†*apotasia (ost?)*: fraetgen-
　　gian.
　appetitus: gidsung. 82.
185 *apparitione*: getiunge. 97.
†*ap[p]aratu*[3]: aexfaru.
†*applare*: eorscripel.
†*apricitas, color*: hio.
†*ap[p]aritio*: gethingio.
190 †*apparatum*: geþrec.
†*appotheca (apotheca)*:
　　winfaet.
　aquilium (aculeus): onga.
　　43.
†*aquemale (aqua(e)manile,
　　-manalis)*: lebel. (cp.
　　1269.)
　aquilae: segnas. 92.
195 †*[h]armonia*: suinsung.
　[h]ariolatus[4]: frihtrung.
　　10.

---

[1] antedo q̄.　　　[2] *from* aporiens, *second* a *above expuncted* e.
[3] *uel* ministratio *added by a corrector.*　　[4] *see p. 2, fn. 8.*

100 †*adepto—adempto: ginumni—.enumini[1].
  adsaeculam (assecula)—*adsexulam: thegn—degn. 77.
  *adepta—adempta: binumni both. 76.
  arcessitus[2] vel evocatus: fetod—*fettad. 222.
  ablata: binumini—binoman. 37.
105 accetum (i): gefetodnae—*gefetatnae. 63.
  amentis: sceptloum both. 156.
  aestuaria: fleotas—fleutas. 95.
  alumne—alumnae: fosturbearn—*foetribarn. 131.
  affectui: megsibbi vel dilectione both. 103.
110 arcibus: faestinnum—fẹstinnun. 223.
  antempna—antemna: segilgaerd both. 165.
  adrogantissime—*adrogantissimae: uulanclicae—gelplih. 85.
  [h]auserunt: naamun—*noumun. 247.
  arcister: strelbora both. 224.
115 aere alieno: gaebuli both. 96.
115a †alum[i]nis: aelifnae.
  anate (amites?): cladẹrsticca—claderstecca[3]. 171.
116a alapiosa (cp. alopecia): calua[4] both. 132.
116b alites (-ter): *challes both. 136a.
  anser: goos both. 172.
  affricus[5]: westsuþwind—uestsuduuind. 102.
  atticus (tac): dora both. 236.

---

[1] now covered.　　[2] ascessitus Erf.　　[3] d from t.　　[4] not
certainly Old English.　　[5] affric;s Erf.

areoli (*-lae*): sceabas. 30.

ardia (*-ea*): hragra *et dieperdulum*. 42.

argella (*-illa*): laam. 48.

200 *argutiae*: thrauuo. 53.

arrius (*varius*): faag. 61.

†*arbutus*: aespe.

†*argutiae*(*-u*(*i*)*tio*?): gleau-
nisse.

†*arx*: faestin.

205 †*archtoes* (*arctos*):
*waegne þixl.

†*artura* (cp. *arcuatus*?):
tot.

argilla: thoae. 3.

arula: fyrponne. 5.

†*artemon*: obersegl, *vel
malus navis*.

210 *armilausia* (*-sa*): serce.
18.

[*h*]*arpago*: awel *vel*
clauuo. 29.

arpa (*harpe*): earngeot.
40 (cp. 233).

anaglosa (*arnoglossa*):
wegbrade. 65.

†*arpia*: ceber.

215 *armus*: boog. 67.

arbatae(*artabae*): sibæd[1].
70.

†*ars plumaria*: uuynde-
creft.

†*archiatros*: healecas.

†*arvina*: risel.

220 †*ardebat*: scaan.

†*ar*[*r*]*ectas*: hlysnendi.

arcessitus: feotod. 103.

arbitus (*arcib.*): faestinnum. 110.

arcister: strelbora. 114.

225 *asilo* (*-us*): briosa. 27.

asses scorteas (*-eos*): liþ-
rine trymsas. 31.

ascella (*axilla*): ocusta.
38.

aspaltum (*aspalathum*?):
spaldur. 54.

ascalonium: ynnelaec. 62.

230 *astu*: facni *vel* fraefeli. 83.

†*ascop*[*er*]*a*: kylle.

†*aspera*: unsmoþi.

†*asapa* (*harpe*?): earngeat.
(cp. 212.)

†*astur*: haesualwe.

235 *atflarat* (*adfl.*): onsueop.
32 (100).

atticus (*tac*): dora. 119.

†*attoniti*: hlysnende,
afyrhte. (cp. 82.)

atqueve: *on suilce. (75.)

auriculum: *dorsos. 39.

240 *auriculum*: earwicga. 44.

†*avus*: aeldra faeder.

auriola: stigu. 45.

[1] *see p. 6, fn. 6.*

120   *Buccula*: bucc—*bua[1]. 338.
      balus (*boia(e)*?): iṣẹrnfetor—isaernfetor. 272.
121a *bothona*[2]—*bothana* (*butina*? *putínē*?): embrin *both*. 308a.
      bothonicula: stappa[3]—stoppa. 309.
      bacidones[4]: redisnae—rẹdisnae. 260.
      bicoca: *hraebrebletae—hebrebletae. 294.
125   *beacita*—*biacita*: *stearno—stẹrn. 284.
      briensis: *handuyrp—*honduyrp. 320.
      bagula[5]: bridils—brigdils[6]. 261.
      basis—*balsis*: teter *both*. 262.
      bobellum (*bovile*): falaed *both*. 310.
130   *bratium* (*c*): malt *both*. 322.
      bradigabo—*badrigabo*: felduuop[7]—*felduus. 323.
      beta (*betula*): berc, *arbor dicitur*[8] both. 285.
      bitumen: lim *both*. 295.
      bulla: sigil *both*. 331.

---

[1] *comes at the end of* b *in Erf.*   [2] *from* bothonia, i *er.*   [3] *first*
a *altered; meant as* o (?).   [4] *foll. by* er. *in Ep.; elsewhere glossed*
botrus, clyster.   [5] *from* bacula *in Ep.*, g *above expuncted* c.
[6] g *from* s.   [7] *beginning of* d *er. between* e *and* l.   [8] berc-
arbdɨ *Ep.*

avellanus: haesl. 50 (cp. 33).

aucupatione: setunge. 72.

245 *ausus*: gedyrstig. 81.

avehit: on weg aferide. 91.

[*h*]*auserunt*: nomun, hlo-dun. 113.

†*avena*: atę.

aul[*a*]*ea*: stregl¹. 9.

250 *a*[*l*]*v*[*e*]*um*: meli. (123.)

†*auspicantur*: haelsadon.

†*auster*: suðuuind.

†*augur*: haelsere.

†[*h*]*ausurae*: brucende.

255 †*aurocalcum* (*orichalcum*): groeni aar.

axungia: rysel. 2.

axredones (*axe.*): lynisas. 8.

†*axredo* (*axe.*): lynis.

axis: aex. 13.

260 *Bacidones*²: raedinne. 123.

bagula: bridels. 127.

balsis: teter. 128.

ballista: staefliðre. 136.

basterna: beer. 137.

265 *bat*[*t*]*uitum*: gebeaten. 140.

baccinia(*va-*): beger. 143.

ballena (*balaena*): horn. 146 (1525).

†*barritus*: genung.

battat: geonath. 149.

270 †*basterna*: scrid.

†*balbus*: uulisp.

balus (*boia*(*e*)?): isern-feotor. 121.

†*ba*[*c*]*chantes*: uuoedende.

†*barat*[*h*]*rum*: dael.

275 †*basis*: syl.

†*ballationes* (cp. *bulla*?): cnop.

†*balbutus*: stom, wlisp.

†*ban*[*dum*]: segn.

†*bapis*: treuteru.

280 †*baruina* (*bargin*(*n*)*a*?): barriggae. (cp. 330?)

†*balneum*: stofa.

†*balatus*: bletid.

†*bariulus* (cp. *varius*): rea-gufinc.

beacita: stearn. 125.

285 *beta* (*betula*): berc, *arbor dicitur*. 132.

aeneficium (*be.*): freomo. 135.

berrus (*verres*): baar. 151.

¹ *from* streal, g *above* a.

² *see p. 12, fn. 4.*

135   *beneficium*: fremu *both*. 286.
       ballista: staeblidrae—steblidrae. 263.
       basterna: beer *both*. 264.
       byssum: *tuum—tuigin. 343.
       bitiligo (*v*): blecthrustfel *both*. 296 (cp. 1069).
140   *battuitum—batuitum*: gibeataen—gebeatten. 265.
       bile (*-is*): atr—*art. 297.
       bubu (*-o*): uuf *both*. 334 (161).
       bucina (*vaccinia*): begir *both*. 266.
       blitum: clatae—clate. 306.
145   *blattis—*blatis*: bitulum *both*[1]. 307.
       ballena (*balaena*): hran—hron. 267.
       broel (*brolium, broilum*): edisc *both*[2]. 324.
       broelarius—broellearius: ediscueard[3]—ediscuard. 325.
       batat—battat: ginath *both*[4]. 269.
150   *bruchus*[5]: cefr *both*. 326.
       berrus (*verres*): baar *both*. 287.
       bruncus—brunchus: uurot—urot. 327.
       buculus (*buccula*)—*baculus*: randbeag—rondbaeg. 335.
       berruca (*v*): uueartae—uaertae. 288 (cp. 1049).
155   *byrseus—*byrreus*: lediruuyrcta—lediruyrhta. 344.
       berna (*v*): higrae—higrę. 290.
       bona: scaet *both*. 311.
       *branc[h]iae—*brancie*: cian *both*. 328.
       burrum: bruun—*bruum. 336.
160   *bubalis* (*-us*)—*babalis*: uusend—uesand. 337.
       bufo (*bubo*)—*bubu*: uuf *both*[6]. (142.)
       boreus (*-as*): eastnorþwind—*eustnorduind. 312.

---

[1] -um *partly lost on hole in MS. in Ep.*   [2] *before* ballena (146)
in Erf.   [3] *from* esd-, s *expuncted and er.*   [4] *er. after* i *in Erf.,*
prob. to make n *from* m.   [5] *curved stroke as of* c *between* r *and* u *in*
Ep.   [6] *after* brunchus (152) *in Erf.*

berruca (v): uearte. 154
(cp. 2088).

†*bellicum*: slag.

290 *berna (v)*: higrae. 156.

bena (avena): atę.

†*becta (ve-)*: *stęrt.

†*bettonica (ve-)*: aturlaðe.

bicoca: haebreblete. 124.

295 *bitumen*: liim. 133.

bitiligo(v): blaecthrustfel.
139 (cp. 2123).

bile (-is): atr. 141.

†*bitulus (betula)*: berc.

†*biothanatas*: seolfbonan.

300†*bitricius (vitricus)*: steopfaeder.

†*birbicariolus (vervecario-
lus)*: werna.

†*bitorius*: erdling.

†*bipertitum*: *herbid.

†*bilance*: tuiheolore.

305†*bibulta*: billeru.

blitum: clate. 144.

blattis: bitulum. 145.

†*blessus (blaesus)*: stom.

308a *bothonia*[1] *(butina?
putínē?)*: embrin. 121a
(cp. 341?).

blohonicula[2]*(bothonicula)*:
stoppa. 122.

310 *bofellum (bovile)*: falud.
129.

bona: scaet. 157.

boreus (-eas): eastnorð-
wind. 162.

†*bobulcus(bu.)*: hriðhiorde.

†*bovestra*: radre.

315†*bacarius*[3]: meresuin.

†*bofor*: lendislieg.

†*bombosa*: hlaegulendi.

†*botrum (botrys)*: clystri.

†*bolides*: sundgerd in scipe
vel metrap.

320 *briensis*: honduyrm. 126
(cp. 1193).

†*bra[c]hiale*: gyrdels.

bratium (c): malt. 130.

bradigabo: felduop. 131.

broel (brolium, broilum):
edisc, deortuun. 147.

325 *broellarius*: ediscueard.
148.

bruchus: cefer. 150.

bruncus: wrot. 152.

bra[n]c[h]iae: cian. 158.

†*brittia*: cressa.

330 †*braugina*: barice. (cp.
280?)

bulla: sigl. 134.

†*bux[us]*: box.

---

[1] *from* bothoma, ni *from* m.
words (bosboris *and* 308a bothonia).
by alph. order.

[2] *preceded by the first two* bo-
[3] *originally* bocarius, *as shown*

Colonus: gibuur—*vicinus*. 493.

contribulus (-is): meeg—*consanguinis*[1]. 495.

165 *calculus*: calc *both*. 345.

clibosum (v)—cliborum: clibecti—*clibectis. 478.

colobium: ham—hom. 494.

caccabum: cetil *both*. 346.

coccum bis tinctum: uuilocread[2]—*uuslucreud. 496.

170 *cados*: ambras *both*. 347.

citropodes (chytropus): crocha *super IIII pedes*—*chroca. 461.

calculus, ratio vel sententia vel: tebelstan *vel lapillus*—*tebiltan
*vel *labillus. 349.

cartellus (tal): windil—*pindil. 348.

*cartilaga (-o)—*cartalago*: naesgristlae *both*. 350.

175 *carbunculus*: spyrng[3]—spryng. 351.

†*celatum—caelatum*: utathrungaen—utathrungen.

cautere (-er), ferrum id est[4]: haa*m*—*fam. 352.

cotizat (cp. *kottizo*): teblith *both*. 497.

178a *cyprinus—*capprinus*: fornaeticli—forneticcli. 627a.

convexum: hualb—*halb. 498.

180 *cercylus—cerciclus (cercurus)*: aesc *vel navis* both. 438.

*chaos—*chos*: duolma—dualma. 457.

conquilium (conchylium): uuilucscel—uuylucscel. 499.

---

[1] *on er.; tail of g still visible below second* n.   [2] *from* -raed, a
expuncted and a *added above the line between* e *and* d.   [3] n *on er.*
[4] id est *not in Erf.*

†*butio (-eo)*: cyta.
bubo: uuf. 142.
335 *buculus (buccula)*: rond-
baeg. 153.
burrum: bruun. 159.
bubulis[1] *(bubalus)*: weo-
send. 160.

buccula: buuc. 120.
†*bucitum (e)*: seotu.
340 †*butio (-eo)*: frysca.
†*bunia*: byden. (cp. 308a?)
†*bubla*: flood.
byssum: tuin. 138.
byrseus: leðeruyrhta. 155.

345 *Calculus*: calc. 165.
caccabum: cetil. 168.
cados: ambras. 170.
cartellus(tal): windil.173.
*calculus, ratio, vel senten-
tia, vel numerus vel*:
teblstan. 172.
350 *cartilago*: naesgristle.
174.
carbunculus: spryng. 175.
cautere (-er): aam. 177.
†*catapulta*: flaan.
†*cabillatio (v)*: glio.
355 *camellea (chamaeleon)*:
wulfes camb. 183.
canes (-is) lingua: ribbe.
184.
calentes: hatende. 206.
caulem: steola. 215 (cp.
432).
†*capulus*: helt.
360 *caumeuniae (cham-)*:
eordreste. 219.

361a †*catabatus (cac(c)a-)*:
romei.
calcar: spora. 226.
cauterium: merciseren.
227.
catasta: geloed. 229.
†*capillatur (-ra)*: faexnis.
365 *capsis (-a)*: cest. 231.
†*carcura (carruca)*: craet.
caractis (cataracta):
uueterþruh. 232.
cariscus: cuicbeam, uuice.
238.
capitium: hood. 239.
370 *camis[i]a*: haam. 244.
carix (-ex): secg. 251.
†*canalibus*: waeterðruum.
cappa: scicging. 245.
castanea: cistenbeam.
249.
375 *calt[h]a*: reade clafre *vel
genus floris*. 250.
†*capistrum*: caebestr[2].

---

[1] *from* bubalis, *second* u *above* a.   [2] *foll. by* er.

camellea (*chamaeleon*): uulfes camb *both*. 355.

canis lingua: ribbae *both*. 356.

185 *cicuta*: hymblicae—huymblicae. 462.

contemptum (*-im*): heruuendlicae—haeruendlicae. 500.

conlatio—*conlato: ambechtae *both*. 501.

**commeatos—commeatus*: sandae[1]—sondae. 502.

contubernalis: gidopta[2]—*gidogta. 503.

190 *conjectura*: resung *both*. 504.

condidit: gisettae—*girette. 505.

convincens: obaerstaelendi—oberstẹlendi. 506.

corben (*-is*): mand—*mondi. 511.

convicta: obaerstaelid—oberstaelid. 515.

195 *concidit*: tislog—*gislog. 516.

conparantem: *gegeruuednae—*gegeruednae. 517.

censores: giroefan—geroefan. 439.

coaluissent: suornodun—*suarnadun. 518.

cuniculos: smigilas—smygilas. 608.

200 *concedam*: lytisna[3] *both*. 519.

conjurati: gimodae—gimode. 520.

contumax: anmod—onmod. 521.

**confussione—confusione*: gimaengiungiae—gemengiungae. 522.

concesserim: arectae[4] *both*. 523.

205 *conpar*: gihaeplice—gihaeplicae. 524.

calentes: haetendae—hattendae. 357.

constipuisse (*tup*)—*constipuissen: *gesuidradrae[5]—*gisudera-
dae[6]. 525.

curiositas: feruuitgeornnis—feruitgernis. 609.

clava: *stegn—stẹng. 480.

210 *convenio*: groetu *vel adjuro*—*gloeto. 526.

---

[1] *from* scandae, c *er*.   [2] *from* gidapta, o *above first* a.
[3] *apparently explains some other word, prob.* fortasse, *which in a possible source occurs adjacent to* concedam.   [4] e *er. after first* a *in Ep.*
[5] *first* e *from* i.   [6] *second* d *from* t.

calcesta: huite clafre. 254.

†*cavanni*: ulae.

cancer: haebrn. 258.

380 *calciculium*: ieces surae.
263.

cardella (*-uelis*): þistel-
tuige. 266 (cp. 397).

cacomicanus (*kakomḗ-
khanos*): logðor. 268.

calomachus (*calamau-
ċus?*): haet. 269 (cp.
570?).

cardu[*u*]*s*: þistel. 271.

385 *castorius* (*castor*): beber.
272.

†*caenum*: wase.

carectum: hreod. 290.

carpella: sadulboga. 283
(cp. 1563).

†*carina*: bythne.

390 *cant*[*h*]*i*: faelge. 292.

cassidele (*-ile*): pung. 297.

cappa: snod. 301.

carpasini (*b*): græsgroeni.
298.

cal[*a*]*metum*: mersc. 289,
302.

395 †*caliga*: scoh.

carbo: gloed. 304.

carduelis: linetuige. 309
(cp. 381).

397a †*caraðrion* (*charadrius*):
laurice[1].

cantarus (*cantharis*):
wibil. 310.

†*caper*: heber.

400 †*callos*: weorras *vel* ill.

†*carula* (*garrula*): crauue.

cartilago: grundsopa.
312.

†*capria* (*-ea*): raha.

†*cauda*: steort.

405 †*caldaria*: cetil.

†*cater* (*ater?*): suearth.

†*cartago* (*sartago*): braad-
ponne.

†*caragios*[2]: lyblaecan.

†*cas*[*u*]*la*: heden.

410 †*canda*: boga.

†*campus*: brogdetende *vel*
cleppetende[3].

†*carbasus*: seglbosm.

†*cautionem*: gewrit.

†*capulum*: helt.

415 †*caumati*: suole. (cp. 458.)

†*caverniculis*: holum.

†*capistrinum*: geflit.

†*cassidis*: helmes.

---

[1] *from* laurici, e *above second* i; *for the lemma cp. p. 26, fn. 1.*
[2] *from* caragius, o *above expuncted* u.   [3] *the glosses apparently*
explain palpitans; *cp. Cp. 1472, the probable source of which is a line*
containing both campus *and* palpitans.

contis: spreotum—spreutum. 527.

condiciones—conditiones: raedinnae—redinnae. 529.

crebrat—crefrat (cribrat): siftit—siftid. 596.

consubrinus (consobrinus): gesuirgion—gisuirgia*n*. 530.

215   *caulem*: stela *both*. 358.

†*clunis*: lẹndnum—*laendum.

coc[h]leae: lytlae sneglas *both*. 531.

crepacula (crepitaculum): claedur, *id est tabula qua a segitibus territantur aves*—cledr. 599.

caumeuniae (cham-)—caumaeuniae: eordrestae—eordraestae. 360.

220   *caustella—clustella*: clustorlocae—clusterlocae. 481.

c[a]erula: haeuui—*haui. 444.

cofinus (ph): mand. 532.

commentariensis[1]: giroefa—geroefa. 533.

*clatrum (clathri)—*cleatrum*: pearroc *both*. 486.

225   *cospis (u)*: palester—*plaster. 534.

calear (calcar): spora *both*. 361.

cauterium: *mearisern—*merisaen. 362.

clabatum (v): *gybyrdid—gebyrdid. 487.

catasta: gloed—geleod. 363.

230   *celox—*caelox*: ceol *both*. 442.

capsis (-a): cest *both*. 365.

caractis—caractes (cataractes): uuaeterthruch—*uaeterthrouch. 367.

cer[v]us: elch *both*[2]. 443.

†*cyat[h]us—*cutus*: bolla—bollae.

235   *color*: aac[3] *both*. 535.

corylus: haesil—haesl. 536.

cerasius[4]—*caerassius (cerasus)*: cisirbeam—cysirbeam. 445.

---

[1] *from* commend- *in Ep.*, t *above* d.   [2] *from* eleh *in Erf.*, c (*or* o?) *above expuncted second* e.   [3] *apparently explains some other word; confusion of* robur *and* rubor?   [4] *might also be read* cerasris.

†*casus*: fer.
420 †*cas[s]is*: ned.
†*casso*: idle.
†*cassium (-is)*: helm.
†*cardo*: heor.
†*caelatum*: agraben[1].
424a †*catagrinas*: bleremina mees[2].
425 †*canthera (-arus)*: trog.
†*callus*: waar.
426a †*calviale*: *cosobri, case[u]s.
†*calvarium*: caluuerclim. (cp. 952, 954, 956.)
†*cardiolus*: uudusnite.
†*callis*: paat.
430 †*capistro*: caefli.
†*calleo*: fraefeleo.
†*cauliculus*: steola. (cp. 358.)
†*carpebat*: sclat.
†*cavernas*[3]: holu.
435 *cartamo (cardamum)*: lybcorn[4]. 279 (459).
†*carc[h]esia*: bunan.
†*cessere*: *onwicum.
cercilus (cercurus): aesc. 180.
censores: geroefan. 197.
440 †*censeo*: doema.

†*ces[s]uram*: *gegandende.
celox: ceol. 230.
cer[v]us: elh. 233.
c[a]erula: heawi. 221.
445 *cerasius (-sus)*: ciserbeam. 237.
c[a]erefolium: cunelle. 246.
cefalus: heardhara. 270.
c[a]epa: ynnilaec, cipe. 286.
c[a]ementum: liim, *lapidum*. 289a.
450 †*cente (ganta)*: wilde goos. (cp. 960, 963.)
†*c[a]elatum*: *abrectat.
†*c[a]espites*: tyrb.
†*cessit*: geeode.
†*cereacus (ceryx)*: hornblauuere.
455 †*cernua*: hald.
†*cerefolium*: cerfelle.
chaus(-os): duolma, *prima confusio omnium rerum*. 181.
chaumos (cauma): suol. 274 (cp. 415).
chartamo (cardamum): lybcorn. (435.)

---

[1] agra:ben   [2] bleremina mees *not certainly Old English*; *for the lemma cp. in other glossaries* catacrina(s), -nis, *explained as* 'hipbone(s)'.   [3] *from* cauernus, a *above second* u.   [4] n *above* er.

cariscus: cuicbeam. 368.

capitium: hood *both*. 369.

240 †*cornicula*: chyae—ciae.

cornacula[1] (*-icula*): crauuae *both*. 537.

crocus—*croccus: gelu—gelo. 598.

culcites (*-ta*): bedd *both*. 610.

camis[i]a[2]—*camissa*: haam *both*[3]. 370.

245 *cappa*: scicing—*scinccing. 373.

c[a]erefolium: cunillae *both*. 446.

corimbus (*y*): leactrocas[4] *both*. 540.

cicuta: uuodaeuistlae—*uuodeuuislae[5]. 463.

castania (*-ea*): *cistimbeam. 374

250 *calt[h]a*: **rede clabre. 375.

carix (*-ex*): **sech. 371.

culmus: uuryd. 612.

cucumis: popeg. 611.

calcesta[6]: huitti clabre. 377.

255 *c[r]abro*: uaeps. 603.

cicad[a]e: haman. 464.

cu[r]culio: æmil. 613 (cp. 484).

cancer: hafaern. 379.

ciconia: storc. 465.

260 *cupa*: bydin. 614.

colobostrum (*colostrum*): beost. 541.

ciscillus: heardheui. 467.

calciculium: **iaces *sura. 380.

cucuzata: laepaeuincæ. 619.

265 *cuculus*: gęc. 618.

---

[1] *from* cornicula *in Ep.*, a *above* i.   [2] ca:misa, ca *on* er.
[3] *second* a *in Ep. altered from* i (*prob. first stroke of an* m).   [4] *might*
also be read leactrogas *in Ep.*   [5] *beginning of gap in Ep., this gloss*
being the last.   [6] calesta, *with* c (*or* o?) *above the line between* l
and e.

460 †*chorus* (*caurus*): eostnorð-
     wind.
     citropodes (*chytropus*):
        chroa, croha. 171.
     cicuta: hymlice. 185.
     cicuta: wodewistle. 248.
     cicad[*ae*]: secggescere *vel*
        haman. 256.
465 *ciconia*: storc. 259.
     cicer: bean. 284.
     cisculus: heardheau. 262
        (cp. 49?).
     cinoglosa (*cynoglossos*):
        ribbe. 280.
     circinno (*circinus*): gabul-
        rond. 293.
470 *circius*: westnorðwind.
        311.
     †*cis*: biheonan.
     †*cimiterium* (*coemeterium*),
        pontiani: licburg, *a no-*
        mine pon' pr' qui con-
        struxit.
     †*circinni* (*cinc-*):windeloc-
        cas.
     †*circinatio*: oefsung.
475 †*cinnamomum*: cymin, *re-*
        sina.
     †*cicuanus* (*ciconia*): higrae.
     †*citonium* (*cydonia*): good-
        aeppel.
     clibosum (*v*): clibecti. 166.
     †*clavia* (*-vus*): borda.

480 *clava*: steng. 209.
     clustella: clustorloc. 220.
     cladica: wefl *vel* owef.
        300 (cp. 2016?).
     †*clinici*: faertyhted.
     †*clavus caligaris* (*-ius*):
        scohnegl.
485 †*clas*[*s*]*is*: flota.
     clatrum (*clathri*): pearuc.
        224.
     clabatum (*v*): gebyrded.
        228.
     †*clus* (*clavus*): teltreo.
     †*clima*: half.
490 †*clavicularius*: caeghiorde.
     †*commis*[*s*]*ura*: flycticlað.
     †*conabulum* (*cunabula*):
        cilda trog.
     colonus: gebuur. 163.
     colobium: hom. 167.
495 *contribulius* (*-is*): meig,
        vel sanguiñ. 164.
     coccum bis tinctum: wio-
        locread. 169.
     cotizat (cp. *kottizo*): teb-
        leth. 178.
     convexu[*m*]: hualf. 179.
     conquilium (*conchylium*):
        wilocscel. 182.
500 *contemtum* (*-im*): *heuu-
        endlice. 186.
     conlato (*-io*): oembecht.
        187.

cardella (*-uelis*): thistil. 381 (cp. 309).

coc[*h*]*leas*: uuylocas. 542.

cacomicamus (*kakomékhanos*): logdor. 382.

calomacus (*calamaucus*): haeth. 383.

270   *cefalus*: heardhara. 447.

carduus: thistil. 384.

castorius (*castor*): bebir. 385.

campos (*compos*): faegen. 543.

camos (*cauma*): suol. 458.

275   *crabro*: hirnitu. 603.

contentus: ginehord. 544.

culix (*-ex*): mich[1], *longas tibias habens.* 617.

commentis: searuum *vel* ordoncu*m*. 545.

cartamo (*cardamum*): lypbcorn. 435.

280   *cynoglossa* (*-os*): ribbae. 468.

co[*ho*]*rs*: *tuuni. 546.

cummi (*g*): teru. 616.

carpella: sadulbogo. 388 (cp. 818).

cicer: bean. 466.

285   *corax*: hraebn. 553.

caepa: cipae. 448.

culinia: *coacas. 620.

crustulla (*crustulum*): halstan. 604.

cemetum (*calam-*): merisc. 394 (302).

289a   *cementum*: lim, *lipidium*[2] (*lapidum*). 449.

290   *carectum*: hreod. 387.

commissuras (*-a*): cimbing. 554.

cant[*h*]*i*: felge. 390.

circinno (*circinus*): gabelrend. 469.

cox (*cos*): huetistan. 555.

295   *coxa*: theoh. 556.

[1] *from* mihc, *final* c *expuncted and* c *added above* i.   [2] *from* lipa-dium, *second* i *over* a.

commeatos (-us): sondę. 188.

contubernalis: geþofta. 189.

conjectura: resung. 190.

505 *condidit*: gesette. 191.

convincens: oberstae-lende. 192.

†*codices*: onheawas.

†*consutum*: gesiowed.

†*corimbos (y)*: bergan.

510 †*commercium*: ceapstou, gestrion.

corben (-is): mand. 193.

†*conpactis*: gegaedradon.

corbus (-is): cauuel. 305.

†*consulo*: frigno.

515 *convicta*: oberstaeled. 194.

concidit: toslog. 195.

conparantem: gegaer-wendne. 196.

coaluissent: suornadun. 198.

concedam: lytesna[1]. 200.

520 *conjurati*: gemode. 201.

contumax: anmood. 202.

confusione: gemengiunge. 203.

concesserim: arecte. 204.

conpar: gehaeplice. 205.

525 *constipuisse (tup)*: gesue-drade. 207.

convenio: ic groetu. 210.

contis: spreotum. 211.

†*contos*: speoru.

condicione: raedenne. 21.2

530 *consobrinus*: gesuigran. 214.

coc[h]leae: lytle sneglas. 217.

coffinus (ph): mand. 222.

commentariensis: geroefa. 223.

cospis (u): palstr. 225 (622).

535 *color*: aac[2]. 235.

corylus: haesl. 236.

cornacula (-icula): crauue. 241.

cornix: crawe. 308.

†*conglutinata*: gelimed.

540 *corimbos (y)*: leactrogas. 247.

colostrum: beost. 261.

coc[h]leas: uuiolocas. 267.

conpos: faegen. 273 (cp. 2157?).

contentus: geneorð. 276.

545 *commentis*: seorwum. 278.

co[ho]rs, numerus mili-tum: tuun. 281.

†*confici*: gemęngan.

[1] *see p. 18, fn. 3.*

[2] *see p. 20, fn. 3.*

†*cervical*: *bol.

cassidele (*-ile*): pung. 391.

carpassini (*carbasinus*): gręsgroeni. 393.

crus: scia. 602.

300   *caldica*: uuefl. 482.

cappa: snod. 392.

cal[a]metum: *merix. 394 (289).

colicum: aebordrotae. 558; cp. 595?

carbo: gloed. 396.

305   *corvis* (*corbis*): couel. 513.

colus: *uuilmod. 559.

conpetum: tuun *vel* ðrop. 557.

cornix: crauua. 538.

carduelis: *linaethuigae[1]. 397 (cp. 266).

310   *cantarus* (*cantharis*): uuibil. 398.

circius: *uuestnorduuid. 470.

cartilago gg.: *grundsuopa. 402.

[1] *followed on the same line by* caradrion (*cp. Cp.* 397a).

†*conpetentes portiunculas*
  i.: gelimplice daele.

†*conpagem*: gegederung.

550 †*coituras*: gegangendo.

†*commanipularius*: ges-
  cota, *vel conscius, socius,*
  collega.

†*consobrinus*: sueor.

  corax: hraefn. 285.

  commis[s]ura: cimbing.
  291.

555 *cox (cos)*: huetestan. 294.

  coxa: thegh. 295.

  conpetum:tuun, þrop. 307.

  colicus: eoburthrote. 303
  (cp. 595?).

  colus: *wulfmod. 306.

560 †*conc[h]is*: scellum.

†*conc[h]a*: mundleu.

†*coagolum(-ulum)*: ceselyb.

†*commolitio*: forgrindet.

†*concisium*: scelle.

565 †*confundit*: menget.

†*commentum*: aþoht.

†*conderetur*: gewarht.

†*conpe[n]dium*: gescroep-
  nis.

†*coleandrum (coria-)*: cel-
  lendre.

570 †*colomata (calliomar-
  chus?)*: haetcolae. (cp.
  383?)

†*concha*: beme.

†*convaluit*: geuaerpte.

†*consors (conc-?)*: orsorg.

†*comitavere*: to geles-
  tunne.

575 †*conclamatus, commotus*:
  loma.

†*concessit*: *geuuatu.

†*commendabat*: trymide.

†*condebitores*: gescolan.

†*concussionibus*: raednisse.

580 †*confoti*: afoedde.

†*convenientes*: seruuende.

†*conlisio*: slaege.

†*cot[h]urno*: wodhae.

†*contio*: gemoot, *convoca-
  tio populi.*

585 †*costa*: rib.

†*contionatur*: maðalade,
  *declamat vel judicat vel
  contestatur.*

†*consobrinus, filius patruelis
  vel*: moderge.

†*confutat*: oberstaelid.

†*conpilat*: stilith.

590 †*cornu*: ceste.

†*con[n]ectit*: teldat.

†*concretum*: gerunnen.

†*conc[h]a*: musclan scel.

†*coccum*: wioloc.

595 †*cocilus (cul)*: ampre. (cp.
  558?)

  crebrat (cribrat): siftið.
  213.

Dulcis sapa : *coerim. 709.

defructum (defrutum): coerin. 628.

315   *dolatum*: gesnidan. 701.

dodrans: aegur. 702.

dumus: thyrnae. 710.

devotaturus: uuergendi. 632.

dromidus (-edarius): afyrid[1] *obbenda. 707.

320   *dromidarius*: se *oritmon. 708.

dalaturae (dolatorium): *braedlaestu *aesc. 703.

[1] āfyrid.

†*crebrum* (*cribrum*): sibi.

crucus (*crocus*): gelo. 242.

crepacula (*crepitaculum*):
   cleadur, *id est, tabula
   quae a segetibus territantur aves*. 218.

599a †*crepundia*: *maenoe.

600 †*cratem*: flecta *vel* hyrþil.

†*crepido*: rimo[1].

crus: scia. 299.

crabro: waefs *vel* hurnitu.
   255, 275.

crustula (*-lum*) *similis*:
   haalstaan. 288.

605 †*crama*: flete.

†*crates*: hegas.

†*cragacus*: styria.

cuniculos: smyglas. 199.

curiositas: feorwitgeornis.
   208.

610 *culcites* (*-ta*): bed. 243.

cucumis: popæg. 253.

627b *Damma, bestia id est*:
   eola. 346a.

defrutum: coerin. 314.

†*detulerat*: brohte.

630 †*delicatus*: wrast.

†*destituit*: obgibeht.

devotaturus: wergendi.
   318.

†*desis* (*-es*): suuẹr.

culmus: *wyrð. 252.

curculio: emil. 257 (cp.
   1003).

cupa: byden. 260.

615 †*cuba* (*p*): tunne.

cummi (*g*): teoru. 282.

culix (*-ex*): mygg, *longas
   tibias habet*. 277.

cuculus: gaec. 265.

cucuzata: lepeuuince.
   264.

620 *culinia*: cocas. 287.

†*cucuma*: fyrcruce.

cuspis: palstr. (534.)

†*cunae*: cildclaðas.

†*curtina* (*cor-*): wagryft.

625 †*culter*: saex.

†*cuneus*: waecg.

†*cuppa* [*ab*] *accipiendo i.*:
   beodbollẹ.

627a *cyprinus*: *fornetedcli.
   178a.

†*desolutus* (*diss-*): onsaelid.

635 †*destituunt*: towuorpon.

†*destitutae*: toworpne.

†*decipula*: bisuicfalle.

decrepita: dobgendi.
   322.

desidebat (*diss-*): unsib-
   bade. 323.

640 †*defatiget*: suenceth.

---

[1] i *and part of* r *on* er.

decrepita: dobendi. 638.

desidebat (*diss-*): unsibbadae. 639.

dos: uuituma. 704.

325 †*delibutus*: gisalbot. cp. 676.

delumentem (cp. *diluo*): thuachl. 641.

ditor: gifyrdro. 678.

depoline: uueftan. 642.

de confugione, statione[1]: *hydde. 643.

330 *disceptant*: flitad[2]. 680.

deliberatio: *ymbdritung. 644.

delicatis et quaerulosis: urastum. 645.

disparuit: *ungiseem uard. 682.

defectura: aspringendi. 646.

335 *decidens*: geuuitendi. 647.

debita pensio: *gedębin gebil. 648.

deditio: hondgong. 649.

difficile: uernuislicæ. 686.

detractavit: forsoc. 650.

340 *devia callis*: horuaeg stiig. 651.

distabueret (*-unt*): *asundum. 683.

deperuntur (*deferuntur*): *meldadum *vel* *roactum. 652.

dehisciat (*dehiscit*): tecinid. 653.

defecit (*disicit*?): *tedridtid. 654.

345 *detritu* (*-a*) *r*[*ub*]*igine*: agnidinne. 655.

345a *dracontia*: *grimrodr[3]. 708a.

digitalium *munusculorum: fingirdoccuna. 687.

346a *damina* (*-mma*), *bestia id est*: eola. 627b.

---

[1] *prob. originally* de confugiendi statione.   [2] *from* flicad, t *above* c.   [3] *see p. 33, fn. 2.*

delumentum (cp. *diluo*):
ðhuehl. 326.

deponile: wefta. 328.

de confugione, statione[1]:
hyðae. 329.

deliberatio: ymbðrio-
dung. 331.

645 *delicatis et querulis*:
wrastum end seobgen-
dum. 332.

defectura: aspringendi.
334·

decidens: gewitendi. 335·

debita pensio: gedaebeni
geabuli. 336.

deditio: *handgand[2]. 337.

650 *detractavit*: forsooc. 339.

devia callus (*-is*): horweg
stig. 340.

defferuntur (*deferuntur*):
meldadun *vel* wroeg-
dun. 342.

dehiscat (*-it*): tocinit. 343.

desicit (*dis-?*): tetridit. 344.

655 *detritu* (*-a*) *r*[*ub*]*igine*: ag-
nidine. 345.

†*dentalia*: sules reost.

†*devinxit*: geband.

†*decerni*: scriben.

†*deglobere* (*u*) *i.*: flean.

660 †*defotabat* (*v*): forsuor.

†*depraehendo* (*pre*): anfin-
do.

†*descivit*: wiðstylde, *pedem
retraxit.*

†*defert*: wroegde.

†*delectum*: cyri, *vel electio.*

665 †*detestare* (*-i*): onseacan.

†*detrimentum*: wonung.

†*degeneraverat*: misthagch.

†*des*[*i*]*isse*: tiorade.

†*degesto* (*dig-*): geraedit.

670 †*decreta*: geðoht.

†*devota*: cystig.

†*difortium* (*v*): weggedal,
repudium.

†*diem obiit*: asualt.

†*dictatorem*: aldur.

675 †*dilotis* (*lat*): todaeldum.

†*delibutus*: gesmirwid. cp.
325·

†*dilatio*: aelding.

ditor: gefyrðro. 327.

†*dispendium*: wom.

680 *disceptant*: flitat. 330.

†*dissimulat*: miðið.

disparuit: ungesene
wearð. 333·

distabuerunt: *asundun.
341.

†*discensor* (*disse-*): unge-
ðyre.

---

[1] *see p. 30, fn. 1* [2] *above* deditio *and* handgand *are added* traditio
and spontane.

Echo: uuydumer. 715.

[*h*]*edera*: uuidouuindae. 717.

empticius: *ceapcnext. 742.

350   *enunum* (*aenulum*): cetil. 749.

ebor (*-ur*): elpendes ban. 712.

erimio: *hindbrere. 758.

expendisse: araebndae. 776.

egerere: *ascrefan. 730.

355   *exundavit*: uueol. 777.

eluderet: auęgdæ. 734.

exercitus (*-iis*): bigongum. 779.

extorti: athraestae. 780.

685 †*dilectum*: meniu, *exercitum.*
difficile: wearnwislice.
338.
digitalium musculorum:
fingirdoccana. 346.
†*disceptavero*: sciro.
†*dicam (-ax)*: quedol.
690 †*dicas (-ax)*: quedole.
†*difinis*: suiðe micel.
†*dispensatio*: scir.
†*dimisis(demissis)*: *asclae-
cadun.
†*dicimenta*: tacne.
695 †*dispectus (desp-)*:
fraecuð.
†*dignitosa*: meodomlice.
†*dis[s]olverat*: ascaeltte.
†*divinos*: uuitgan.

†*distitutum (dest.)*: ofge-
fen.
700 †*distentus*: aðegen.
dolatum: gesniden[1]. 315.
dodrans: egur. 316.
dolatura (-orium): braad-
lastęcus. 321.
dos: wituma *vel* uuetma.
324.
705 †*domatis*: huses.
†*dolones*: hunsporan.
dromidus (-edarius): afy-
red olbenda. 319.
dromidarius: se eorod-
mon. 320.
708a *dracontia*: gimrodr[2].
345a.
dulcis sapa: caerin. 313.
710 *dumus*: þyrne. 317.

Eatenus: oð ðaet.
ebor (-ur): elpendbaan.
351.
†*ebredio (e radio?)*:
hrisle.
ebulum: walhwyrt. 393.
715 *echo*: wudumer. 347.
echinus, piscis vel: scel.
376.

[h]*edera*: uuduwinde.
348.
[h]*eder[a]*: ifegn. 392.
†[a]*edilitatem*: hámscire.
720 †*edissere[re]*: asaecgan.
effos[s]is: ahlocadum.
364.
†*enebata*[3] (*enervata*): asuond[3].

---

[1] ni *on er.* [2] gimro. dĩ., *i.e. apparently* gimro *dicitur; meant as*
gimrodor, *used several times elsewhere to explain* dracontia? [3] *these
two words added above a gloss* effeta: languida.

exposito: geboronae[1]. 781.

360   *emolomentum* (*-umentum*): fulteam. 743.

exaltavit (*exhalavit*): stanc. 782.

eviscerata: aeohed. 768.

[*a*]*egre*: erabedlicae. 729.

effossis: achlocadum. 721.

365   *expendisse*: throuadae. 783.

expedierunt: aręddun. 784.

exito (*-u*): *stęb *vel perditio*. 785.

exoleverunt: *gesuedradum. 786.

ex falange (*ph*): ob threatae. 787.

370   *evertigo* (*e vestigio*), *statim vel*: an landae. 769.

exauctoravit: *giheldae. 788.

expilatam: aritrid. 789.

expeditio: *fetd[2]. 790.

elegio (*log*?): geddi. 733.

375   *egesta*: ascrepaeni. 731.

echinus, piscis vel: scel. 716.

extentera (*exint-*): anseot. 791.

emlemma (*emblema*): fothr. 744.

[*h*]*eptasyllon* (*ph*), VII *folia id est*: *gilodusrt. 753.

380   *exagium*: handmitta. 793.

extale (*-is*): *snaedil *vel* thearm. 794.

emunctoria: *candelthuist. 745.

ephilenticus (*epilepticus*): uuoda. 754.

excolat: siid. 800.

385   *exta*: bęcdermi. 801.

electirum (*electrum*): elothr. 735.

eptafolium (*heptaphyllon*): sinfullae. 755.

[*h*]*elleborus*: *poedibergæ. 736.

epimemia (*meni*): nest. 756.

---

[1] *apparently explains* concepto, *which in the probable source occurs in the same sentence as* exposito.   [2] *from* fertd, r *expuncted*.

†*effetum*[1] : ortudri.

eftafolium (heptaphyllon): sinfulle. (755.)

725 *eftafylon (heptaphyllon)*: gelodwyrt. (753.)

†*efficaciter, velociter*: fromlice.

†*efficax, expeditus*: from.

†*effectum*: deid.

[*a*]*egre*: earfedlice. 363.

730 *egerere*: ascrepan. 354.

egesta: ascrepen. 375.

†[*a*]*egra*: slaece.

elogio: geddi. 374.

eluderet: auuægde. 356.

735 *electrum*: elotr. 386.

[*h*]*el*[*l*]*eborus*: þung, woedeberge. 388.

†*elogia*: laac.

†*elegans, loquax*: smicre.

†*eliminat*: aðytið.

740 †*elimat*: gesuirbet.

†*empta*: geboht.

empticius: ceapcneht. 349.

emolumentum[2] : lean, fultum. 360.

emblema: fothr. 378.

745 *emunctoria*: candeltuist. 382.

†*emaones*: scinneras.

†*emenso*: oberfoerde.

†*enervat*: asuond.

enum (aenulum): cetil.350.

750 †*enucleata*: geondsmead.

†*enixa*: beorende.

†*enixa est, genuit agnam i.*: ceolborlomb.

[*h*]*eptasyllon (ph)*: gelodwyrt. 379 (725).

epilenticus (epilepticus): woda. 383.

755 *eptafolium (heptaphyllon)*: sinfulle. 387 (724).

epimenia: nest. 389.

ependiten (ependytes): cóp. 390 (760).

erimio: hindberge. 352.

†*erenis (Erinys)*: haegtis, furia.

760 *erenditen (ependytes)*: cop. (757.)

erpica: egðe. 395.

erpicarius: egðere. 396.

[*a*]*erugo*: rust. 397.

†*errabiles*[3] : huerbende.

765 †*ericius*: iil.

[*a*]*esculus*: boece. 391.

†*essox (esox)*: laex.

eviscerata: athed. 362.

e vestigio: on lande, on laste. 370.

---

[1] *from* effetrum, r *expuncted.* *first* u. [3] *from* errabilis, e *above second* i.

[2] *from* emulumentum, o *above*

390   *efetidem (ependytes)*: cop. 757.
             [a]esculus, ob (ab) edendo: *beccae. 766.
             [h]edera: ifeg. 718.
             ebulum: uualhuyrt. 714.
             exactio: gebles monung. 813.
395   *erpica*: egdae. 761.
             erpicarius: egderi. 762.
396a   *expediam*[1]: *arectio. 813a.
             [a]erugo: rost[2]. 763.

[1] a *from another letter.*   [2] *end of gap in Ep.; begins again with*
the gloss filoxsenia: philosophia.

770 †*evidens*: seotol.

†*eurynis* (*Erinys*): wal-
cyrge.

†*eumenides*: haehtisse.

†*expeditus*: abundęn.

†*eximet*: alieset.

775 †*exegestus*: gebero. (cp.
957.)

expendisse: araefnde. 353.

exundavit: auueol. 355.

†*experimentum*: andwis-
nis.

exercitiis: bigangum.
357.

780 *ex*[*t*]*orti*: aðręsti. 358.

exposito: geborone[1]. 359.

exaltavit (*exhalavit*):
stonc. 361.

expe[*n*]*disset*: ðrowode.
365.

expedierant: araeddun.
366.

785 *exito* (*-u*), *perditio*: endi-
staeb. 367.

exoleverunt: gesueðra-
dun. 368.

ex phalange: of ðreote, of
foeðan. 369.

exauctoravit: geheende.
371.

expilatam: aþryid, ary-
trid. 372 (cp. 817).

790 *expeditio*: faerd. 373.

exintera: ansceat. 377.

†*explodit, excludit*: atynið.

exagium: andmitta. 380.

extale (*-is*): snaedilþear*m*.
381.

795 †*exilia*: gestinccum.

†*expeditis*: gearuum.

†*exta*: iesen.

†*exenium* (*xenium*): laac.

†*exactor*: scultheta.

800 *excolat*: siid. 384.

exta, praecordia: baecþe-
arm. 385.

†*examus*[*s*]*im*: geornlice,
*absolute, certe, vel ex-
quisite.*

†*exorbitans*: asuab.

†*exalaparetur*: suungen.

805 †*extipices* (*extispices*): hael-
sent.

†*expensa*: daeguuini[2].

†*ex*[*s*]*erta lingua*: naecad
tun*ge*.

†*exces*[*s*]*us*: egylt.

†*exigebant*: araefndun.

810 †*expeditionibus*: ferdun.

†*examen*: suearm.

---

[1] *see p. 34, fn. 1.* [2] *may explain some other word* (*perhaps*
stipendium, *which in a possible source occurs in the same sentence as*
expensa).

Facitiae (*facetiae*): gliu *both*. 825.

fiber: bebr *both*. 867.

400 †*flustra, undae vel—*frustra, unde vel*: hraen—*raen.

forfices: sceroro *both*. 898.

fovit (*-et*): feormat—*caeormad[1]. 899.

**fiscilla*—*fiscella*: taenil—tenil. 868.

flavum vel fulfum (*v*): read—reod. 887.

405 *fibrae*: librlaeppan *both*. 873.

fastidium: ciisnis—*ciinis. 829.

†*fax*: fæcilae—faecile.

fibula: sigil *both*. 874.

†*furca*: uueargrod—uaergrod.

410 *fibula*: hringiae—hringae. 874.

fenicia[2]—*finicia* (*phoeniceus*): baeso—beoso[3]. 877.

flegmata (*ph*): horh *both*. 888.

frugus (*-gi*): uncystig *vel* heamol—uncystig *vel* *healful. 917.

frixum: afigaen—afigen. 918.

415 *ferinum* (cp. *-a*): hold *both*. 853.

**fraximus*—*fraxinus*: aesc—*aastc. 920.

fagus[4]: boecae—boecce. 828.

---

[1] d *from* t.   [2] e *v. faint.*   [3] *after* fibula: sigil (408) in *Erf.*
[4] *from* fragus *in Ep.*, ꞃ *er.*

†*extorres*: wraeccan.
exactio: geabules mo-
nung. 394.
813a *expediam*: arecio. 396a.
†*excubias*: weardseld.
815 †*expendere*: to aseodenne.
†*exugia*: gescincio.
expilatam: arydid. cp.
372 (cp. 789).

†*expraesserunt* (*e*): areh-
tun.
†*exerceri*: wesan draegtre.
820 †*exercitatae*: ðare getyh-
tan[1].
†*expeditio*: hergiung.
†*exactum*: baedde.
†*expeditus*: snel, *velox, fortis.*

†*Favor*: herenis.
825 *facetia*[2]: glio. 398.
†*falc[o]*: walhhabuc.
fasces, libri: goduueb[3].
441.
fagus: boece. 417.
fastidium, odium: cymnis.
406.
830 *fasianus* (*ph*): worhona.
424.
†*fascia*: sweðel[4].
famfaluca (*pomphólyx*):
faam, leasung. 426.
†*fasciarum*: suaeðila.
falcis: wudubil, siðe, rift-
ras. 430.
835 *famfaluca* (*pomphólyx*):
wapul. 447.
falcastrum: wudubil. 449.

fa[v]onius: westsuðwind.
452.
†*fastinatio*[5] (*fascinatio*):
malscrung.
†*falarica*: *ægtęro.
840 †*falanx*[6] (*ph*): foeða.
†*farius* (*v*): faag.
†*facessit*: sueðrað.
†*farsa*: acrummen.
†*favo* (*faba*): bean.
845 †*fasces*: cynedomas.
†*fastu*: uulencu.
†*fabrile*: smiðlice.
†*farelas* (*phalerae*): hryste.
†*falerata* (*ph*): gehyrsti.
850 †*fer[r]uginius* (-*eus*): greig.
†*ferox*: roeðe, *ferae
similis.*
†*ferculum*: disc, *vasculum.*

---

[1] *perhaps intended to explain* excitatae.   [2] *from* facitia, e *above
first* i.   [3] *perhaps intended to explain* purpura, *which in a possible
source occurs in the same line as* fasces.   [4] *MS.* fascias: weðel.
[5] *from* festinatio, *first* a *above* e.   [6] fa:lanx.

fusarius—*fagus: uuananbeam—uuonanbea*m*. 935.

fulix: ganot *vel* dopaenid *both*[1]. 936.

420   *filix*: fearn—*feran. 871.

fraga: *obtt—*obea. 919.

ficetula (d): sugga—sucga. 878.

fringella[2] *(-illa)*: finc *both*. 921.

fasianus (ph)—*fassianus: uuorhana—uuorhona. 830.

425   *furuncu[lu]s*: mearth—meard. 937.

famfaluca (pomphólyx): leasung *vel* faam—laesung *vel* faa*m*.
     832.

fungus: suamm—sua*m*m. 938.

furfures: siuida *both*. 940.

†*fitilium (vitellus)*: aegergelu.

430   *falces—falcis (falx, falcis)*: uudubil, sigdi[3], riftr—uuidubil,
     sigdi, riftr. 834.

430a *fucus*: fex *both*[4]. 934.

flabanus: suan *both*. 889.

flabum—flavum: gelu *both*. 890.

furvum: bruun *both*. 931.

fibrans[5] *(v)*: risaendi—*ripendi. 879.

435   *fenus*: spearuua—spearua. 855.

foederatas: gitreeudae—getreudæ. 900.

funestavere[6]: *smitor—smiton. 941.

frons—*fros: hleor *both*[7]. 923.

funestissima[8]: tha deatlicostan—da deudlicustan. 942.

440   *framea*: aetgaeru—*aetgaru. 922.

fasces—*faces: goduuebb[9]—*guoduueb. 827.

---

[1] *the order of the last seven in Erf. is*: frugus, fraxinus, fagus:
boecce, frixum, ferinum, fagus: uuonanbeam, fulix.   [2] *from*
frincella *in Ep.*, g *above* c.   [3] *er. between* i *and* g?   [4] *after*
fiscella (403) *in Erf.*   [5] fi:::brans *Ep.*   [6] *curved stroke as of*
c *between* u *and* n *in Ep.*   [7] h *in margin in Ep.*   [8] *curved*
stroke as of c *between* f *and* u *in Ep.*   [9] *see p. 39, fn. 3.*

ferinum (cp. -*a*): hold.
  415.

†*feriatus*: gerested.

855 *fenus*: spearua. 435.

†*foenus*[1]: borg.

†*foederatus*[2]: getriowad.

†*faecce*: maere.

†*fespa* (*v*): waefs.

860 †*fefellit*: uuegið.

  ferula: aescŏrote. 450.

  [*fellitat*: *suggit*[3]. 455.]

†*fellus* (*felis*): catte.

†*f[a]enum*: graes.

865 †*ferrugine*: iserngrei.

†*ferruginem, obscuritatem
  ferri i.*: omei.

  fiber: bebr. 399.

  fiscilla (-*ella*): taenil. 403
    (cp. 872).

†*fida*: stearn.

870 †*fibra*: þearm.

  filix: fearn. 420.

†*fiscillus* (-*ella*): stictenel.
    (cp. 868.)

  fibrae: librlaeppan. 405.

  fibula: hringe, sigl. 408,
    410.

875 †*fiscillis* (-*ellis*): sprinclum.

†*filum*: ðred.

  finicia (*phoeniceus*): beo-
    su. 411.

ficetula (*ficedula*): sugga.
  422.

fibrans (*v*): risende. 434.

880 *finiculus* (*faeniculum*):
    finulae. 451.

†*fiscalis r[a]eda*: *gebelli-
    cum wægnfearu.

†*fimum*: goor.

†*fictis*: facnum.

†*fistulis*: þeotum.

885 †*figite*: suiðigað.

†*filiaster*: steopsunu.

  flavum, fulvum: read.
    404.

  flegmata (*ph*): horh. 412.

  flabanus: suan. 431.

890 *flabum* (*v*): geolu. 432.

†*flagris*: suiopum.

  flamma: blęd. 445.

  floccus: loca. 448.

†*flavescit*: glitinat, *albescit*.

895 †*flagrans* (*fr.*): stincendi.

†*flebotoma* (*phlebotomus*):
    blodsaex.

†*fortuna*: wyrd.

  forfices: scerero. 401.

  fovet: feormat, broedeth.
    402.

900 *foederatas*: getreuuade.
    436.

  fornicem: bogan. 442.

---

[1] *originally* fenus, *as shown by alph. order.*   [2] *originally* federa-
tus, *as shown by alph. order.*   [3] *represents Lat.* sugit.

fornicem: bogan *both*[1]. 901.

†*feriatis, quietis vel securis vel*[2]: restaendu*m*—restendu*m*.

†*facundia, eloquentia vel*: *þoot—*puood.

445   *flamma*: blaeed—bled. 892.

fragor: suoeg *both*. 925.

famfaluca—fanfaluca (*pomphólyx*): uuapul *both*. 835.

floccus: loca *both*. 893.

falcastrum: uuidubil *both*. 836.

450   *ferula—*ferola*: aescthrotae—aescdrotae. 861.

finiculus (*faeniculum*): finugl *both*. 880.

fa[v]onius: uuestsuduuind. 837.

fornix[3]: boga *super columnis* both. 909.

follis: blestbaelg *both*. 910.

455   [*fellitat*: suggit—suggid[4]. 862.]

Gurgulio: throtbolla—ðrotbolla. 1000.

[1] *from* bogant *in Erf.*, t *expuncted.*   [2] feriatus quietis securis *uel Erf.*   [3] *from* fornax *in Ep.*, i *above expuncted* a.   [4] *preceded by expuncted* r; d *from* t; *for both glosses see p. 41, fn. 3.*

†*formido*: anoða.

†*forfex*: isernsceruru.

†*fors*: wyrd.

905 †*forceps*: tong.

†*fornacula*: cyline, heorðe.

†*foras* (*-os*): bolcan.

†*fortex* (*v*): edwelle.

fornis (*-ix*): bogo, *super columnis*. 453.

910 *follis*: blaesbaelg. 454.

†*fornaculum* (*-la*): here.

†*formaticus* (*-um*): cese, *a forma*.

†*fronulus*: linetuigle.

†*frat*[*r*]*uelis*: geaduling.

915 †*frat*[*r*]*uelis*: suhterga.

†*frat*[*r*]*uelis*: broðorsunu.

frugus (*-gi*): uncystig, heamul. 413.

frixum: afigaen. 414.

fraga: obet. 421.

920 *fraxinus*: aesc. 416.

fringella (*-illa*): finc. 423.

921a †*frutectum*: lose, *locus ubi ponunt*.

framea: ætgaeru. 440.

f[*r*]*ons*: hleor. 438.

†*fretus*: bald.

925 *fragor*: suoeg, cirm. 446.

†*fraudulenter*: faecenlice.

†*frontuosus* (*frontosus*): bald.

†*frutina*: fultemend.

†*fuscinula*[1]: awel.

930 †*furcimen* (cp. *furca*?): waergrood.

furbum (*v*): bruun. 433.

931a †*fundi*: *grundus.

†*funalia*: *con*del.

†*fusum*: spinel.

†*fucus*: faex[2], taelg. 430a.

935 *fusarius*: wananbeam. 418.

funix (*fulix*): gonot *vel* doppaenid. 419.

furuncu[*lu*]*s*: mearð. 425.

fungus: suom. 427.

†*funda*: liðre.

940 *furfures*: sifiðan. 428.

funestavere: smiton. 437.

funestissima: ða deadlicustan. 439.

†*funalia, cerei*: waexcondel.

†*ful*[*i*]*gine*: *sooth.

945 †*furia*: haehtis.

†*Gargarizet*: gagul suille.

†*garrit*: gionat.

†*gannatura*: gliu.

galla: galluc. 466.

[1] *from* fiscinula, *first* u *above expuncted first* i.   [2] *not certainly* Old English.

gurgustium: cesol *both*. 1001.

gilvus: gelu *both*. 966.

gibbus—**gypbus*: hofr—*hosr. 969.

460   *gipsus*—*gypsus* (*gypsum*): sparaen—sparen. 968.

glarea—**glare*: cisil—cisal. 975.

glumula[1] (cp. *gluma*): scalu *both*. 976.

gladiolum: segg—secg. 977.

gramen: quiquae[2]—quicae. 989.

465   *genistae*—*geniste* (*-a*): broom *both*. 959.

galla: galluc *both*[3]. 949.

grassator: ferhergend—ferhergend. 990.

garbas: sceabas *both*. 951.

grallus (*graculus*): hrooc *both*[4]. 991.

469a *genisculas*—*genisculae*: muscellas—muscellae. 960a.

470   *glis*: eglae—egilae. 973.

galmaria: caluuaer—caluuer. 952 (cp. 476).

glomer (*-us*): cleouuae—cleuuue[5]. 979.

glaucum: hęuui *vel* grei—*hauui *vel* grei. 981.

gracilis: smael—*smal[6]. 992.

475   *glus* (*gluttus*?): frecnis *both*. 980.

galbalacrum—*galmaria*: caluuaer—caluuer. 956 (cp. 471).

galmum: molegn—moleng. 953.

globus: leoma—leuma. 974.

gregariorum: *aedilra *both*. 993.

480   †*genuino*: gecyndilican[7] *both*.

gladiatores: caempan—cempan. 984.

†*genas*—**genus*: hleor *both*.

gilvus: falu *both*. 970.

gurgulio (*curculio*): aemil *both*. 1003 (cp. 257).

485   *gelum*: frost—*frots. 964.

---

[1] *Erf. perhaps* glamula.   [2] *from* cuiquae, *first* q *above* c.
[3] c *from* s *in Erf.*   [4] h *in margin in Ep.*   [5] *or* ol-?   [6] *after*
galmum (477) *in Erf.*   [7] e *from* i *in Ep.*

950 †*gar[r]ula*: crauue.
  garbas: sceabas. 468.
  galmaria: caluuer. 471
    (cp. 427, 956).
  galmum: moling. 477.
953a†*galmulum*: molegnstycci.
  †*galmilla*: liimcaluuer. cp.
    486 (cp. 427).
955 †*gabea* (*gavia*): meau.
  gabalacrum: calwer. 476
    (cp. 427).
  †*gestus*: gebero. (cp. 775.)
  †*generosus*: aeðile.
  genista: brom. 465.
960†*gente* (*ganta*): wilde goos.
    (963; cp. 450.)
960a *genisculus* (-*las*):
    muscellas. 469a.
  †*genuino*: tusc, *naturale*.
    (cp. *Erf.* 487.)
  †*genas*: heagaspen.
  †*gente* (*ganta*): wilde goos.
    (960; cp. 450.)
  gelum: forst. 485.
964a †*gener*: *adam.
965 †*geumatrix*: geac.
  gilvus: geolu. 458.
  †*gillus* (*gilvus*): grei.
  gipsus (*gypsum*): spaeren.
    460.
  gippus (*bb*): hofr. 459.
970 *gilvus*: falu. 483.
  †*gilbus*: gyrno.

  †*gingria*: spon.
  glis: egle. 470.
  globus: leoma. 478.
975 *glarea*: cisilstan. 461.
  glumula (cp. *gluma*?):
    scala. 462.
  gladiolum: saecg. 463.
  †*glitilia*: clife.
  glomer (-*us*): *clouue.
    472.
980 *glus* (*gluttus*?): frecnis.
    475.
  glaucum: heauui, grei.
    473.
  †*glandula*: cirnel.
  †*glebo*: unwis.
  gladiatores: cempan. 481.
985 †*gluten*: teoru.
  †*gripem* (*gryps*): gig.
  †*grillus* (*y*): hama.
  †*gremen* (*gremium*): faethm.
  gramen: quice. 464.
990 *grassator*: forhergend.
    467.
  grallus (*graculus*): hrooc.
    469.
  gracilis: smel. 474.
  gregariorum: *unaeðilsa.
    479.
  †*gregatim*: wearnmelum.
995 †*grus, gruis*: cornoch.
  †*gravis* (*grus*): cornuc.
  †*graffium* (*ph*): gref.

†*galmilla—gamilla*: liimmolegn—limmolegn[1]. cp. 954.
†——*genuinum, intimum vel dens id est*: tusc[2]. cp. 961.

**Hebitatus—hebetatus*: astyntid *both*[3]. 1012.
hastilia telorum: scaeptloan[4]. 1005.
490   *hebesceret*: asuand—*ansuand. 1013.
hebitavit (bet)—*habitavit: aslacudae *both*. 1014.
habitudines: geberu *both*. 1006.
hyadas (-es): raedgaesram—redgaesram. 1035.
horno: thys geri *both*. 1028.
495   *hiulca*: cinaendi—cinendi. 1020.
hibiscum: biscopuuyrt *both*. 1021.
horodius (erōdiós): uualhhebuc—uualhhaebuc. 1016
hirundo: sualuuae—sualuae[5]. 1022.

---

[1] *after* gracilis (474) *in Erf.*   [2] *from* tunsc, n *expuncted.*
[3] astyn::: tid *Ep.*   [4] *apparently explains some other word, probably* amentis; *cp. EE* 106, *the probable source of which is a sentence containing both* hastilia telorum *and* amentis.   [5] *from* sualnuae, n *expuncted.*

†*grunnire*: grunnettan.
†*graticium (cr.)*: wag-
    flecta.
1000 *gurgulio*: ðrotbolla. 456.
    gurgustium: ceosol. 457.

†**gurgustiore* (*-tio*): ce-
    tan.
gurgulio (*curculio*): emil.
    484 (cp. 613).
†*gunna*: heden.

1005 *Hastilia telorum*: scaept-
    loan[1]. 489.
    habitudines: geberu.
    492.
    †*harundo*(*arundo*), *canna*:
        hreod.
    †*haustum*: drync.
    †*habenis*: gewaldleðru*m*.
1010 †*habile*: lioðuwac.
    †*heus*: geheres thu.
    hebitatus (*bet*): astyntid.
    488.
    hebesceret: asuand. 490.
    hebitabit (*hebetavit*): as-
        clacade. 491.
1015 †*heia* (*eja*): welga.
    herodius(*erōdiós*): walch-
        habuc. 497.
    †*helleborus*: woidiberge.
    †*herinis* (*Erinys*): walc-
        rigge.
    †*hebetat*: styntid.

1020 *hiulca*: cinendi. 495.
    hibiscum: biscopuuyrt.
    496.
    hirundo: sualuue. 498.
    †*histrix* (*hystrix*): iil.
    †*hinnitus*: hnaeggiung.
1025 †*hy*[*ae*]*na*: naectgenge.
    †*holor* (*olor*): suan.
    †*hora* (*ora*): sueg.
    horno: þys gere. 494
    (1030).
    †*hoctatus*: gelaechtrad.
1030 *horno*: þys gere. (1028.)
    †*holido* (*olido*): fule.
    †*honeraria* (*oneraria*):
        hlaestscip.
    †*huscide* (*viscide*): tolice.
    (cp. 2170.)
    †*humase* (*-re*): bimyldan.
1035 *hyadas* (*-es*): raedgas-
        ram[2]. 493.
    †*hymen*[*a*]*eos*: hęmedo.

1 *see p. 46, fn. 4.*   2 *first a on er.*

Indruticans: uuraestendi—*uraesgendi. 1045.

500 *inhians*: gredig *both*. 1046.

inluvies secundarum: hama, *in quo fit parvulus*[1] *both*. 1049.

inpetigo—*inpegit: tetr[2]—*teg. 1047 (cp. 766).

intestinum: thearm *both*. 1058.

interamen (*interaneum*): innifli—inifli. 1059.

505 †*ilium*: neuunseada—*naensida.

instites (*-a*): suedilas *both*. 1060.

intexunt: auundun *both*. 1062.

increpitans: hlaeodrindi—*hleodendri. 1065.

inlex: tyctaend, *anbinliciendi—tychtend, *ab inliciendo*. 1063.

510 *infestus*: flach *both*. 1066.

†*intercaeptum—*interceptum*: araepsid—arepsit.

infandum: maanful—*meinfol*. 1069.

inlecebris: tyctinnum *both*. 1070.

ingratus: lath—laad. 1071.

515 *inritatus in rixam*: gigremid—gigremit. 1073.

incitamenta: tyctinnae *both*. 1074.

516a *iota*: soctha *both*. 1151.

jungetum (*juncetum*): riscthyfil—*rycthyfil. 1159.

intula (*inula*): uualhuuyrt—uualhuyrt. 1075.

inprobus: gimach—gemach. 1076.

520 *ingruerit*: anhriosith—onhrisit. 1077.

intractabilis: unlidouuac—*unliduuuac. 1079.

*incomodum—*incommodum*: unbryci—*unbrycci. 1050.

interceptum est: raebsid uuaes—repsit uaes. 1084.

†*insimulatione*: uuroctae—uurochtae.

525 *inpendebatur*: gibaen uuaes[3]—geben uaes. 1086.

interpellari: raefsed—refset[4]. 1087.

industria: *geeornnissae[5]—*gyrnissæ. 1088.

---

[1] *from* paruulis *in Ep., third* u *above* i.   [2] e *partly on* er. *after first* t.   [3] *curved stroke as of* c *between the* u*'s*.   [4] de er. *before* refs&.   [5] ge:eor:nnissae.

Ibices: firgengaet. 560.

†*idoneus*: *oxstaelde.

†*igni (-em) sacrum*: oman.

1040 *ign[i]arium*: aalgewerc.
556.

†*ilia*: midhridir, nioðan-
weard hype.

†*illi[n]c*: þanan.

†*imbricibus*: þaectigilum.

†*inergumenos (energoúme-
nos)*: wodan.

1045 *indruticans*: wraestendi[1].
499.

in[h]ians: gredig. 500.

inpetigo: teter. 502 (cp.
1550).

†*inextricabilis*: untosli-
ten.

inluvies secundarum:
hama, *in quo fit par-
vulus*. 501.

1050 *incommodum*: unbryce.
522.

†*inprovisu (-o)*: feringa.

†*infestatio*: unlioþuwac-
nis.

†*infula*: uueorðmynd.

†*inminente*: aetweosen-
dre.

1055 †*infestus (infectus)*: ge-
menged.

†*ingesta*: ondoen.

†*inola (-ula)*: eolene.

intestinum: þearm. 503.

interamen (cp. *intera-
neum*): innifli. 504.

1060 *instites (-a)*: sueðelas.
506.

†*infima*: niol.

intexunt: wundun. 507.

inlex: tyctendi. 509.

†*interim*: þrage.

1065 *increpitans*: hleoþrendi.
508.

infestus: flach. 510.

†*interceptum*: arasad.

†*interceptio*: raepsung.

infandum: mánful. 512.

1070 *inlecebris*: tychtingum.
513.

ingratus: la·ð[2]. 514.

†*incuda (incus)*: onfilti.

inritatus: gegremid. 515.

incitamenta: tyhtinne.
516.

1075 *intula (inula)*: uualh-
wyrt. 518.

inprobus: gemah. 519.

ingruerit: onhrioseð. 520.

†*inruens*: þerende.

intractabilis: unlioþu-
wac. 521.

---

[1] *from* wraestende, i *above final* e.   [2] ð *from* d.

inpendebat: saldae—*saltae. 1089.

in dies crudesceret: a fordh—a *forthe. 1090.

530 *in transmigratione—in transmigrationem*: in foernissae—in
        *fornissæ. 1091.

iners: asolcaen—asolcæn. 1092.

interventu: þingungae—*ingungae. 1093.

inlectus: gitychtid—getyctid. 1094.

interlitam[1]: bismiridae—bismirida. 1095.

535 *inpactae*: *anslegaengrae—aslegenræ. 1096.

indigestae: unofaercumenrae—unofercum*enr*æ. 1097.

innitentes[2]: uuidirhliniendae—*uuidirlinienti. 1098.

insolesceret[3]: oberuuaenidae—oberuenedæ. 1099.

inpulsore: baedendrae—bedændræ. 1100.

540 *infractus*: giuuaemmid—geuemmid. 1101.

inopimum: unaseddae—*unasettæ. 1102.

inditas: þa gisettan[4]—ða *gisettai. 1103.

infici: gimaengdae—gimengdæ. 1104.

index: taecnaendi, torctendi—taecnendi, torchtendi. 1105.

545 *inpostorem—*inposterem*: bisuicend—bisuiccend. 1106.

inter primores: *bituicn aeldru*m*—bituichn ældru*m*. 1107.

intercapido (-*edo*)—*intercapito: fristmearc—*fritmaerc. 1108.

insolens: feruuaenid—*feruendid. 1109.

in curia: in maethlae—in medlæ. 1110.

550 *in mimo*: in gliuuae, *quod tamen ad mimarios vel mimigraphos*[5]
        pertinet both. 1112.

jurisperiti: redboran *both*. 1160.

invisus—*invissus: laath—lath. 1113.

in aestivo caenaculo[6]: uppae, *ubi*[7] *per aestatem frigus captant*[8]—
        yppe. 1114.

---

[1] interlitan *Erf*.   [2] inniten̄t *Erf*.   [3] *from* insolescerit *in*
Ep., *third* e *above expuncted second* i.   [4] gise:t.   [5] mimi-
grafos *Ep*.   [6] caenaculi *Ep*., -li *partly on* er. *before* uppae.
[7] *om. in Erf*.   [8] capiatur *Erf*.

1080 †*inmunes*: orceas.
    †*in procinctu*: in ðeg-
       nunge.
    †*intercepit*: rᶒfsde.
    †*intercepit*: fornoom.
    interceptum est: raefsit
       waes. 523.
1085 †*insimulatione*: feringe.
    inpendebatur: geben
       waes. 525.
    interpellare (-i): raefsit.
       526.
    industria: geornis. 527.
    inpendebat: salde. 528.
1090 *in dies crudesceret*: a
       *forht. 529.
    in transmigrationem: in
       foernisse. 530.
    iners: esuind, asolcen.
       531.
    interventu: þingunge.
       532.
    inlectus: getyhtid. 533.
1095 *interlitam*: bismiride.
       534.
    inpactae: onligenre¹.
       535.
    indigestae: unobercum-
       enre. 536.
    innitentes: wiðerhlin-
       gende. 537.

    insolesceret: oberuue-
       nide. 538.
1100 *inpulsore*: baedendre.
       539.
    infractus: ungeuuem-
       mid. 540.
    inopimum: unasaedde.
       541.
    inditas: ða gesettan. 542.
    infici: gemengde. 543.
1105 *index*: tacnendi, torc-
       tendi. 544.
    inposterem (impostor):
       bisuuicend. 545.
    inter primores: *bitun
       aeldrum. 546.
    intercapido (-edo): first-
       maerc. 547.
    insolens: foruuened. 548.
1110 *in curia*: in maeðle.
       549.
    incuba (-bus): maere.
       558.
    in mimo: in gliowe. 550.
    invisus: lath. 552.
    in [a]estivo cenaculi (-o):
       yppe, *ubi per [a]esta-
       tem frigus captant.*
       553.
1115 *involuc[r]us (cp. -um)*:
       uulluc. 557.

----

¹ *perhaps intended to explain* pactae *or* compactae.

juvar (*b*): leoma *vel* earendil—leoma *vel* oerendil. 1161, 1166.

555   *isic* (*esox*): leax—lex. 1155.

ign[*i*]*arium*: algiuueorc—algiuerc. 1040.

involuc[*r*]*us*[1] (cp. *-um*)—**invociucus*: uulluc *both*. 1115.

incuba (*-bus*): mera, *vel satyrus*[2]—merae, *vel* **saturnus*. 1111.

involuco (cp. *-lvulus*)—**involucu*: uuidubindlae—**uuydu-
          blindæ. 1116.

560   *ibices*: firgingaett *both*. 1037.

*infridat—*infrigidat*: caelith—cælid. 1119.

isca (*esca*): tyndirm—tyndrin[3]. 1156.

---

¹ c *from* s.   ² y *on* er.   ³ *after* isic (555) *in Erf.*

involuco (cp. *-lvulus*):
uudubinde. 559.

†*inquilinis* (*-us*): genaeot.

†*indolis* (*-es*): hyhtful *vel*
ðiendi.

infri[gi]dat: kaelið. 561.

1120 †*inruit*: raesde.

†*inpingit*: smat, gemaer-
code¹.

†*incentor*: tyhtend.

†*incantata*: gegaelen.

†*incantatores*: galdriggan.

1125 †*infestationes*: tionan.

†*intercapidine* (*-edine*):
ginnisse.

†*inundatio*: gyte.

†*incurrus* (*incursus*): ongong.

†*inbuit*: onreod.

1130 †*infa[u]stum*: sliden.

†*inruptio*: ongong.

†*innixus*: strimendi. (cp.
1404.)

†*incanduit*: auueoll.

†*ineptus*: gemędid.

1135 †*intrinicio* (*internecio*):
forsliet.

†*in sirtim* (*y*): in sondge-
wearp.

†*innitor*: onhlingu².

†*inficio*: blondu.

¹ *confusion with* pingit?
³ *or* interneci[v]um bellum?

†*infula*: uyrðo.

1140 †*inmoratur*: wunat.

†*infectum*: geblonden.

†*indomitus*: wilde.

†*instincta*: onsuapen.

†*intransmeabili*: unofer-
foere.

1145 †*inbellem*: orwige.

†*internicium* (*internecio*),
*bellum*³ *dicitur quo*
nullus remanet: ut-
cualm.

†*[h]in[n]ulus*: hindcaelf.

†*in catamo* (*tom*): in bęce.

†*initiatum*: gestoepid.

1150 †*intimandum*: to cyðenne.

iota: sochtha. 516a.

†*jovem*: þuner.

†*irridabant* (*irritabant*):
tyhton.

†*irritum*: forhogd, *ina-*
nem.

1155 *isic* (*esox*): laex. 555.

isca (*esca*): tyndrin.
562.

†*istic*: uueðer.

†*istuc*: hider.

jungetum (*juncetum*):
riscðyfel. 517.

1160 *jurisperiti*: redboran.
551.

² *from* onhlingo, u *above final* o.

Lebes—*leves: huuer *both*. 1197.

lepor, subtilitas vel: uuoþ—*vel pro*[1] uod. 1196.

565   *lagones—lagonas* (*ligones*): mettocas *both*. 1211 (586).

liburnices (*-cas*): gerec *both*. 1212.

labarum[2]: seng—segn. 1167.

lurcones, avidi vel: sigiras—*lurcones*: sigiras, *vel avidi*. 1241.

larbula (*v*): egisigrima *both*[3]. 1168.

570   *lunules* (*-as*): menescillingas—meniscillingas. 1242.

lituus, baculum augurale in prima parte curvum[4], *id est*: crycc
       both. 1222.

lacerna: haecilae *vel* lotha[5]—hecile *vel* lotha. 1169.

lumbare: gyrdils *vel* broec—gyrdils, broec. 1244.

573 a *la[n]x*: heolor—eolor[6]. 1169a, 1177 (607).

luculentum (*-tiam?*): torchtnis—torhtnis. 1243.

575   *lymphatico*: *uuoendendi—uuodenti. 1263.

livida[7] *toxica*: tha uuannan aetrinan—tha uuannan *etrinani.
       1215.

ludi   litterari[i]—ludi   *litterali: staebplegan—*scæbplega.
       1245.

liquentes—*linquentes: hlutrae *both*. 1216.

lenoc[in]ium—lenotium: *thyctin *vel* scocha—tyctin *vel* scocha.
       1199.

580   *lacessit*: graemid—gremid. 1170.

lenta, tarda vel: toch—*thoch. 1198.

---

[1] þ.   [2] *bow of first a rubbed or partly er. in Ep.; resembles* o.
[3] *from* egisigrimma *in Erf., first* m *expuncted.*   [4] *nasal stroke cut
off by binder in Ep.*   [5] th *from* d.   [6] *after* lacerna (572)
in Erf.   [7] d (? *expuncted and*) *erased between first* i *and* v *in Ep.*

jubar: earendel. 554.
†*jugum*: cnol.
†*junctura*: foeging.

†*juventus*: midferh.
1165 †*juncus*: risc.
jubar: leoma. 554.

Lab[a]rum: segn. 567.
larbula (v): egisgrima.
 569.
lacerna: haecile *vel* loða.
 572.
1169a *la[n]x*: *heholor. 573a,
 607 (1177).
1170 *lacessit*: gremið. 580.
laogoena (lagena): crog.
 584.
†*latrina*: genge, groepe,
 atque ductus, cloacas.
†*[a]laudae*: laurice.
lacessitus: gegremid. 593.
1175 *laexiva (lixivia)*: laeg.
 591.
1175a †*lacesso*: *suto.
laquear: first, hrof. 595.
lanx: heolor. 573a, 607
 (1169a).
lanucar (lacunar): flode[1].
 597.
lactuca: þuðistel. 601.
1180 †*lacunar*: *hebenhus.
lapatium (lapathum): lelodrae. 606.

†*lacerta*: aðexe.
larus: meau. 610.
lappa: clibe. 613.
1185 †*latex*: burne.
1187 †*laena*: rift.
†*labat*: weagat.
†*lana*: uul.
1190 †*laquearia*: firste.
†*latratus*: bercae[2].
†*laudariulus* (cp. *lari-
 dum?*): frecmase.
†*ladascapiae, briensis i.*:
 hondwyrm. (cp. 320.)
†*lanterna*: lehtfaet.
1195 †*lacessere*: gremman.
lepor: wooð. 564.
lebes: huer. 563.
lenta: toh. 581.
lenocinium: tyhten. 579.
1200 †*legit, collegit*: lisit.
lembum (limbus): listan.
 583.
legula (lig.): gyrdils-
 hringe. 582 (1226).
lendina (lens): hnitu[3].
 590.

[1] *appears to explain* lacuna.
[3] *from* hutu, ni *above first* u.

[2] *from* baercae, *first* a *expuncted*.

legula (i)—**legu*: gyrdislrhingae—gyrdilshringe. 1202.

lembum (limbus): listan *vel* thres[1]—listan *vel* ðres. 1201.

lagoena (-ena): croog *both*. 1171.

585 *lutrus*[2] *(-a)*: otr—**octur*. 1246.

ligones—**lagones*: mettocas—**metocas*. 1211 (565).

lucius: haecid *both*[3]. 1247.

lucanica: maerh—mærh. 1249.

lurdus (lordós)—**lurdur*: laempihalt—**lemphihalt*. 1250.

590 *lendina*[4] *(lens)*: hnitu *both*. 1203.

lexiva (lixivia): leag—læg. 1175.

lupus: baers *both*. 1251.

lacessitus: gigraemid—gigremid. 1174.

lien: **multi*—milti. 1217.

595 *laquear*: fierst—**firt*. 1176.

ludaris: steor *both*. 1252.

lacunar: flodae[5] *both*. 1178.

levir: tacor *both*. 1204.

lolium: atae—atte. 1235.

600 *lodix*: lotha *both*. 1237.

lactuca: þuþistil—**popistil*. 1179.

liciatorium—**licitorium*: hebild[6] *both*. 1219.

lihargum (lithargyrus): slęgu—slægu. 1230.

licidus—*lucidus (liqui-?)*: huet—huaet. 1223.

605 *lectidiclatum (lac tud-?)*—*lectidicladum*: githuornae fleti—
        githuorne fleti. 1205.

lapatium (lapathum): lelodrae *both*. 1181.

lanx: helor *both*. 1169a, 1177 (573a).

lepus, leporis[7]: hara—hæra[8]. 1206.

---

[1] *curved stroke as of* c *between* h *and* r.   [2] *from* lotrus *in Erf.*,
u *above* o.   [3] h *added in margin in Ep.*   [4] *first* n *from* m
in Ep.   [5] *see p. 55, fn. 1.*   [6] *word* er. *before* hebild *in Ep.*
[7] læporis *Erf.*   [8] *Erf. adds* quae cum intro canit, *evidently taken
from the gloss* liciter: qui cum lituo canit (*four glosses on* in *Ep. but om.
in Erf.*).

levir: tacur. 598.

1205 *lectidiclatum* (*lac tud-*?): geþuorne flete. 605.

lepus, leporis: hara. 608.

lentum vimen: toh gęrd. 614.

†*lenticula*: piose.

†*lesta*: borda.

1210 †*lenirent*: afroebirdun.

ligones: meottucas. 565, 586.

liburnices (*-cas*): gerec. 566.

†*libor* (*v*): uuam.

ligustrum: hunigsuge. 615.

1215 *livida toxica*: ða wonnan aetrinan. 576.

liquentes: hlutre. 578.

lien: milte. 594.

†*libertabus*: frioletan.

liciatorium: hebelgerd. 602.

1220 *limax*: snegl. 611.

†*limphaticus* (*y*): woeden-di. (cp. 1263.)

lituus: cryc. 571.

licidus (*liqui-*? *luc-*?): huæt. 604.

†*libertus*: frioleta.

1225 †*linter*: baat.

lingula (*ligula*): gyrdils-hringe. (1202.)

†*limus*: laam.

†*limbus*: ðres, liste. (cp. 1264.)

†*liberalitas*: roopnis.

1230 *li*[*t*]*harg*[*yr*]*um*: slaegu. 603.

†*linea*: waebtaeg.

†*licium*: hebeld.

†*licia*: hebeldðred.

†*lima*: fiil.

1235 *lolium*: ate. 599.

†*lotium*: hlond.

lodix: loða. 600.

†*locusta*: lopust.

†*luscus*: anege.

1240 †*lu*[*r*]*cor*: freceo.

lurcones: siras. 568.

lunulus (*-as*): menescil-lingas. 570.

luculentum (*-tiam*?): torhtnis. 574.

lumbare: gyrdils, broec. 573.

1245 *ludi litterari*[*i*]: staef-plagan. 577.

lutraos (*lutra*): otr. 585.

lucius: haecid. 587.

†*lupatis*: bridelsum.

lucanica: mærh. 588.

1250 *lurdus* (*lordós*): lemp-halt. 589.

lupus: brers. 592.

ludarius: steor. 596.

†*lacuna[r]*: hrof[1] *both.*

610 *laris (-us)*: *men—meu. 1183.

  limax: snel—snegl. 1220.

  lumbricus: regenuuyrm—regnuuyrm. 1253.

  lappa: *cliþae—clifae. 1184.

  lentum vimen: toch gerd—*thoh gerd. 1207.

615 *ligustrum*: hunaegsugae—hunegsugae. 1214.

  Mordicos (-cus): bibitnae[2] *both.* 1319.

  manipulatim: threatmelum—*theatmelum. 1265.

  mendacio conposito[3]: geregnodae[4]—*geradnodae. 1301.

  molestissimum: earbetlicust[5]—*easbedlicust. 1320.

620 *municeps[6]*: burgleod, *a mu[ni]cipio.* 1334.

  munifica: cistigian[7]. 1335.

  monarchia: anuuald—anuald. 1321.

  mirifillon (myriophyllon), millefolium[8]: geruuae—geruȩ. 1315
      (639).

  murica: gespan, *aureum in tunica[9]*—gespon. 1336.

625 *modioli*: nabae—nebæ. 1322.

  mancus[10]: anhendi—anhaendi. 1266.

  mafortae—maforte (mafors): scybla[11] *both.* 1267.

  morgit (mulget): milciþ—milcid. 1323.

  mossiclum—mossuclum (cp. *muscus*): ragu *both.* 1324.

630 *mimoparo (myo-)*: thebscib—thebscip. 1316.

---

[1] h *added in margin in Ep.*; hroflititen *Erf. from* liciter *in Ep. (see
p. 56, fn. 8).*   [2] *perhaps explains* corrosos, *which in the probable
source occurs adjacent to* mordicus.   [3] conpsito *Erf.*   [4] eg
from e.   [5] c *from* s.   [6] *curved stroke as of* c *between* m *and*
u *in Ep.*   [7] *Lat. originally* magnifica?; *for this and the fore-
going Erf. has only* munificit.   [8] e *er. between* m *and* i *in Ep.*
[9] tonica *Erf.*   [10] mncus *Erf.*   [11] *from* scibla: *Ep.,* y *above* i
and letter er. *after* a.

lumbricus: regnwyrm.
612.
†luteum: crohha.
1255 †lupercal: haerg.
†lumbus: side.
†luscinia: naectegale.
†luscinius: forsc.
†lupus: wulf.

1260 †lupa: wylf.
†lupinare (-anaria?):
uulfholu.
†lumbulos: lendebrede.
lymphatico: woedendi.
575 (cp. 1221).
†lymbo (i): ðresi. (cp.
1228.)

1265 Manipulatim: þreat-
melum. 617.
mancus: anhendi. 626.
maforte (mafors): scyfla.
627.
manica: glof. 631.
manile: lebil. 633 (cp.
193).
1270 manitergium (nut): lin.
634.
†margo: obr.
malagma: salf. 635.
malus: apuldur. 636.
†mandras: eouuistras.
1275 †maceratus: þreatende.
mastigium: suiopan.
641.
manubium: waelreaf.
642.
manticum: hondful
beowes. 645.
†masca: grima.
1280 mascus: grima. 646.

marsopicus: fina. 648.
†marsuppia (marsupium):
ceodas.
marruca: snegl. 651.
majales (-is): bearug.
652.
1285 mango: mengio. 659.
maulistis (maulistēs):
scyend. 654.
mastic[h]e: huitcudu.
655.
malva: hocc, cottuc, vel
gearwan leaf. 656.
mar[r]ubium: biowyrt
vel hune. 657.
1290 matrix: quiða. 661.
†massa: clyne.
†mapalia: byre.
mars, martis: tiig. 663.
†magalia: byre. 155.
1295 †macilentus: gefaested.
†manere: bidan.
†madidum: obðaenit.

manica[1]: gloob—glob. 1268.

momentum: scytil *both*. 1325.

manile: lebil *both*. 1269; cp. 193.

manitergium—manutergium: liin—*lim. 1270.

635   *malagna—malagma*: salb *both*. 1272.

malus: apuldur—*apuldro. 1273.

martus—myrtus: uuyr *both*[2]. 1356.

melarium: milscapuldr—*milcapuldr[3]. 1302.

†*millefolium*[4]: gearuuae.

640   *molibus*: ormetum *both*. 1326.

mastigia: suipan—*suibæ[5]. 1276.

manubium—manuvium: uuaelreab—uuelreab. 1277.

melodium (-*ia*): suinsung—*ruinsung. 1303.

mustacia (cp. *mústax*)—*murtacia*: granae—granæ. 1343.

645   *manticum*: handful *beouuas—handful beouaes. 1278.

mascus (cp. -*ca*)—*marcus*: grima *both*[6]. 1280.

mergulus: scalfr *both*. 1304.

*marsopicus—*marpicus*: fina—*pina. 1281.

musiranus (*mus araneus*): screuua. 1344.

650   *mustella*: uuesulae *both*. 1345.

maruca: snegl[7]. 1283.

majalis: bearug. 1284.

mordacius: clofae—clofæ. 1327.

maulistis (*maulistḗs*): scyhend. 1286.

655   *mastic*[*h*]*e*: huuitquidu. 1287.

malva: cotuc *vel* geormantlab[8]. 1288.

marrubium[9]: hunae *vel* biouuyrt. 1289.

657a   *merx*: merze. 1304a.

---

[1] i *above er. in Ep.*   [2] *after* melarium (638) *in Erf.*   [3] milc-
apuldŕ.   [4] *curved stroke as of* c *between* m *and* i *in Ep.*   [5] *after*
malagma (635) *in Erf.*   [6] *after* myrtus (637) *in Erf.*   [7] *prec.*
by er.   [8] *curved stroke as of* c *between* r *and* m.   [9] *from*
murrubium, a *above expuncted and er. first* u.

†*madefacta*: geuueted.

†*machinamenta*: orðonc.

1300 †*mantega* (*-tica*): taeg.
(cp. Cp.[1] 20.)

mendacio conposito: ge-
regnade. 618.

melarium: mircapuldur.
638.

melodium (*-ia*): suin-
sung. 643.

1303a †*mea[n]dro*: bordan.

mergulus: scalfur. 647.

1304a *merx*: mertze. 657a.

1305 †*m[a]ereo*: groeto.

merula: oslę. 665.

megale (*mugalê*): hearma. 666.

†*medulla*: merg.

†*mercurium*: Woden.

1310 †*mentagra*[1]: bituihn.

†*merga* (*-us*): scraeb.

†*metricius*(*-cus?*): meder-
wyrhta.

†*milvus*: glioda.

†*milium* (*mille*): miil.

1315 *mirifillo* (*myriophyllon*):
gearwe. 623.

mimopora (*myoparo*):
ðeofscip. 630.

†*minaci*: hlibendri.

†*mitra*: haet.

mordicos(*-cus*): bibitne[2].
616.

1320 *molestissimum*: earbetlicust. 619.

monarchia: anuualda.
622.

modioli: *habae. 625.

morgit (*mulget*): milcit.
628 (cp. 1347a).

mosiclum (cp. *muscus*):
ragu. 629 (1332).

1325 *momentum*: scytel. 632.

molibus: ormetum. 640.

mordacius: clouae. 653.

†*movebor*: styrið.

†*moles*: falthing.

1330 †*molos[s]us*: roðhund.

†*morenula* (*mur-*): eil.

mosicum: ragu. (1324.)

†*mora* (*-rum*): heorot-
berge.

municeps: burgliod. 620.

1335 *munifica*[3]: cystigan. 621.

murica: gespon. 624.

†*murenula*: bool.

†*muluctra* (*mulctra*): ce-
oldre.

†*munila* (*monile*): baeg.

1340 †*muscipula*: muusfalle.

†*mucro*: mece.

mugil: haeced. 660.

---

[1] *elsewhere explained as 'toes'.*
p. 58, fn. 7.

[2] *see p. 58, fn. 2.*   [3] *see*

mulio: horsthegn. 1346.

margo (*mango*): mengio. 1285.

660   *mugil*: haecid—hecid. 1342.

matrix: quiða. 1290.

†*mergus*: scalfr.

mars, martis: tiig *both*. 1293.

mus, muris: mus *both*. 1348.

665   *merula*: oslae *both*. 1306.

megale (*mugalê*): hearma *both*. 1307.

Nausatio (cp. *nausea*), *vomitus*[1] *vel*: uulatung—uulating. 1357.

naviter: horsclicae *both*. 1358.

ninguit: *hsniuuith—sniuidh. 1379.

670   *nomisma—nomysma*: mynit—munit. 1383.

nux: hnutbea*m*—hnutbeam. 1394.

nigra spina: slachthorn—slachdorn. 1380 (cp. 957).

noctua: naechthraebn, *ali*[2] *dicunt* nectigalae—necthraebn,
         *nacthegelae. 1384.

†*nycticorax*—*nicticorax*[3]: naechthraebn—*nethhræbn.

675   *netila* (*nitela*): hearma *both*. 1369.

nasturcium (*nasturtium*): tuuncressa—leccressae. 1359.

nap[*h*]*t*[*h*]*a*: blaec teru *both*. 1360.

nugacitas—*nugatitas*: unnytnis *both*. 1395.

non subs[*i*]*civum*[4]: unfaecni—unfecni. 1386 (cp. 938).

680   *negotio—negotia*: unemotan—*unemo. 1371.

nebulonis[5]: scinlaecean—scinlecan. 1372.

nimbus: storm *both*. 1378.

nequiquam[6]—*nequicquam*: holunga *both*. 1373.

nepa: habern—hafern. 1370.

---

[1] fomitus *Erf.*   [2] alii *Erf.*   [3] *the first* c *looks like an un-*
finished x.   [4] subciuu*m Erf.*   [5] *from* nebolonis *in Ep.*, u *above*
first o.   [5] *curved stroke as of* c *between first* u *and* i.

mustacia (cp. *mústax*):
    granae. 644.
musiranus (*mus araneus*):
    screauua. 649.
1345 *mustela*[1]: uueosule. 650.
    mulio: horsðegn. 658.
    †*mugil*: heardhara.
1347a †*mulgit* (*-get*): milcit.
    (cp. 1323.)
    mus, muris: muus. 664.

    Nausatio (cp. *nausea*):
    uulatunc. 667.
    naviter: horsclice. 668.
    nasturcium[2] (*t*): tuun-
    cressa. 676.
1360 *nap[h]t[h]a*: blaec teoru.
    677.
    nap[h]t[h]a: tynder.
    685.
1361a *navat*: *frangat. 685a.
    navus (*nanus*), *pumilio*:
    duerg. 686.
    napis (*-us*): naep. 687.
    †*nazarei*: loccas.
1365 †*nabulum* (*naulum*): fere-
    scaet.
    †*naviter*: suiðfromlice.
    †*neptam* (*naphtham*): tyn-
    dre.

†*multabitur*: uuitnath.
1350 †*murilium*: byrgen.
    †*musca* (*masca*): eges-
    grima.
    †*musica*: myrgnis.
    †*murice*: wurman.
    †*musca*: flege.
1355 †*murus* (*morum*): braer.
    myrtus: uuir. 637.

†[*nectar, mel, vel vinum*
    vel: **carere*[3].]
    netila (*nitela*): hearma.
    675.
1370 *nepa*: haebern. 684.
    negotia: unemetta. 680.
    nebulonis: scinlaecan.
    681.
    nequiquam: holunga.
    683.
    †*netum*: gesiuwid.
1375 †*nervus*: sionu.
    †*necabantur*: aqualdun.
    †*nitorium*: spinil.
    nymbus[4] (*i*): storm. 682.
    ninguit: sniuwið. 669.
1380 *nigra spina*: slaghðorn.
    672 (cp. 1898).
    †*nixu*: werðeode.

---

[1] mustel: a.   [2] *from* nastarcium, u *above expuncted second* a.
[3] *prob. represents Lat.* carenum.   [4] *originally* nimbus, *as shown*
by alph. order.

685   *nap[h]t[h]a¹, genus fomenti, id est*: tyndir—*ryndir. 1361.
685a *navat*: *frangat *both*. 1361a.
      nanus vel pumilio²: duerg *both*. 1362.
      napi (-us): naep—nep. 1363.
      nodus: ost *both³*. 1387.

      Oscillae—oscille (-a): totridan *both*. 1466.
690   *oscitantes*: ganaendae—ganendæ. 1467.
      origanum: uurmillae—uurmillæ. 1452.
      osma (osmé): suicae *both*. 1468.
      oppillavit: gigiscdae—giscdae⁴. 1447.
      obliquum: scytihalt—*sestihalth. 1403.
695   *obnixus*: strimaendi—strimendi. 1404.
      obreptione: criopungae—criupungae. 1405.
      oridanum (origanum): elonae *both⁵*. 1453.
      orcus—orci (-a? urceus?): orc *both*. 1454.
      opere plumario⁶: bisiuuidi uuerci—*bisiuuisidi uerci. 1450.
700   *olor*: suan *both*. 1436.
      obuncans: genicldae—*gensccilde⁷. 1408.
      o[b]ligia: nettae—*nectae. 1437.
      obestrum: beost—*beoth. 1406.
      ogastrum: aeggimang—aeggimong. 1435.

---

¹ *first a from* e *in Erf.*   ² *punilio Erf.*   ³ *after* nequicquam (683) *in Erf.*   ⁴ g̅ (*between columns*) scdae.   ⁵ *second*
e *from another letter in Erf.*   ⁶ plumari *Ep.*   ⁷ *fourth letter
meant as* y?

†*noctua, ulula*: ule.
nomisma: mynit. 670.
noctua: naehthraefn.
673.
1385 †*navalia (nov-)*: faelging.
non subs[i]civum: un-
faecni. 679 (cp. 1950).
nodus: wrasan, ost. 688.
†*notae*: speccan.
†*notatus*: oncunnen.
1390 †*noverca*: steopmoder.
†*no[r]ma*: rihtebred.

†*Obolitio*: eðung[1].
1400 †*obsides*: gislas.
†*obrizum (y)*: smaete
gold.
†*obriguit*: gefreos.
obliquum: scytehald.
694.
obnixus: strimendi. 695.
1405 *obreptione*: criopunge.
696.
obestrum: beost. 703.
†*optimates*[2]: gesiðas.
obuncans: genyclede.
701.
obtenuit (tin): forcuom,
bigaet. 706.
1410 *obnixe*: geornlice. 708.

†*numularius, nummorum
praerogatur (-or)*:
miyniteri.
†*nurus*: snoro.
nux: hnutbeam. 671.
1395 *nugacitas*: unnytnis.
678.
†*nucl[e]i*: cirnlas.
†*nullo negotio*: naenge
earbeðe.
†*numquid*: ne huru is.

†*obunca*: crump.
†*obvix (obvius)*: wiðerstal.
obligamentum: lyb,
lybsn. 711.
†*obstruit*: fordytte.
1415 †*object[a]e*: ongen sette.
†*objectus*: uuitsetnis.
†*obruere*: oberuurecan.
†*obsedatus (sid)*: gislhada.
†*obturat*: *folclaemid.
1420 †*obtinuit*: ofercuom.
†*objectionibus*: gestalum.
†*obnoxius*: scyldig.
†*obex*: ogengel.
†*obicula*: geocstecca.
1425 *occupavit*: onette. 712.
†*ocreis*: baangeberg.

---

[1] *intended to explain* abolitio?
by alph. order.

[2] *originally* obtimates, *as shown*

705 *oresta*: thres *both*. 1455.
  obtenuit (tin): bigaet *both*. 1409.
  ordinatissimam: *ŏ gisettan—*a *girettan. 1458.
  *obnixe—*obnixae*: geornlice—*geornlicet. 1410.
  omnimoda (-o): oeghuuelci ŏinga¹—oeghuelci *hadga. 1442.
710 *orbita*: huueolrad—*hueolraat. 1459.
  *obligamentum—*oblicamentum*: lybb—*libb. 1413.
  occupavit: onettae—*onete. 1425.
  †*occas*: fealga. cp. 1427.
  ortigomera (ortygometra): edischaen—*edischenim. 1460.
715 *occiput—*occipud*: hreacca—hrĕca. 1429.
  ostriger: bruunbesu—bruunbesu. 1469.
  †——*occupavit*: *geomette.
  olor graece, latin² cignus (y): aelbitu—*ĕbitu. 1439.
  [*omentum*: *maffa³—*naffa³. 1443.]
720 †*occipitium*: *snecca.

---

¹ ŏi:nga; i *from* n?   ² ḡr latin· *Ep.*; ḡ latinae *Erf.*   ³ *represents Lat.* mappa.

†*occa*: faelging. cp.
713.

†*occubuit (-bavit)*: ge-
crong.

occiput: hrecca. 715.

1430 †*occabat*: egide.

†*ocearium (acia-)*: staeli.
(55.)

†*offendit*: moette.

†*offirmans*: claemende.

†*officit*: werdit.

1435 *ogastrum*: aeggimong[1].
704 (1438, cp. 105).

olor: suon. 700.

o[b]ligia: nettae. 702.

olgastrum: aeggimong.
(1435.)

olor, cicnus (y): aelbitu.
718.

1440 †*olim*: singale.

†*olastrum*: staeb.

omnimodo: oeghwelce
ðinga. 709.

[*omentum: maffa*[2].
719.]

†*omer (omen)*: hael.

1445 †*onocratallus (onocro-
talus)*: feolufer.

†*op[p]ilavit*: forclaemde.

oppilavit, clausit: ge-
giscte. 693.

†*opinare (-i)*: resigan.

[1] first g on er.

†*op[p]ortunitatem*: ge-
hydnis.

1450 *opere plumario*: bisiudi
werci. 699.

†*oppilatae*: bisparrade.

origanum: wurmille.
691.

oridanum (origanum):
eolone. 697.

orcus (-a? urceus?): orc.
698.

1455 *oresta*: ŏres. 705.

†*[h]or[r]ipilatio*: celi-
wearte.

†*orcus*: ðyrs, heldiobul.

ordinatissimam: þa
gesettan. 707.

orbita: hueolrád. 710.

1460 *ortigomera (ortygometra)*: edischen. 714.

†*oratores*: spelbodan.

†*ordinatus*: gehaeplice.

†*or[diens?]*: onginnendi.

†*orion*: eburðring.

1465 †*orbitae*: last.

oscillae (-a): totridan.
689.

oscitantes: geongendi.
690.

osma (osmẽ): suice. 692.

ostriger: bruunbeosu.
716.

[2] see p. 66, fn. 3.

—— *Procuratio*: *scur. 1625.

promulserit (*perm*-): lithircadae—lithircadæ. 1626.

profusis—*profussis*: genyctfullum—genyctfullum. 1627.

promulgarunt: scribun *both*. 1628.

725 *provehit*: gifraemith—gifremit. 1629.

perfidia: treulesnis *both*[1]. 1533.

pro captu: faengae *both*. 1630.

pro (*per*) *maritima*: saegesetu—*saegaesetu. 1631.

percommodo[2], *matunos*—*percommoda, matutinos*: sua cendlic, morgenlic—sua cendlic, *morgendlic. 1534/5.

730 *praetextatus*—*pretextatus*: gigeruuid—*gigarauuit. 1632.

partim: sume daeli—sumae dæli. 1471.

pudor: scamu—*scoma. 1679.

propropera[3] (*praep*-)—*propepera*: fraehraedae *both*. 1633.

privigna, filia sororis, id est: nift *both*. 1634.

735 *palpitans*: brocdaettendi—*brogdaethendi. 1472.

piraticum—*piraticam*: uuicingsceadan—uuicingsceadae. 1579.

percrebuit: mere uueard—mere uuard. 1536.

perduellium (-*io*): þorgifect—*dorhgifecilae. 1537.

proscribit: ferred. 1635.

740 *paludamentum, genus vestimenti bellici, id est*: haecilae—hecæli. 1474.

per seudoterum—*per seuduterum* (*pseudothyrum*): þorh ludgaet —dorh ludgaet[4]. 1538.

percitus: hraed[5]—*hrad. 1539.

propensior[6]: tylg *both*. 1636.

profligatus—*profligatis*: forsleginum—*faerlslaegmum. 1637.

745 *pel[l]ices*: cebisae—*caebis. 1540.

phisillos (*Psylli*): leceas *both*. 1578.

praerupta: staegilrae—stegelræ. 1638.

---

[1] u *er. between second e and s in Ep.*   [2] *third o unclear.*   [3] a *damaged.*   [4] *follows* percitus (742) *in Erf.*   [5] h *added in margin in Ep.*   [6] *or from* us *in Erf.*

1470 †*Patrimonium*: gestrion.
partim: sume daeli. 731.
palpitans: brogdetende.
735.
particulatim: styccime-
lum. 751.
*paludamentum, genus
vestimenti bellici*: hae-
cile. 740.
1475 †*patrocinium*: mundbyrd.
†*paranimphus* (*y*): dryht-
guma. (1514.)
†*pal*[*a*]*estra*: plaega.
†*pastinare*: settan.
†*palatina*: raecedlic.
[1479a †*panice*: *ru seam*[1].]
1480 *parcae*: wyrde. 764.
parcas: burgrune. 761.
1481a *parabsides* (*rops*): gauu-
tan. 764a.
†*palearibus*: deadraege-
lum.
†*palas*: scoble.
papilio: fiffalde. 768.
1485 *papula*: wearte. 771.
pampinus: *crous. 773.
papilivus (*papyrus*):
*wiolucscel. 781.
palingenesean (*palin-*

genesia): edscaeft.
783.
paneta (*patina*): holo-
ponne. 784.
1490 *paneta* (*patina*): disc.
786.
†*paupilius* (*papyrus*):
scaldhulas.
papula: spryng. 791.
†*pandis*: geapum.
†*patruus*: faedra.
1495 †*patruelis*: faedran sunu.
†*patruelis*: geaduling.
†*paxillum, palum*: naegl.
†*panpila*: wibl.
†*panuculum* (*panuncula*):
uuefl.
1500 †*palagra* (*poda-*): ecilma.
†*pascsos* (*passus*): geros-
cade.
pastinaca: walhmore.
794.
papirum (*y*): eorisc. 795.
pangebant: faedun[2]. 797.
1505 *palla*: rift. 801.
parula (cp. *parus*):
mase. 806.
papilio: buterflege. 817.
paliurus: sinfulle. 819.
pavo: pauua. 826.

---

[1] *prob. not Old English; for* puniceum: roseam? *Cp. the all-Latin entry in Cp. and EE* phanicem [phanicæn *Erf.*] (*for* phoeniceum): roseum.   [2] *apparently intended to explain* pingebant.

probus: ferth—fert. 1639.

proterunt[1]: treddun—*treodun. 1640.

750 *permixtum* (*-im*): gimengidlicę—gimaengidlicæ. 1542.

particulatim: styccimelum—*scyccimelum. 1473.

proterentem: naetendnae *both*. 1641.

pertinaciter[2]: anuuillicae *both*. 1543.

penduloso[3]: halði[4]—*hahdi. 1541.

755 *pessum*: spilth *both*. 1544.

petisse: sochtae—*scochtae. 1545.

per anticipationem: þorch obust—dorh obust. 1546.

provectae[5]: frodrae *both*. 1642.

provectae[5]—*provecta*: gifraemid—gifremid. 1643.

760 *per vispellones* (*vespill-*): þorch[6] byrgeras—dorh *buyrgenas.
     1547.

parcas: burgrunae—burgrunæ. 1481.

pliadas (*-es*): sifunsterri—*funsterri. 1599.

perpendiculum: colþred—coldraed. 1548.

parcae—*parce*: uuyrdae *both*. 1480.

764a *parabsides* (*rops*)—*parapsidam*: gabutan *both*. 1481a.

765 [*im*]*petigo*: tetr *both*. 1550 (cp. 502).

puncto, foramine, in quo pedes vinctorum[7] *tenentur*[8] *in ligno
    cubitali*[9], *spatio*[10] *interjecto, id est*: cosp *both*. 1680.

pulenta (*polenta*): briig *both*. 1681.

papilio—*papilici*: fifaldae—uiualdra. 1484.

pice, sevo (*b*): unamaelti *sperwi—*cinamelti *spreui. 1581.

770 *pustula*: angseta[11]—*angreta. 1682.

papula: uueartae—uearte. 1485.

praxinus (*fraxinus*): aesc—esc. 1651.

pampinus—*panipinus*[12]: cros—*crous. 1486.

---

[1] perterunt *Erf.*   [2] pertinatiter *Erf.*   [3] penduloro *Erf.*
[4] *or for* pendulos: ohaldi (*cp. Cp.* 1572, *EE* 838)?   [5] *from* pro-
fectae *in Ep.*, u *above* f.   [6] c *half* er.   [7] uinctoriu*m Erf.*
[8] tenetur *Erf.*   [9] cubitalis *Erf.*   [10] spacio *Erf.*   [11] an:gseta.
[12] *second* i *from* a.

1510 †*passus*: faeðm *vel* tuegen
   stridi.
palumbes: cuscote. 829.
pastellus (-*illus*): hunig-
   aeppel. 830.
pansa: scaffoot. 832.
†*paranymphus*: dryht-
   guma. (1476.)
1515 †*parumper*: huonhlot*um*.
papaver: popei. (1621.)
†*pariter*: gelice.
†*paruca* (cp. *parus*):
   hicae.
†*palpant*[*i*]*um*: olecten-
   dra.
1520 †*palmula*: steorroðor.
†*parricidio*: megcualm.
†*paciscitur*: geðingadon.
†*palagdrigus*(*podagricus*):
   ecilmehti.
†*pantigatum* (*pantaga-
   thus*): uuduhona.
1525 *palina* (*balaena*): hran.
   (267.)
†*paleae*: aegnan.
†*pabulatores*: horshior-
   das.
†*passim*: styccimelum.
†*part*[*h*]*ica*: reodnaesc.
1530 †*perstrenue*:fromlice.(cp.
   1917.)

†*pedisequa*: ðignen.
†*perpessum est*: aðroten
   is.
perfidia: treuleasnis.
   726.
1534/5 *percommoda, matutinos*:
   sua cenlic, morgenlic.
   729.
percrebuit: mere wearð.
   737.
perduellium (-*io*): þorh-
   gefeht. 738.
per seudoterum (*pseudothyrum*): ðorh lud-
   gæt. 741.
percitus: hraed. 742.
1540 *pel*[*l*]*ices*: cebise. 745.
penduloso (-*ulo*): haldi[1].
   754.
permixtum: gemenget-
   lic. 750.
pertinaciter: anuuillice.
   753.
pessum: spilth. 755.
1545 *petisse*: sohte. 756.
per anticipationem: ðorh
   obst. 757.
per vispellones (*vespill*-):
   ðorh byrgeras. 760.
perpendiculum: colðred.
   763.

[1] *see p. 70, fn. 4.*

perna: flicci *both*. (804) 1551.

775   *pituita*: gibrec—gibreec. 1580.

pres et vas—praes et vas: byrgea *both*. 1652.

pus: uuorsm—*uuorsin. 1683.

pedo[1] *vel paturum*: fetor *both*. 1552.

praetersorim—praetorsorum: paad *both*. 1654.

780   *prifeta*: thriuuuintri steor—*triuumtri steur. 1655.

papiluus[2] (*papyrus*): ilugsegg—*ilugseg. 1487.

pun[c]tus: brord—broord. 1685.

palingenesean—palingeneseon (-esía): edscaept *both*. 1488.

patena (-ina): holopannae. 1489.

785   *pingit*: faehit—*faethit. 1582.

patena (-ina): disc *both*. 1490.

pila: thothor—*thorr. 1584.

*prorigo—prurigo: gycinis *both*. 1658.

pittacium: clut *both*. 1585.

790   *ptysones (ptisanas)*: berecorn[3] berendae[4]—berecorn beren-
        dæ[4]. 1677.

papula vel pustula: spryng *vel* tetr *both*. 1492.

populus: birciae *both*. 1609.

plantago vel septenerbia (septemnerva)—plantaga vel septinerbia:
        uuaegbradae—uuegbradæ. 1601.

pastinaca—*pastinacia: uualhmorae *both*. 1502.

795   *paperum—papirum (papyrus)*: eorisc *both*. 1503.

pictus acu—*pictis acu: mið naeðlae[5] asiuuid—mid nedlæ
        asiuuid. 1591.

pangebant: faedun[6]—*fædum. 1504.

polimita (lym): hringfaag—*hrnigfaag. 1612.

pronus: nihol *both*. 1659.

---

[1] *vertical stroke between* d *and* o *in Ep.*   [2] papil:uus *Ep.*
[3] *from* bericorn, *second* e *above* i.   [4] *apparently an erroneous ex-*
planation of feriente, *which follows* ptisanas *in the probable source.*
[5] na *from* m.   [6] *see p. 69, fn. 2.*

†*per hironiam* (*ironiam*):
ðorh hosp.

1550 [*im*]*petigo*: teter. 765
(cp. 1047).

perna: flicci. 774.

pedo, vel paturum: feo-
tur. 778.

†*perpendiculum*: pundur.

†*penuria*: weðl.

1555 †*percellitur*: bið slaegen.
(cp. 1565.)

†*pervicax*: ðroehtig.

†*pero*: himming.

†*pessum*: clifhlep.

pessul[*us*]: haeca. 803.

1560 *peducla* (*pediculus*): luus.
812.

petra[1] *focaria, i. silex*:
flint. 805.

pendulus: ridusende.
816.

pella: sadulfelge. 818
(cp. 388).

pecten: camb. 825.

1565 †*percellitur*: slaegen. (cp.
1555.)

†*pes*: fot.

†*perstant*: tioludun.

†*persolvio* (-*vo*): ic
ðrouuio.

petulans: wraene. 835.

1570 *perpendit*: aehtað. 836.

perstromata, ornamenta:
steba[2]. 837.

pendulus: ohældi. 838.

†*pellis*: fel.

†*perpes*: hraed[3].

1575 †*petuita* (*pi.*): sped.

†*pectica*: slahae.

†*philosophus*: uðuuta.

phisillos (*Psylli*): leceas.
746.

1578a *phitecus* (*pithecus*): apa.
827.

piraticam: wicincscea-
ðan. 736.

1580 *pituita*: gebrec. 775.

pice, saevo (*sebo*): una-
maelte smeoruue.769.

pingit: faehit. 785.

†*pistrimum* (-*num*): cofa.

pila: thothr. 787.

1585 *pittacium, osperi* (*hōspe-
rei*?): clut, cleot.
789.

†*pisum*: piosan.

†*pistrilla*: cofincel.

†*pillentes* (*pile-*): bere.

†*pirus*: pirge.

1590 †*pinus*: furhwudu.

pictus acu: mið nethle
asiowid. 796.

---

[1] *from* patra, e *above expuncted first* a.   [2] *not certainly Old English.*   [3] *apparently intended to explain* praepes.

800   *prodimur*: birednae—biraednae. 1661.

     palla: rift—*ritf. 1505.

     platisa—platissa (*-essa*): flooc—floc. 1602.

     pessul[*us*]: haca *both*. 1559.

     perna: *flicii. (774) 1551.

805   *petra focaria*: flint *both*. 1561.

     parrula: masae *both*. 1506.

     porfyrio (*ph*)—*porfirio*: felofor—*felusor. 1613.

     picus: fina *vel* higrae *both*. 1592.

     porcopiscis: styria *both*. 1614.

810   *porcaster*[1]: foor—for. 1615.

     porcellus: faerh *both*. 1616.

     peducla (*pediculus*): luus *both*. 1560.

     pulix[2] (*-ex*): fleah—*floc. 1684.

     proflicta (*-igata*): forslaegẹn *both*. 1662.

815   *proventus*: spoed *both*. 1663.

     pendulus[3]: ridusaendi[4]—ridusendi. 1562.

     papilo (*-io*): buturfliogae—*buturfliogo. 1507.

     pella: sadulfelgae *both*. 1563 (cp. 283).

     palurus—palliurus (*paliurus*): sinfullae—sinfullæ. 1508.

820   *pix, picis, id*: pic[5] *both*. 1593.

     pollux (*-ex*): thuma—thumo. 1617.

     prunus: plumae *both*. 1664.

     pullis—pollix.(*pollis = pollen*): grytt *both*. 1620.

     **popaver—*papaver*: popaeg—*papoeg. 1621.

825   *pecten*: camb *both*. 1564.

     *pavo—*paud*: pauua *both*. 1509.

     phitecus (*pithecus*): apa—*capa. 1578a.

     progna—progina (*Procne*): suualuae[6]—suualuuæ. 1665.

---

[1] *er.* (s?) *between* o *and* r *in Ep.*   [2] *from* pulux *in Ep.*, i *above* expuncted *second* u.   [3] pend: ulus *Ep.*   [4] ri: dusaendi *Ep.* [5] x *er. between* i *and* c *in Erf.*   [6] *dot above* e.

picus: higre, fina. 808.

pix, picis: pic. 820.

†*pilus*: her.

1595 †*piceca*: neb.

†*piscis*: fisc.

†*pistillus*: gnidil.

†*plunas* (*prunus*): plum-
treu.

pliadas(*-es*): sibunsterri.
762.

1600 †*plumum* (*prunus*): plu-
mae. (cp. 1664.)

plantago: uuegbrade.
793.

platisa (*-essa*): flooc.
802.

†*plect*[*u*]*ra*: auunden.

†*pla*[*n*]*taria*: setin.

1605 †*plus minus*: ymb ðæt.

†*polenta*: smeodoma.

†*postena*: boga.

†*portio*: hlyte.

populus: birce. 792.

1610 †*politis*[1]: smoeðum.

†*portentum*: scin.

pilimita[2] (*polym-*):
hringfaag. 798.

porfyrio (*ph*): feolufer.
807.

porcopiscis: styrga. 809.

1615 *porcaster*: foor. 810.

porcellus: faerh. 811.

pollux (*-ex*): ðuma. 821.

†*poleo* (*-io*): scaebe.

†*pollinis*: gruiit.

1620 *pollis*: grytt. 823.

popaver (*pa*.): popæg.
824 (1516).

†*posthumus*: unlab.

†*pons*: brycg.

†*procax*: huuæl.

1625 *procuratio*: sciir. 721.

promulserit (*perm-*):
liðercade. 722.

profusis: genyhtfullum.
723.

promulgarunt: scribun.
724.

provehit: gefremið. 725.

1630 *pro captu*: fenge. 727.

pro (*per*) *maritima*: sae-
geseotu. 728.

praetextatus: gegeruuid.
730.

propropera (*praepro-
pera*): fraehraeðe. 733.

privigna: nift. 734 (cp.
1655a).

1635 *proscripsit*: faerred. 739.

propensior: tylg. 743.

profligatis: forslaege-
num. 744.

---

[1] po: litis.   [2] *originally* polimita, *as shown by alph. order.*

palumbes—*palumpes: cuscutan—cuscotae[1]. 1511.

830 *pastellas—pastellus (pastillus)*: hunaegaepl[2]—*cænegaepl.
   1512.

pulium—puleum (pulegium): duuergaedostae—duergaedostae.
   1686.

pansa: scabfoot—scaabfot. 1513.

†*pituita*: gillistrae.

†——— *pedetemptim, caute, quasi pede temptans vel*: fotmelum[3].

835 *petulans vel spurcus*[4]: uuraeni—ureni. 1569.

perpendit: aectath—aechtath. 1570.

perstromata, ornamenta: stefad *brum[5]—staefad *brum[5].
   1571.

pendulus: ohaelði—oheldi. 1572.

838 a†———*peltam, auram*: del.

---

[1] *after* paud (826) *in Erf.* [2] g *above er.*; *second* e *from another*
letter. [3] *Ep. has only the Latin*: pedetemtim caute quasi temtans
pede. [4] purcus *from* purcos *Erf., second* u *above* o. [5] *not*
certainly Old English.

praerupta: staegilre. 747.

probus: ferht. 748.

1640 *proterunt*: tredun. 749.

proterentem: naetendne.
752.

praefectae (*provectae*):
frodre. 758.

profecta (*provecta*): ge-
fremid. 759.

†*praecipitat*: ascufið.

1645 †*praecipita*: afael.

†*praefaricator* (*v*): recci-
leas.

†*praestantior*: fromra.

†*praesidium*: spoed.

†*praestante*: fremmen-
du*m*.

1650†*proteri*: brecan.

praxinus (*fr.*), *viridus*
(*-is*), *color*[1] *vel*: aesc.
772.

1651a †*prosapia*: ob cniorisse.

pr[*a*]*es et vas*: byrga.
776.

†*pruina*: hrim.

pretersorim: paad. 779
(1676).

1655 *prifeta*: *ŏriuuintra
steor. 780.

1655a †*prifignus* (*v*): nefa. (cp.
1634.)

†*provehitur*: fremid.

†*prunas*: gloede.

prurigo: gycenis. 788.

pronus: nihold. 799.

1660 †*pronuba*: heorðsuaepe.

prodimur: birednae. 800.

proflicta (*-igata*): for-
slaegen. 814.

praeventus (*pro*): spoed.
815.

prunus: plumę. 821.

1665 *progna* (*Procne*): suu-
aluue. 828.

†*praesorium* (*press-*):
pund.

†*prorostris*[2]: haehsed-
lum.

†*praeceps*: trondendi.

†*procus*: brydguma.

1670 †*prodigus*: stryndere.

†*praesum*[*p*]*tio*: fore-
nyme.

†*propugnaculum*: briost-
biorg.

†*proveho*: fyrŏru.

†*proceres*: geroefan.

1675 †*propero* (*-e*?): hraeðe.

praetersorium: paad.
(1654.)

ptysones (*ptisanas*): berecorn beorende[3]. 790.

---

[1] *the last two words are apparently intended to explain* prasinus.
[2] *two words* (pro r.)?   [3] *see p. 72, fn. 4.*

Qualiis[1]—qualus: mand *both*. 1689.

840 *quisquiliae*: *aehrian—*ægrihan. 1696.

quadripertitum: cocunung *both*. 1690.

quacumquemodo[2]—quocumquemodo: *gihuuuelci uuaega—gihuelci uuegi. 1700.

quacumque: suae suithae—suue suidae. 1691.

quantisper—*quantusper: suae suithae—suue *sidae. 1692.

845 *quoquomodo—*quoquemodo*: aengi þinga—aengi dinga. 1701.

quin etiam: aec þan—aec don. 1695.

quaternio—quaterno: quatern—quaterni. 1693.

quinquefolium: hraebnęs foot—hræfnæs foot. 1697 (1084).

**quiquenervia—quinquenervia*: leciuuyrt—leciuyrt. 1698.

850 *Renunculus*: lundlaga[3] *both*. 1712.

radium: hrisil—hrisl. 1704.

rictus: graennung[4]—*graemung. 1738.

runcina—*runtina: locaer *vel* sceaba *both*. 1755.

rabulus (-a): flitere in *ebhatis *both*. 1705.

855 *rema (rheuma)*: stream *both*. 1714.

r[h]euma: gibrec—gebrec. 1717.

roscinia (luscinia): nectaegalae—*necegle. 1746.

---

[1] *might also be read* qualns.   [2] a *from* o.   [3] *from* lunolaga *in Ep.*, d *above* er. o.   [4] graen:n.

†*putamina*: hnyglan.
pudor: scomo. 732.
1680 *puncto*: cosp. 766.
pulenta (*polenta*): briig.
767.
pustula: oncgseta. 770.
pus: *uuorm. 777.

pulix (*-ex*): flęh. 813.
1685 *pun*[*c*]*tus*: *brond. 782.
pulleium (*pulegium*):
duergedostle. 831.
†*pullus*: brid.
†*pulla*: blaco.

Qualus: mand. 839.
1690 *quadripertitum*: cocunung. 841.
quacumque: suae suiðe.
843.
quantisper: suae suiðe.
844.
quaternio: quatern. 847.
†*quadrare*: *geeblicadun.
1695 *quin etiam*: aec ðon.
846.

quisquiliae: aegnan.
840.
quinquefolium: hraefnes
foot. 848.
quinquenervia: leciwyrt.
849.
†*quintus*: giululing.
1700 *quocumque modo*: ge-
hwelci wega. 842.
quoquomodo: aenge
þinga. 845.

† *Raster* (*rastrum*): egiðe.
†*rancidis*: bitrum.
radius: hrisl. 851.
1705 *rabulus* (*-a*): flitere in
eobotum. 854.
rationat[*i*]*o*: ambaect.
866.
†*rabies*: geris.
rancor: troh. 874.

rastros: mettocas. 878.
1710 *ramnus* (*rhamnos*):
ðeofeðorn[1]. 880.
†*radio*: gabulrond.
renunculus: lundlaga.
850.
†*retentare*: stouuigan.
rema (*rheuma*): stream.
855.

[1] ðeofe:ðorn.

resina: teru *both*. 1716.

respuplica (respublica): cynidom *both*[1]. 1719.

860   *rien (renes)*: lęndino—lendino. 1740.

*radinape—*rodinare*: lelothrae—lelothre. 1747.

rostrum: neb *vel* scipes[2] celae—neb *vel* scipes cæle. 1748.

robor (-ur): aac *both*. 1749.

reciprocato: gistaebnęndrae—*gistaebnen. 1721.

865   *reclines*: suae haldae—*suuaeldae[3]. 1722.

rationat[i]o[4]: ambect—*ambaet. 1706.

recessus: helustras *both*. 1723.

rostratum: tindicti *both*. 1750.

relatu: spelli *both*. 1720.

870   *remota*: framadoenre—*framadoændrae. 1724.

rigore: heardnissae *both*. 1742.

reserat: andleac *both*. 1725.

rostris: foraeuuallu*m* *vel* tindu*m*—foreuuallu*m* *vel* tindum.
       1751.

rancor: throh, *vel invidia*[5], *vel odium*—throch. 1708.

875   *remex*: roedra *both*. 1726.

rumex (-en): edroc *both*. 1756.

ridimiculae—ridimiculi (redimicula): cyniuuithan *both*. 1743.

rastros, ligones, id: mettocas—*metticas. 1709.

ruscus (-um): cnioholaen—*cniolen. 1759.

880   *ramnus (rhamnos)*: thebanthorn—*thebanthron. 1710.

---

[1] i *from* o *in Erf.*
also be read suuoeldae.
Ep.

[2] sci: : es, *with* p *above the* er.
[4] *second* o *from* i *in Ep.*

[3] *might*
[5] inui : dia

1715 †*refugium*: geberg.

    resina: teoru. 858.

    r[h]euma: gebrec. 856.

    †*reses*: slaec.

    †*respuplica* (*b*): cyne-
doom. 859.

1720 *relatu*: spelli. 869.

    reciprocato: gestaef-
nendre. 864.

    reclines: suae halde.
865.

    recessus: heolstras. 867.

    remota: from adoenre.
870.

1725 *reserat*: onlaec. 872.

    remex: roeðra. 875.

    †*repagula*: sale.

    †*reciprocis*: wrixlindum.

    †*relatio*: eðcuide.

1730 †*retorto*: geðraune.

    †*renis* (*-es*): heðir.

    †*rediv[iv]a*: aettaelg.

    †*reverant* (*ne.*): spunnun.

    †*respectus*: etsith.

1735 †*reponile*: gearnuuinde.

    †*reciprocatu* (*-to? -tum?*):
uurixlende.

    †*retiunculas* (*ra.*): re-
sunge.

    rictus: grennung. 852.

    †*rimosa*: cionecti.

1740 *rien* (*renes*): laendino.
860.

†*rima* (*rhythmus*): getael.

rigore: heardnisse.
871.

ridimiculae (*redimicula*):
cynewiððan. 877.

†*rigentia*: forclingendu.

1745 †*ripariolus*: staeðsuual-
we.

roscinia (*luscinia*): naectegale. 857 (cp. 52).

rodinope: lelothrae.
861.

rostrum: neb *vel* scipes
caeli. 862.

robor (*-ur*), *arbor*: aac.
863.

1750 *rostratum*: tindecte.
868.

rostris: foreuuallum *vel*
tindum. 873.

†*roscido*: deawe.

†*rostri* (*-a*): tindas.

†*rotnum*: nabogar.

1755 *runcina*: locer, sceaba.
853.

rumex (*-en*): edric. 876.

†*rubigo*: brond, oom.

†*ruber*: read.

ruscus (*-um*): cnioholen.
879.

1759a †*rubisca*: saeltna.

1759b †*rubisca*: raedda, *rabi-
sca.*

Salebrae: thuerhfyri *both*. 1761.

sibba (*fibula*?): sigil *both*. 1856 (cp. 408).

scalbellum—scabellum (*scalpellum*): bredisern—bredisaern. 1793.

scrobibus: furhum *both*. 1793a.

885   *sartago*: bredipannae—*breitibannæ. 1762.

sarcinatum: gisiuuid[1]—gesiuuid[1]. 1763.

sarculum, ferrum, id[2]: uueadhoc *both*. 1764.

sternutatio: fnora—*huora. 1909.

sarta tecta: gifoegnissae—*gefegnessi. 1765.

890   *sentina*: lectha, *ubi multae aqu*[a]*e colliguntur in navem*[3]—lechta. 1833.

*scalprum—*scalbrum*: byris, *vel ut* *ali thuear*m*—byris, *vel ut alii* duæram. 1795.

salix: salch—salh. 1767.

sambucus: ellaen—ellae. 1775.

scirpea: *lerb, *de qua mat*[t]*a conficitur*—lebrae. 1804.

895   *serpillum* (*y*): bradae leac—brade lec[4]. 1835.

stabula: seto *both*. 1903.

surum (*-a*): sparuua—sparua. 1944.

sagulum: loda *both*. 1779.

struere: stridae—streidæ. 1910.

900   *seditio*: unsibb—unsib. 1836.

secessum—secessus: helostr *both*. 1838.

sc[a]*ena*: sceadu[5] *both*. 1801.

sanguinis: *cneorissa—cneorissae. 1780.

†*scina* (*scaena*?): grima *both*. (953.)

905   *seta*: byrst *both*. 1837.

---

[1] *apparently intended to explain* sartum; *cp. Cp.* 1773 *and the all-Latin gloss in Cp.* sarcitum (*for* sartum): consutum. [2] surculum id *est* ferru*m Erf.* [3] ubi multae aquae colligu*ntur* in una*m* naue*m Erf.* [4] *foll. on the same line by* sylenoru*m*. [5] *from* sceado *in Ep.*, u *above* o.

1760 †*Sab[u]lo*: molde.
      salebrae: þuerhfyri. 881.
      sartago: brediponne.
      885.
      sarcinatum: gesiouuid¹.
      886 (1774).
      sarculum: uueodhoc.
      887.
1765 *sarta tecta*: gefoegnisse.
      889.
      †*saevo (sebo)*: *unslit
      smeoro. (cp. 1846.)
      salix: salh. 892.
      †*sagax*: gleu.
      †*sarmentum*: spraec.
1770 †*salibaribus (iva)*: mið-
      lum.
      †*sarcofago (sarcophagus)*:
      licbeorg.
      †*sacellorum*: haerga.
      †*sarcio*: siouu.
      sarcinatum: gesiowid.
      (1763.)
1775 *sambucus*: ellaern. 893.
      †*sandalium*: scete, loða.
      †*sambucus (-ca)*: suegl-
      horn.
      †*salum*: haeb.
      sagulum: loða. 898.

1780 *sanguinis*: cniorisse.
      903.
      sardinas: heringas. 909.
      saginabant: maestun.
      930.
      sandix: uueard. 950.
      sardas: smeltas. 949.
1785 †*saliunca*: sure.
      salum: seeg *vel mare*.
      966.
      salsa: sure. 973.
      †*sarabar[a]e*: braeccę²
      dicitur.
      †*satiare*: asoedan.
1790 †*sacra, orgia*: edmelu.
      †*scolonia (ascalonia)*:
      cipe.
      †*scabellum*: windfona³.
      scalpellum: bredisern.
      883.
1793a *scrobibus*: furum. 884.
      †*scopa[e]*: besma.
1795 *scalprum*: byrs *vel*
      þuarm. 891.
      †*scamma*: feld.
      †*saltuum*: feltha.
      †*Scylla*: eduuelle⁴.
      †*scansio*: scyrft.
1800 †*sceptra*: onwald.

---

¹ *see p. 82, fn. 1.*   ² *not certainly Old English; cp. the all-Latin
gloss in EE* sarabarę [-bara *Erf.*]: braccae lingua [lingui *Ep.*] Persarum.
³ *apparently intended to explain* flabellum.   ⁴ *prob. intended to
explain* Charybdis.

scarpinat: scripit haen—scripit hæn. 1805.

†*scalpellum*: byris *both*.

sturnus: staer—*sterm. 1911.

scorelus: emer *both*. 1810.

910 *sardinas*—*sandinas*: heringas *both*. 1781.

scira (sciurus): aqueorna—aquorna. 1811.

scrofa: sugu—*ruga. 1812.

strigia—*striga*: haegtis—hegtis. 1913.

913a *scabris, pisces similes*: lopostris. 1813a.

sullus (húllos?): otor—otr. 1945.

915 *suspensus*: anhaebd—anhæbd. 1947.

scnifes (scinifes, ciniphes): mygg—mycg. 1814.

sinapio (sinapi): cressae—cressa. (922) 1860.

sicalia (sec-)—*sycalia*: rygi—*ryg. 1861.

simbulum—*symbulum* (*symbolum*): herebaecon—herebecon. 1873.

920 *scilla*: gladinae—gledinae. 1815.

sequester: byrgea *both*. 1840.

—— *sinapio*: cressae. (917.)

situla—*situlae*: ambaer—ember. 1859.

stornus (stur-)—*stronus*: dropfaag—*drofaxg. 1914.

925 *sualdam (valvam)*: durhere[1] *both*. 1948 (cp. 1053).

sella: sadol—satul. 1839.

scasa (scaria?): eborthrotae *both*. 1816; cp. Cp[1]. 27.

strepitu: brectme *vel* cliderme—*bretme *vel* clidrinnae. 1916.

stipatoribus: ymbhringendum—ymbdringendum. 1915.

930 *saginabant*: maesttun—*mestum. 1782.

semigelato—*semigelatu*: halbclungni *both*. 1844.

spatiaretur—*spatiareti*: suicudae *both*. 1893.

squalores: orfiermae—orfermae. 1902.

suffragator[2]: mundbora *both*. 1949.

---

[1] du: rhere *Ep.*   [2] *second* a *from* o *in Erf.*

scena: scadu. 902.

†*scotomaticus*: staerblind.

†*scalpro*: bore.

scirpea: lebr. 894 (cp. 1823).

1805 *scarpinat*: scripið. 906.

†*scalpellum*: bor.

†*scaturit*: criid.

†*scoria*: sinder.

†*scurra*: scond.

1810 *scorelus*: omer. 909.

scirra (*sciurus*): aqueorna. 911.

scrofa: sugu. 912.

†*scara*: scaed. (cp. 1801 ?)

1813a *scabri, pisces similes*: lopostum. 913a.

scniphes (*scinifes, ciniphes*): mygg. 916.

1815 *scilla*: glaedine. 920.

scasa (*scaria*?): eborðrote. 927 (cp. Cp[1]. 27).

scindulis: scidum. 943.

†*scena*: uuebung.

scrobibus: groepum. 948.

1820 †*scalmus*: thol.

sc[h]eda(-*dia*?): taeg. 964.

scienices (*scenicus*): scinneras. 952.

scirpea: eorisc[1], leber. 960 (cp. 1804).

scalpula (*scapulae*): sculdur. 963.

1825 †*scaphum* (-*a*): scip.

sciphus (*y*): bolla. 965.

†*scintella* (-*illa*): spærca.

†*scalpio* (*scalpo*): scriopu.

†*sc[a]evum*: goduureci.

1830 †*scabro*: unsmoeði.

†*scenis*: scinnum.

1831a †*scafus* (*p*): huma.

†*semispatium* (-*spatha*): þeohsaex.

sentina: lectha. 890.

†*sentes*: ðornas.

1835 *serpillum* (*y*): bradelaec. 895.

seditio: unsib. 900.

seta: byrst. 905.

secessus: heolstr. 901.

sella: sadol. 926.

1840 *sequester*: byrga. 921.

†*sclabrum* (*fl*-): uuind.

†*scalpo*: clawe.

†*scuporum* (*scopulorum*?): hliuða.

semigelato: halfclungni. 931.

1845 *ser[i]o*: eornisti. 945.

sevo (*sebo*): smeoru. 944 (cp. 1766).

serum: hwæg. 979.

†*sensim*: softe.

[1] s *on er.*

935 †*suffragium—subfragium*: mundbyrd *both.*
    sollicitat: tychtit[1]. 1883.
    spiculis: flanum—flanum. 1894.
    subs[i]civum: faecni *both.* 1950 (cp. 679).
    *sinuosa—*sinuossa*: faetmaendi—faedmendi. 1862.
940 *successus*: spoed *both.* 1951.
    *sublustris—*sublustrus*: sciir *both.* 1952.
    sopitis[2]: ansuebidum—*ensuebitum. 1882.
    scindulis: scidum—scidum. 1817.
    sevo (sebo): smeruui *both.* 1846.
945 *serio*: eornęsti—eornesti. 1845.
    strenuae: framlicae—fromlicae. 1917.
    spina: bodęi *both.* 1891.
    *scrobibus—*scropibus*: groepum *both.* 1819.
    sardas: smeltas *both.* 1784.
950 *sandix*: uueard *both.* 1783.
    soccus: sooc *both.* 1879.
    scienicis (scenicus): scinneras—*scineras. 1822.
    †*scina (scaena?) nitatio*[3] *(imit-?) vel*: grima *both.* (904.)
    stiria: gecilae—gecile. 1919.
955 *sponda*: selma *both.* 1895.
    spina alba: haeguthorn—heguthorn. 1897 (cp. 19).
    spina nigra: slaghthorn—salachthorn. 1898 (cp. 672).
    singultus: iesca *both.* 1865.
    stabulum: falaed *both.* 1920.
960 *scirrpea—scirpea*: eorisc *both.* 1823.
    sabulcus—subulcus: suan—*suam. 1953.
    stagnum: staeg *vel* meri *both.* 1921.
    scapula (-ae): sculdur—*sculdra. 1824.
    sc[h]eda: *teac—teag. 1821.
965 *scifus—sciffus (scyphus)*: bolla—bollae. 1826.

---

[1] tyctit, *with* h *written above* c.   [2] p *from* b *in Erf.*   [3] *cp.*
the all-Latin gloss in Cp. scina: nititio.

senon: cearricgge. 968.

1850 senecen (senecio): gunde-
suilge. 976.

†sepeliant: onsuebbað.

†sermo: sprͅc.

†sedulium: rægu.

†senex: ald.

1855 †senior: aeldra.

sibba (fibula?): sigl. 882
(cp. 874).

†singultat: sicetit vel
gesca slaet.

†sicomoros (sycomorus):
heopan.

situla: omber. 923.

1860 sinapian (sinapi):
cressa. 917.

sicalia (sec-): ryge. 918.

sinuosa: faeðmendi. 939.

†simpla: anfald.

†sirina (siren): mereme-
nin.

1865 singultus: gesca. 958.

†sinnum (sinum): *cirm[1].

†siliqua: pisan hosa.

sisca: sniðstreo. 973 (cp.
Cp[1]. 27).

sinfoniaca (symphonia-
ca): belone. 975.

1870 †signaum (signum): segn.

†simultas: unsib.

†sinopede (pid): redestan.

simbulum (symbolum):
*herebenc. 918
(1971).

†sinus: byge.

1875 †sinus: faeðm.

smus (sinus): wellyrgae.
969.

†socrus: sueger.

†socer: *sur.

soccus: socc, slebescoh.
951.

1880 †solisequia (solsequium):
sunfolgend.

†sopio: suebbo.

sopitis: onsuebdum. 942.

sollicitat: tyhteð. 936.

sorix (-ex): mús. 977.

1885 sortem: wyrd, condi-
cionem. 980.

†sortilegos: hlytan[2].

†sollicito: tyhto.

†solvat: *ondest.

†sollicitare: tyhtan.

1890 †soricarius: mushabuc.

1890a†sopor: *momna.

spina: bodeg. 947.

†spicas: ear.

spatiaretur: suicade.
932.

spiculis: flanum. 937.

---

[1] i.e. cirin; or signum: cirm?

[2] from hlutan, y above u.

salum: segg—seg. 1786.

stilium vel fusa: spinil *both*. 1922.

senon: cearruccae—cearricae. 1849.

smus (sinus)—simus: uuellyrgae *both*. 1876.

970   *slens—splenis (splen, splenis)*: milti *both*. 1896.

spatula: bed *both*. 1899.

suesta—sivesta: suina suadu *both*. 1954.

sisca—sista: snidstreo[1]—snidstreu. 1868; cp. Cp[1]. 27.

salsa: surae *both*. 1787.

975   *sinfoniaca[2] (symphoniaca)*: belonae *both*. 1869.

senecen (-io): gundaesuelgiae—gundaesuelgae. 1850.

sorix[3] (-ex), id est: mus *both*. 1884.

stilio (stellio) vel vespertilio[4]: hreathamus *both*. 1924 (cp. 1098).

seru[m]: huaeg *both*. (982) 1847.

980   *sortem, condicionem[5], id*: *uuyd—uyrd. 1885.

†*sc[a]evus[6], strabus, torbus (v), id est[7]*: sceolhegi—sceolegi. 1939.

serum, liquor casei, id: huaeg—huuaeg. (979.)

---

[1] s:::nidstreo.   [2] sinfroniaca *Erf*.   [3] sorid *Erf*.
[4] stilio uespertilio *Erf*.   [5] conditionem *Erf*.   [6] s:ceuus *Ep*.,
with horizontal stroke well below er.   [7] id *Erf*.

1895 *sponda*: benc, selma.
955.
splenis: milte. 970.
spina alba: haeguðorn.
956 (cp. 114).
spina nigra: slahðorn.
957 (cp. 1380).
spatula (*spart-?*): bed.
971.
1900 †*spiramentum*: hol.
†*spiato*: matte.
squalores: orfeormnisse.
933.
stabula: seto. 896.
†*stiba* (*v*): handle.
1905 †*stabulum*: stal.
†*strigillum* (*strigilis*):
screope.
†*stragua* (*stragulum*):
strel.
†*stuppa*: heordan.
sternutatio: fnora. 888.
1910 *struerer*: streide. 899.
sturnus: staer. 608.
†*strues*: heap.
striga: haegtis. 913.
stornus (*stur-*): dropfaag. 924.
1915 *stipatoribus*: ymbhrin-
gend*um*. 929.
strepitu: braechtme. 928.

strenue: fromlice. 946
(cp. 1530).
†*strictis*: getogenum.
stiria: gecilae. 954.
1920 *stabulum*: falaed. 959.
stagnum: mere. 962.
stilium: spinel. 967.
†*stertens*: hrutende.
stilio (*stellio*): hraeðemuus[1]. 978 (cp.
2103).
1925 †*s[t]uppa*: ecambe.
†*st[r]angulat*: wyrgeð *vel*
smorað.
†*stricta mac[ha]era*: geto-
gone sueorde.
†*stamen*: wearp.
†*sternit*: gehnægith.
1930 †*strenas*: lybesne.
†*stellatus*: astaenid.
†*strut[h]io*: stryta[2].
†*stigmata*: picung.
†*stomachum*: maga.
1935 †*strigillus* (*-ilis*): aera,
aeren screop.
†*ste[r]nax*: wurpul.
†*stiga*: gaad.
†*sturfus* (*sturnus*): fina.
strabus: scelege[3]. 981.
1940 †*subplaudans*: gelpende.
†*suffundit[4]*: ablendeð.

---

[1] *lemma confused with* vespertilio; *cp. EE.*   [2] y *on er.*   [3] ge *on er.*   [4] *subject in the probable source is* glaucoma.

Trux palpitat[1], *vel*: *hunhieri—unhyri. 2040.
tonica polimita (*tunica polymita*): hringfaag, *a rotunditate cir-*
  culorum—*hrinfag. 2029.
985   *torta*: auunden *both*. 2030.
tonsa: rothor—*rohr. 2031.
titio: brand—brond. 2018.
trutina vel statera: helor *both*. 2041.
trulla: crucae *both*. 2051.

                    [1] palpitrat *Erf*.

†*surculus*: tuig, ouu-
    aestm.
†*susurio* (cp. *susurro*):
    wrohtspitel.
surum(-*a*): spearua. 897.
1945 *sullus* (*húllos*?): ottor.
    914.
†*subarrata*: geuuetfaes-
    tae.
suspensus: ahaefd. 915.
sualdam (*valvam*): dur-
    here. 925 (cp. 2075).
subfragator: mundbora.
    934.
1950 *subs*[*i*]*civum*: *fraecni.
    938 (cp. 1386).
successus: spoed. 940.
sublustris: scir. 941.
subulcus: *snan. 961.
suesta: suina sceadu.
    972.
1955 †*surgit*: waexit.

†*sulforia* (*sulfurea*): suefl-
    sueart.
†*suspenderat*: awenide.
†*sucini*: glaeres.
†*subigo*: wrotu.
1960 †*sub cono*: under haeh-
    nisse.
†*sudum*: lybt, *siccum*.
†*sutrinator*: scoere.
†*subsannat*: hospetęt.
†*suffocacium*: cecil.
1965 †*subjugatis*: geðedum.
†*suis* (*sus*): suin.
†*suaeder*: butan toðum.
1967a †*sunt*: sint.
†*suellium* (*suillus*?): sui-
    nin.
†*subtalaris*: steppescoh.
1970 †*sup*[*p*]*uratio*: gelostr.
symbulum (*symbolus*):
    herebæcun. (1873.)

Taxus: iuu. 1005.
talpa: wond. 1014.
taculus (*taxu*-): brocc.
    1008.
1975 *talpa*: wondeuueorpe.
    1045.
tabunus (*tabanus*):
    briosa. 1016.

tapetsa (*tapete*): rye.
    1020.
tab[*l*]*etum*[1]: bred. 1023.
talumbus: gescadwyrt.
    1032.
1980 *taxatione*: raedinne.
    1035.
tabuisset: asuond. 1036.

---

[1] *or* tapetum, *i.e.* -te?

990   *traductus*: georuuierdid *both*. 2042.
      Tempe: scaedugeardas—sceadugeardas. 1998.
      trop[a]ea, signa vel: sigbeacn—*beanc. 2043.
      tortum (-ta): coecil *both*. 2032.
      troc[h]leis, rotis modicis vel: stricilum *both*. 2044.
995   *triplia—triblia*[1] *(trýblion)*: lebil *both*. 2045.
      *tignarius—*trigrarius*: hrofuuyrcta—*hrofhuyrihta. 2020.
      testudo: *borohaca *vel* sceldreda *vel* *ifaenucæ—*brodthaca
         vel sceldhreða *vel* *fænucæ. 1999.
      tessera: tasol, *quadrangulum*[2]—tasul. 2000.
      tertiana: *lectinadl—lenctinadl. 2001.
1000   *tubo*[3]*—tuba (-us)*: thruuch—thruch. 2067.
      tragelafus[4] *vel platocerus (platyceros)*: elch *both*. 2054.
      torquet[5]*—*torquetur*: uuraec *both*. 2033.
      tridens: maettoc—mettoc. 2047.
      tilia: lind *both*. 2019 (cp. 1017).
1005   *taxus*: iuu *both*. 1972.
      tremulus: aespae—espę. 2048.
      thymus (-um): haeth—haedth. 2012.
      toculus—taculus (taxu-): brocc—*broa. 1974.
      trifulus—trufulus: felospraeci—*feluspreici. 2049.
1009a   *tabula—tabulo*: fala *both*. 2067a.
1010   *terrebellus—terebellus (-bra)*: nafogar[6]—*naboger[7]. 2002.
      turdella: throstlae *both*. 2068.
      *tilaris—*itilaris*: lauuercae—lauuercæ. 2026.
      turdus: scric—*screc. 2069.
      talpa: wand—uuond. 1973.
1015   *tincti (tinca)*: sli *both*. 2021.
      tabu:us—tabanus: briosa *both*. 1976.
      tilio (-a): lind *vel* baest—lind *vel* best. 2019, 2022 (cp. 1004).

---

[1] b *from* p.   [2] quadrungulu*m Erf.*   [3] *from* tabo, u *above*
er. a.   [4] tragelafb*us Ep.*   [5] ue *no longer visible.*   [6] *from*
nabfogar, b *expuncted.*   [7] b *from* o.

tantisper: ðus suiðe.
1037.
taberna: winaern. 1040.
†*talaria*: feðrhoman.
1985 †*taurus*: fear.
†*taxaverat*: gierende¹.
†*talus*: oncleouue.
†*tabulata*: ðille.
†*tala (tela)*: webgerodes.
1990 †*tabulamen[tum]*: ðille.
†*taeni[i]s*: ðuaelum.
†*tegula*: tigule.
†*t[a]edis*: blesum.
†*teter*: duerc.
1995 †*territorium*: lond.
†*tentigo*: gesca.
†*tentorium*: geteld.
Tempe: sceadugeardas.
991.
testudo: bordðeaca. 997.
2000 *tessera*: tasul. 998.
tertiana: lenctinald. 999.
terebellus (-bra): nabo-
gaar. 1010.
tenticum(cp. *tendicula*?):
sprindel. 1025.
telum (-a): web. 1026.
2005 *textrinum*: webb. 1030.
*termofilas (Thermopy-
las)*: faesten. 1042.

temonibus: þixlum. 1043.
teres: siunhuurful. 1047.
†*temperiem*: uueder.
2010 †*tehis (thecis?)*: tegum,
fodrum.
†*teloniaris (telonarius)*:
uuicgeroebum.
thymus(-um): haet. 1007.
†*tholus*: hrof.
†*thadalus*: brooc. (cp.
1974?)
2015 †*thessera (te-)*: beeme.
†*titica*: uuefl. (cp. 482?)
†*tisifone (ph)*: uualcyrge.
titio: brond. 987.
tilia: lind. 1004, cp.
1017.
2020 *tignarius*: hrofuuyrhta.
996.
tincti (tinca): sli. 1015.
tilio (-a): baest. 1017.
tignum: tin. 1024.
titule: gata loc. 1028.
2025 *tibialis*: *baanrist. 1031.
tilares: lauricae. 1012.
tipo (typhon): draca, *vel
inflatio*². 1048.
†*tigillum*: first.
2028a †*tinnulus a tinniendo
dicitur id est*: eran.

¹ *possibly for* gierendende, *and perhaps intended to explain* usurpans,
which in a possible source occurs in the same sentence as taxaverat.
² *last word perhaps suggests* typhus, *rather than* typhon.

tuber, tumor vel: suollaen—*assuolla*n*. 2071.

**toreum*—*toreuma*: eduella—eduelli. 2034.

1020   *tapeta*[1] (*-e*): ryae—*hryhae. 1977.

transtrum: ses *both*. 2050.

trulla: scofl—*scolf. 2051.

tab[*l*]*etum*[2]—**tebe*: bred *both*. 1978.

tignum: tin *both*. 2023.

1025   *tenticum* (cp. *tendicula*?): sprindil *both*. 2003.

telum (*-a*): uueb *both*. 2004.

t[*h*]*orax*: felofearth—felufrech. 2035.

titule—*titulae*: gata loc—gatan loc. 2024.

tudicla—*tudica* (*tudicula*): thuerae—thuere. 2072.

1030   *textrina*: uueb—uuẹb. 2005.

tibialis: baanrift—baanryft. 2025.

talumbus: giscaduuyrt[3]—*gescanuuyrt. 1979.

torrentibus: *streum—*streaumu*m*. 2036.

tuta: orsorg *both*. 2070.

1035   *taxatione*: raedinnae—redinnae. 1980.

tabuisset[4]: asuand—*assuant. 1981.

tantisper: þus suiþae—dus suidae. 1982.

tutellam (*tutela*): *sclindinnae[5]—scildinnae. 2073.

**triquarum*—*triquadrum* (*triquetrus*): ðrifedor—*trifoedur.
     2052.

1040   *taberna*: uuinaern[6] *both*. 1983.

trans: biginan—bigenan. 2053.

termofilas—*termopilas* (*Thermopylas*): faestin *vel* anstigan—
    *festis *vel* anstiga. 2006.

temonibus: dislum—dixlum. 2007.

†*tabida et putrefacta*: afulodan, asuundnan, *aduinendanan[7]—
    afulat[8] ond asuunden.

---

[1] *first a from* e *in Erf.*   [2] *see p. 91, fn. 1.*   [3] gi *in margin.*
[4] i *unclear in Ep.*   [5] sclindi::nnae.   [6] uuinaernˊ *Ep.*
[7] *between the lines above* (-fa)cta afulodan a(suundnan).   [8] ā fulat.

tonica polimita (tunica
polymita): hringfaag,
a rotund' circu'. 984.

2030 *torta*: auunden. 985.

tonsa: roðr. 986.

tortum (-ta): coecil. 993.

torquet: uuraec. 1002.

toreuma: eduuaelle.
1019.

2035 *t[h]orax*: feoluferð.
1027.

torrentibus: streamum.
1033.

†*torosa*: sionuualt.

†*toga*: goduuebbe.

†*torquent*: þrungun.

2040 *trux*: *unhiorde. 983.

trutina: heolor. 988.

traductus: georuuyrde.
990.

trop[a]ea: sigebecn. 992.

troc[h]leis: stricilum.
994.

2045 *triplia (trýblion)*: lebl.
995.

†*trajectus*: ðorhbrogden.

tridens: auuel, meottoc.
1003.

tremulus: aespe. 1006.

trufulus: feluspreci.
1009.

2050 *transtrum*: saes. 1021.

trulla: cruce, turl, scofl.
989, 1022.

triquadrum (triquetrus):
ðrifeoðor. 1039.

trans: bigeonan. 1041.

tragelaphus: elch. 1001.

2055 †*trulla*: ponne.

†*transfert*: geuuendit.

†*tribuli*: braere.

†*tranant*: ðorhsuimmað.

†*tripes*: stool.

2060 †*tria*: huice.

†*tractibus*: naescum.

†*trita*: ðrostle. (cp. 2063,
2068?)

†*truitius*: ðraesce. (cp.
2062?)

†*traigis*: higrae.

2065 †*tricent[ur]*: aelden.

†*tubera*: clate.

tubo (-us): ðruh. 1000.

2067a *tubolo*: fala. 1009a.

turdella: ðrostle. 1011.

turdus: scric. 1013.

2070 *tuta*: orsorg. 1034.

tuber, tumor: asuollen.
1018.

tudic[u]la: thuaere.
1029.

tutellam (tutela): scil-
denne. 1038.

tuber: hofer. 1046.

1045   *talpa*: uuandaeuuiorpae¹—uuondæuuerpe. 1975.
        tuber: ofr *both*. 2074.
        teres: sinuurbul²—*sinuulfur. 2008 (cp. 154).
        [*tipo* (*typhon*): *droco³—draco³. 2027.]

        Verruca: uueartae—uuertae. 2088.
1050   *via secta*: iringaes uueg—*iuuuringes⁴ uueg. 2118.
        verbere torto⁵: *auundre suipan—auundenre suipan. 2087.
        venabula (*-um*): eborspreot *both⁶*. 2089.
        valba⁷ (*v*): durheri *both⁸*. 2075 (cp. 925).
        ventriculus, stomachus⁹ avis vel: cesol *both*. 2090.
1055   *vescada¹⁰*: mundle:¹¹—munleuu. 2091.
        ur::: *lum—urciolum* (*eo*): crucae—cruce. 2165.
        vicat:*m—vicatum* (*ficatum*): libr *both¹²*. 2119.
        vestibulum: cebęrtuun—*caebertuum. 2094.
        volvola (*convolvulus*): *wiuwindae, *herba similis hederae¹³, quae
                vitibus et frugibus circumdari solet—uuidubindae. 2158.
1060   *vittas¹⁴*—*vitas*: thuelan. 2120.
        vulgo, passim vel: oghuuaer—oeghuuer. 2173.
        vitelli: suehoras—sueoras¹⁵. 2121 (cp. 1099).
        **uscidae¹⁶*—*viscide*: *tholicae—*tochtlicae. 2170.
        venetum¹⁷: geolu—*geholu. 2095.
1065   *vatilla* (*batillum*): gloedscofl *both*. 2076.
        villis: uulohu*m*—uulohum. 2122.

        ¹ n *v. faint.*   ² *from* sinuurful, b *above* f.   ³ *apparently*
        Lat.   ⁴ iuuar-, *with third* u *written above* a.   ⁵ torta *Ep.*
        ⁶ *letter* (f?) *er. between first* e *and* b *in Ep.*   ⁷ *illeg. in Ep.*
        ⁸ *from* duerheri *in Ep., first* e *expuncted* (*and er.?*).   ⁹ -entric-
        no longer legible in Ep., and o *from* a.   ¹⁰ *last* a *illeg. in Ep.*
        ¹¹ *first stroke of* u (?) *visible after* e.   ¹² *comes at the end of* u *in Erf.*
        ¹³ hedere *Erf.*   ¹⁴ ta *faint.*   ¹⁵ *apparently explains* uxoris . . .
        fratres, *which in the probable source occurs adjacent to* Vitellios (*the
        brothers-in-law of Brutus*).   ¹⁶ *only top of* u *still visible.*   ¹⁷ *Ep.*
        uene:um.

2075 *Valba* (*valva*): durheri.
1053 (cp. 1948).
vatilla (*batillum*): gloedscofl. 1065.
varix: ampre. 1073.
varicat: stridit. 1086.
vangas: spadan. 1087.
2080 *vadimonium*: borg,
gilefde[1]. 1089, 90.
†*vatilla* (*batillum*): isern
scobl.
†*vanus*: gemaeded.
†*vapore*: acthmc.
†*vanna* (*-us*): fon.
2085 †*vacca*: cuu.
†*vada brevia*: geuueada.
verbere torto: *awun-
dere suiopan. 1051.
verruca: wearte. 1049
(cp. 288).
venabula (*-um*): eobor-
spreot. 1052.
2090 *ventriculus*: *ceonsol.
1054.
vescada: mundleu. 1055.

†*veror*: witro.
†*vexilla*: seign.
vestibulum: caebrtuun.
1058.
2095 *venetum*: geolu. 1064.
vertigo: eduuelle. 1068.
†*vectis*: *seng.
vespas: uuaefsas. 1071.
verberator[*i*]*um*: corthr.
1074.
2100 *verberatrum* (*-tum*?):
flete. 1075 (cp.
1205?).
vesica: bledre. 1077.
2101a *verbenaca*: sura *magna*.
1077a.
veneria: smeoruwyrt.
1078.
vespertilio: hraeðemuus.
1098; cp. 978.
†*vernaculus*: frioleta.
2105 †*vecors*: gemaad.
†*vernacula*: menen.
vetellus: sueor[2]. 1099
(cp. 2121).

[1] *second word prob. attached to wrong lemma; cp. EE.*
p. 96, fn. 15.

[2] *see*

unibrellas (*umb*.): stalu to fuglum[1]—stalu to *fluglum. 2153.

vertigo: edwalla—edualla. 2096.

vitiligo[2]: blectha *both*. 2123 (cp. 139).

1070   *vitricius* (*vitricus*): steupfaedaer[3]—*staupfotar. 2124.

vespas—*vespa*: waeffsas—uuaeps. 2098.

vorago: hool *both*. 2159.

varix[4]: amprae—omprae. 2077.

verberatorium: cortr—cordr. 2099.

1075   *verberatrum* (*-tum*?): fleti—*fletu. 2100 (cp. 605?).

urna: ambaer—*ombar. 2166.

vessica (*vesica*): bledrae *both*. 2101.

1077a *verbenaca*—*verbaeraca[5]: *sura *magna* both. 2101a.

veneria: *speruuuyrt—smeruuuyrt. 2102.

ulmus: elm *both*[6]. 2149.

1080   *villosa*: ryhae *both*. 2126.

villa (*-us*): linnin ryhae—linin ryhae. 2128.

viburna (*-um*): uuiduuuindae—uuidubindae. 2129.

viscus: mistil. 2127.

quinquefolium: hraefnaes fot. (848.)

1085   *vicium* (*vicia*): fuglaes bean—*flugles bean. 2125.

varicat: stridit *both*. 2078.

vangas: spadan *both*[7]. 2079.

virecta: quicae[8]—*cuique. 2130.

verecundiae[9] *concesserim*: gilebdae—*gilepdae. 2080.

1090   *vadimonium*—*vadi: borg *both*. 2080.

vitiatum: auuaerdid[10]—auuerdid. 2131.

vibrat[11] *vel dirigat* (*-it*): borᴇttit—boretit. 2147.

vitiato oculo: unþyctgi[12] egan—undyctgi ægan. 2133.

---

[1] *first* u *from* l.   [2] *Ep*. uitil: go (*or* uicil: go).   [3] da *v. faint.*
[4] *curved stroke as of* c *between* r *and* i *in Ep*.   [5] *from* uerbærata, c
above expuncted t.   [6] *followed on same line by* umguentum *in*
Erf.; *cp. Cp*. 2154.   [7] *after* uirecta (1088) *in Erf*.   [8] *from*
cuicae, q *above first* c.   [9] uericundię *Ep*.   [10] auuaerdi: : d;
i *uncertain*.   [11] uimbrat *Ep*.   [12] *from* unþyotgi, c *above* t.

†*vertil* (*-tile*?): huerb.
  (cp. Cp¹. 32.)
†*veniculum* (*veh.*): wægn.
2110 †*vertiginem*: suinglunge.
†*vesper*: suansteorra.
†*veterno*: faecnum.
†*vermis*: eorðmata.
†*ve*[*r*]*miculus*: cornuur-
  ma.
2115 †*verbi gratia*: uuordes
  intinga.
†*violenter*: roeðelice.
†*viti*[*li*]*ginem*: bleci.
  via secta: iringes uueg.
  1050.
  vicatum (*f.*): libr. 1057.
2120 *vittas*: thuelan. 1060.
  vitelli: sueoras¹. 1062
  (cp. 2107).
  villis: uulou*m*. 1066.
  vitiligo: blectha. 1069
  (cp. 296).
  vitricius (*vitricus*):
  steopfaeder. 1070.
2125 *vicium* (*-ia*): fugles
  bean. 1085.
  villosa: rye. 1080.
  viscus: mistel. 1083.
  villa (*-us*): linin ryee.
  1081.
  viburna (*-um*): uudu-
  uuinde. 1082.

2130 *virecta*: quicae. 1088.
  vitiatum: awerded. 1091.
†*vibrat*: brogdetteð.
  vitiato oculo: unðyhtge
  egan. 1093.
†*virgultum*: gerd.
2135 †*viscera tosta*: gebreded
  flaesc.
†*vibice*: lelan.
†*vinco*: obersuiðo.
†*viresceret*: greouue.
†*viscellum* (*jus-*?): broht.
2140 †*viscera*: tharme, thumle.
†*vimen*: wearp. (cp.
  1928?)
†*villus*: uuloh.
†*virgo*: unmaelo.
†*vitulus*: caelf.
2145 †*vitula*: cucaelf.
†*vistula* (*fi-*?): suge-
  sweard.
  vibrat: borettið *vel*
  diregað (*dirigit*). 1092.
†*ultroque citroque*: hider
  ond *hider.
  ulmus: elm. 1079.
2150 †*ulula*: ulae.
†*umbilicus*: nabula.
†[*h*]*umecta*: gibrec.
  unibrellas (*umbell-*): stalu
  to fuglum. 1067.
†*unguentum*: smeoru.

¹ *see p. 96, fn. 15.*

†*vesica*[1]: blegnae—blegnæ.

1095   *undecumque*[2]: huuanan[3] huuoega—huuonan huuoega. 2155.

usurpavit[4]: agnaettae—agnetæ. 2171.

uris: uru*m both*. 2167.

vespertilio: hreadaemus—hreadam*us*[5]. 2103 (cp. 978).

—*vetellus*: sueor[6]. 2107 (cp. 1062).

---

[1] u *and* s *unclear.*   [2] undecūq:: *Ep.*   [3] huu:anan.
[4] usurpau:t *Ep.*   [5] *Ep. ends with the gloss* ueterator: stroffosus,
astutus.   [6] *see p. 96, fn. 15.*

2155   *undecumque*: huonan-
          huegu. 1095.
       †*unguana (ungula)*: naegl,
          speru.
       †*voti compos, volo ornatus
          i.*: fægen.
       volvola (convolvulus):
          uuduuuinde. 1059.
       vorago: hool. 1072.
2160 †*voragine*: suelgendi.
       †*voti[v]um*: oestful[1].
       †*voluma*: gorst.
       †*vordalium (formalium?)*:
          laesti.
       †*vox*: stebn.

2165   *urciolum (eo)*: waeter-
          cruce. 1056.
       urna: amber. 1076.
       uris: urum. 1097.
       †*verticeta*[2] *(urticeta)*: net-
          lan.
       †*urguet*: threatade.
2170   *uscide (viscide)*: tohlice[3].
          1063 (cp. 1033).
       usurpavit: agnette.
          1096.
       †*utensile*: geloma.
       vulgo, passim: oeghuer.
          1061.
       †*uxorius*: ceorl.

2175 †*[h]ymnus*: loob.   2175a†*zizania*: laser.

---

[1] o *subpuncted.*   [2] *originally* urticeta, *as shown by alph. order;*
cp. the all-Latin gloss in Cp. urticeta: loca ubi urticae nascuntur.
[3] *gloss written over er.*

II

INSCRIPTIONS

(NORTHUMBRIAN)

1. Franks Casket, British Museum and Museo Nazionale, Florence
c. 700

Lid[1]:   'ægili' (*panel*)

Front: 'fisc flodu ahof   on fergenberig
warþ gasric grorn   þær he on greut giswom
hronæs ban'

'mægi' (*panel*)

Back: 'her fegtaþ titus end giuþeasu' HIC FUGIANT
HIERUSALIM 'afitatores'

'dom'   'gisl' (*panels*)

Left side: 'romwalus and reumwalus twœgen gibroþær
afœddæ hiæ wylif in romæ cæstri oþlæ unneg'

Right side[2]: 'her hos sitaþ   on harmberga
ægl[æ][3] drigiþ   swa hiri ertæ egi sgræf
sarden sorga   ænd sef/a torna'

'risci'   'bita'   'wudu' (*panels*)

---

[1] *the main texts are all cut continuously on borders surrounding the carved pictures on the various faces of the casket, but those on the front and right side have here been set out as lines of alliterative verse; words marked 'panel' are found on prepared spaces within the pictures.*   [2] *the runes on this side which are here printed in italics are in 'code'; those here transcribed as a and æ have also been read as æ and a respectively.*
[3] *this rune broken.*

2. Ruthwell Cross, Dumfries
? *c.* 750

East face.

North-east: '[+ond]geredæ hinæ ḡod almeȝttig (39)[1]
þa he walde on ḡalḡu gistiḡa (40)
[m]odig fo[r]*e* [allæ] men (41)
[b]ug[a] . . . .' (42)

South-east: '[ahof] ic riicnæ k̄yniŋc (44)
heâfunæs hlafard hælda ic ni dorstæ (45)
*b*ismærædu uŋk̄et men ba ætḡad[re] ic
[wæs] *mi*þ blodæ bistemi[d] (48)
bi[ḡot] . . . .' (49)

West face.

South-west: '[+]krist wæs on rodi (56)
hweþræ þer fusæ feârran kwomu (57)
æþþilæ til anum ic þæt al bi*h*[eâld] (58)
sa*r*[æ] ic w[æ]s mi[þ] so*r*ḡum gidrœ[fi]d
h[n]aḡ [ic] . . .' (59)

North-west: '*mi*þ strelum giwundad (62)
alegdun hiæ hinæ limwœrignæ gistoddu*n*
him [æt his] licæs [hea]f[du]m (63)
[bi]*h*eâ[l]du[n] *hi*[æ] þe[r heâfunæs] . . .
. . . .' (64)

East face, top: '. . . . . dægisgæf . . . . .'

Cross-head: '[m/æ]fauœþo'[2]

---

[1] *the figures refer to the corresponding lines of 'The Dream of the Rood', from the Vercelli Book; the runic texts are carved continuously.*
[2] *three further runes are faintly visible, perhaps* 'cl' *and* 'æ'; *the runes on one panel of the south face are the remains of a Latin phrase, probably* '. . . m[a]*r*[ia] m*a*[t]er dominnæ . . .' (*i.e.* Maria mater domini).

3. Dewsbury Cross Fragment, Yorks.

8th to 9th century

. . . . RHTAE BECUN AEFTER BEORNAE GIBIDDAD D*A*ER
SAULE

4. Falstone Stone, Northumberland

8th to 9th century

+*E* . . . . . . *TA. AEFT*[AER] HROETHBERH*T*. BECUN AEFTAER EOMA
'+ . . . . æftær   roe . . . . . tæ *bec*un æftær   e . . .

GEBIDAED DER SAU[LE]
geb . . . æd þe. saule'

5. Thornhill Cross Fragments, Yorks.

8th to 9th century

(I) '+[e]þelbe[rh]t: settæfter eþelwini: . . .'
(II) '+êâdred sete¹ æfte êâteʒnne'
(III) '+jilsuiþ: arærde: æft[e] berhtsuiþe· bekun on bergi
       gebid/daþ þær: saule'

6. Yarm Cross Fragment, Yorks.

8th to 9th century

. . . . *M*BEREHCT + SĀC² + ALLA + SIGNUM AEFTER
HIS BRE/ODER ASSETAE +

---

¹ *prec. by a mark which may be intended as* 'i'.   ² *Old English*
sacerd *or Latin* sacerdos.

III

NORTHUMBRIAN FRAGMENTS

1. Memoranda on Northumbrian History

*(Cambridge Univ. Lib. MS. Kk. 5. 16 ['Moore'], fol. 128v.
c. 737.)*

Anno DXLVII[1] Ida *regnare coepit, a quo regalis* Nordanhym-
bro*rum prosapia originem tenet, et* XII *annos in regno permansit.*
Post hunc Glappa I *annum*, Adda VIII, Aedilric IIII, Theodric
VII, Friduuald VI, Hussa VII, Aedilfrid XXIIII, Aeduini XVII, 5
Osuald VIIII, Osuiu XXVIII, Ecgfrid XV, Aldfrid XX, Osred XI,
Coinred II, Osric XI, Ceoluulf VIII. *Baptizavit Paulinus ante*
annos CXI. *Eclypsis ante annos* LXXIII. Penda *moritur ante annos*
LXXIX. *Pugna* Ecgfridi *ante annos* LXIII; Ælfuini *ante annos*
LVIII. *Monasterium* aet *Uiuræmoda *ante annos* LXIIII. *Cometae* 10
visae ante annos VIII; *eodem anno pater* Ecgberct *transivit ad*
Xpm'. Angli in Brit' ante annos CCXCII.

[1] X *from* C.

2. Cædmon's Hymn

(Cambridge Univ. Lib. MS. Kk 5. 16 ['Moore'], fol. 128v.
c. 737.)

Nu scylun hergan[1]   hefaenricaes uard,
metudæs maecti   end his modgidanc,
uerc uuldurfadur,   sue he uundra gihuaes,
eci dryctin[2],   or astelidæ.

5   He aerist scop   aelda barnu*m*
heben til hrofe,   haleg scepen.
Tha middungeard[3]   moncynnæs uard,
eci dryctin,   æfter tiadæ
firum foldu[4],   frea allmectig.

10   *Primo cantavit* Caedmon *istud carmen.*

(Leningrad Public Lib. MS. Q.v.I.18, fol. 107. c. 746.)

Nu scilun herga   hefenricæs uard,
metudæs mehti   and his modgithanc,
uerc uuldurfadur,   sue he uundra gihuæs,
eci dryctin,   or astelidæ.

5   He ærist scop   aeldu barnum
hefen to hrofæ,   halig sceppend.
Tha middingard   moncynnæs uard,
eci dryctin,   æfter tiadæ
firum foldu,   frea allmehtig.

3. Bede's Death-song

(St. Gall MS. 254, p. 253 [fol. 127]. 9th century.)

Fore the*m*[5] neidfaerae   naenig uuiurthit
thoncsnotturra   than him tharf sie,
to ymbhycggannae,   aer his hiniongae,
huaet his gastae   godaes aeththa yflaes

5   aefter deothdaege   doemid uueorthae.

---

[1] *from* hergen, a *above expuncted second* e.   [2] yc *from* in.
[3] *first* d *from* n.   [4] fold^v.   [5] th'e.

4. Leiden Riddle

(Univ. of Leiden MS. Voss. Lat. 4⁰. 106, fol. 25v.
Early 9th century.)

Mec se ueta[1] uong,   uundrum freorig,
ob his innaðae   aerest[2] cend[æ][3].
[Ni] uuat ic mec *biuorthæ   uullan fliusum,
herum ðerh hehcraeft   hygiðonc[um min].
Uundnae me ni biað ueflæ,   ni ic uarp hafæ,   5
ni ðerih ðreatun giðrae[c]   ðret me hlimmith.
Ne me hrutendu   hrisil scelfath,
ne mec ouana   aam sceal cnyssa.
Uyrmas mec ni auefun   uyrdi craeftum,
ða ði *goelu godueb   geatum fraetuath.   10
Uil mec huethrae[4] suae ðeh   uidæ ofaer eorðu
hatan mith hęliðum   hyhtlic giuæd[e].
Ni *anoegun ic me aerigfaerae   egsan brogum,
ðeh ði n[ume]n [siæ]   niudlicae[5] ob cocrum.

5. Proverb

(Vienna National Bibliothek MS. Lat. 751 [Theol. 259],
fol. 34. 9th century.)

Memento Saxonicum verbum:

Oft daedlata   domę foręldit,
sigisitha gahuem: suuyltit thi ana.

---

[1] *foll. by two* (?) *letters, perhaps erased.*   [2] *or* aerist?   [3] e
uncertain (æ?)   [4] huctrae (c *a faded* e?), *with traces of* h *above* t.
[5] *or* nuid-?

IV

LIBER VITAE

(Cotton MS. Domitian A. vii, fols. 15 ff. First half of 9th century. Northumbrian.)

Nomina regum vel ducum

Eduini. osuald. osuio. ecgfrith. alchfrith. aelfuini. anna. oslaf.
eðilred. eðilberct. milred. beornhaeth. berctred. altfrith.
alduini. eaduulf. coenred. osred. osric. beornred. tilfrith.
5 berctred. eadberct. helmuald. coenred. cynimund. beornred. ecgberct. aeðilmod. ceolbald. casaer. friðubald. eanred.
alchmund. aeðilbald. sigred. osuulf. suiðberct. eðilberct.
eðilberct. eanbald. ricuulf. unust. aelfuald. cuthuulf. eadberct.
pleguulf. eadred. sigsceat. aelfsig. uulfheard. uernfrith. hysca.
10 cyniuulf. earduulf. alduulf. brorda. eadbald. uigfus. uulfhaeth.
helmbaed. helmgils. sigberct. cynibald. uulfheri. beornuini.
helpric. helmuini. ceoluulf. sigberct. eanred. eðilred. osfrith.
torctmund. aluuini. eðiluulf. mægenfrith. aelfuald. karlus.
custantin. sigred. sigred. osberct. tonduini. alduulf. eadred.
15 siguulf. sigred. sigred. alduulf. uada. heaðured. eanred. eadred.
uulfred. ofa. aelfred. beorn. ecgbercht. uoenan. eanred.

Nomina reginarum et abbatissarum

Raegnmaeld. eanfled. iurminburg. aelfled. oeðilburg. cuthburg. nunnae. pendgith. inguburg. ualdgith. aluburg. badu-
20 gyth. eaðryð. uincðryð. bilsuið. aestorhild. uilcumae. eðilgyth.
osgyth. ricfolcyn. eðilhild. eangyth. eðilgyth. haðuburg.
blaedsuith. eadgyð. cyniburg. osgyth. tatsuið. uerburg. osburg.
hungyth. hrothuaru. cuoenburg. berchtae. aebbę. burgðryð.

ðingu. heregyð. cyniðryth. uilcumae. burgðryð. uilðryth.
ecgsuith. scirburg. uilsuith. cyniðryth. ceolðryth. eafu. uilgyth. 25
redburg. redgyth. cuoenðryth. ricðryth. ythsuið. cyniburg.
aldðryth. berctsuið. hildiðryth. berctgyth. edgyth. uerngyth.
tidburg. uilgyth. ecgburg. alchsuið. osburg. tatae. cyniðryð.
huitae. uictgyth. hildiburg. uernðryth. ricðryth. aluburg.
cuoendryth. cuoemlicu. aebbino. aluburg. beorngyth. hroeð- 30
burg. aluchburg. friðhild. eðilburg. bothild. heregyth. heaburg.
eanburg. aldburg. uerburg. sigðryth. cyniburg. redburg.
helmðryth. uernðryth. eðilðryth. altðryth. eðilðryth. uulfgyth.
cuthburg. cuoenðryth. altsuith. aelfgyth. haðugyth. berctðryth.
altðryth. eðilðryth. eadburg. burgsuith. altðryth. saegyth. 35
tidburg. beorngyth. eardgyth. aldgyth. beorngyth. berctuaru.
beorngyth. cyniðryth. aelfgyth. aelfled. saeðryth. eanðryth.
uulfhild. osðryth. uilðryth. uilsuið. eaðryth. tondburg.
eanðryth. aelfðryth. badugyth. siguaru. berctfled. eafu.
ecguaru. *ostðryth. badu. eanburg. eatðryð. ecgsuið. eaðryð. 40
uilgið. badusuið. cyniðryd. uilburg. hildigið. eadu. eardgyð.
haðugið. edildryð. redburg. daegburg. uilburg. cynidryð.
uynburg. hroeðgifu. aelfdryð. eatðryð. eandryð. hygðryð.
eadburg. hygburg. berhtgið. eadburg. beorngið. osgið.
hleoburg. hroeðgeofu. badusuið. saeðryð. osðryð. alburg. 45
cynidryð. uichtburg. bettu. uulfhild. uildryð. alburg. eatcume.
sigburg. seliburg. berhtðryð. eðilu. beonnu. tidcume. eðilsuið.
eandryð. eatdryd. hildidryð. osgid. eardgið. eandryð. ecgburg.
tidhild. sigðryð. cynigyð. osgeofu.

Nomina anchoritarum 50

Oediluald *pr'*. uermund *pbr'*. baldhelm *pbr'*. feligeld *pbr'*.
uichtbercht *pr'*. haemgils *pbr'*. eaduald *pbr'*. herebercht *pr'*.
boesel *pbr'*. herefrid *pbr'*. aethuini *pbr'*. eadhelm *pbr'*. balthere
pbr'. tiluini *pbr'*. fronka *pbr'*. aldbercht *pr'*. echha *pbr'*. tilfrith
pbr'. aldhaeth *pbr'*. agustinus *pbr'*. bilfrith *pbr'*. hadured *pbr'*. 55

uilthegn *pbr'*. garuulf *pbr'*. cuthred *pbr'*. wulfsig *pr'*. hadumund *pr'*. uigbercht *pr'*.

Nomina abbatum gradus *pbratus

Ceolfrið *pbr'*. bacga *pbr'*. elias *pbr'*. haduberct *pr'*. aldhelm
60 *pbr'*. eatfrith *pbr'*. herefrith *prb'*. garuald *pbr'*. tatbercht *pbr'*.
thrythred *pbr'*. heardred *pbr'*. uichthaeth *pbr'*. cynibercht
pbr'. eorpuini *pbr'*. huaetberct *pbr'*. uilbercht *pbr'*. ceolbercht
pbr'. alchmund *pbr'*. aldred *pbr'*. frehelm *pbr'*. tatuini *pbr'*. uic-
bercht *pbr'*. hygbercht *pbr'*. cynidegn *pbr'*. siguini *pbr'*. cyni-
65 uulf *pbr'*. uernbercht *pbr'*. eanuulf *pbr'*. balduini *pbr'*. uulfsig
pbr'. cyniheard *pbr'*. hunsig *pbr'*. botuini *pbr'*. baldhere *pbr'*.
albercht *pbr'*. botuulf *pbr'*. eaduald *pbr'*. uilfrith *pbr'*. torchtuini
pbr'. uulfheard *pbr'*. uulfsig *pbr'*. uichtred *pbr'*. sigred *pbr'*.
hunuini *pbr'*. bressal *pbr'*. beornfrið *pbr'*. headured *pbr'*. edil-
70 hech *pbr'*. frioduuini *pbr'*. berchtred *pbr'*. siguulf *pbr'*. cuthfrith
pbr'. eanbercht *pbr'*. saeuald *pbr'*. tatuini *pbr'*. reduulf *pbr'*.
uilferð *pbr'*. aelfuulf *pr'*. berchtuini *pr'*. ecgheard *pr'*. saered
pr'. ecgred *pr'*. eanuulf *pr'*. earduulf *pr'*. ecgred *pr'*. ecgheard
pr'. eadmund *pr'*. eaduulf *pr'*.

75   Nomina abbatum gradus diaconatus

Beornuini *diac'*. berchthun *dia'*. cuthbercht *dia'*. cuthere
dia'. sigbercht *dia'*. uulfheard *dia'*. alchuini *dia'*. eaduald *dia'*.
ecguulf *diaco'*.

Nomina abbatum

80   Biscopus. cudda. oshere. aesturuini. siguini. billing. utta.
bacga. forthuio. friodumund. hunuald. billing. ecguald.
theodric. hiudu. inuald. cynibercht. maesuith. uilhelm. til-
bercht. hygbald. buna. eanmund. hroðfrith. ethilbald. uigfrith.
herebald. beadheard. aluuini. ricred. maeginuald. cuthuini.

eadbercht. milred. osmund. altfrith. beornuini. redbald. eat- 85
frith. eðilmund. berchtuini. cuthgar. heardred. eadbald.
gefuini. uilbercht. pymma. beornfrith. hygbercht. eadberct *rex.*
beorn. bada. eðilheard. suiðuulf. uulfhaeth. aelberct. alduini.
bosa. helmuini. tilfrith. cynigils. eðiluald *rex.* alchmund.
leofuini. eanuulf. eanbercht. eaduulf. burghelm. berchtuulf. 90
uilred. uernbercht. eatðegn. saebercht. osuulf. torchtmund.
ofa. eduini. eanulf. eðilbald. burghelm. alubercht. cynibald.
ecga. eadbercht. beornheard. aelfsig. osbald. berchtred. tatuulf.
heardberct. berchtuulf. reduulf. eanfrith. huaetred. uulfsig.
beodufrith. osbercht. alduulf. huaetberht.   95

Nomina praesbyterorum

Demma. suiðbald. echha. hemma. scenuulf. ceolfrith. tathysi.
dremka. ceolgar. alda. coenhere. tilisi. tidhere. maeðhelm.
tulla. uulsig. tidhere. sigbald. bron. drycghelm. echha. frood.
uiuti. uendilbercht. faelfi. tiduald. beadufrith. heaðuberct. 100
daeghelm. cuthbercht. tella. coenhere. *aldceord. hygbald.
beda. ceolbercht. aescuald. suiðmer. eanfrith. ini. eðilheard.
hyni. hemma. tatberct. ceolhaeth. badumund. tella. hiuddi.
ultan. londfrith. guthfrith. dycgfrith. cynimund. hygbald.
hyssa. suitha. biscop. beoduca. tilthegn. uicfrith. adding. 105
plecgils. eaduald. ingild. uigbald. hiordi. aldhelm. inuald. tilisi.
hildiberct. tiluini. bercht. ceolhere. londberct. pectuald.
berctuald. dremca. beda. badumund. suiðgils. hysimonn.
uilberct. helmuald. torchtmund. deduc. ðingfrith. londberct.
tilberct. eaduald. cuthuulf. tiluini. bilhelm. daegfrið. betscop. 110
helmuini. eatfrith. deneberct. liodberct. cynhelm. uitgils.
frioðuuald. tilisi. cuðgar. eðilberct. eðilberct. egilmund. cynimund. maethcor. streonberct. eðilberct. hroeðlac. aluberct.
tatberct. tidbald. folcuini. hearduini. beoduuini. bothelm.
berchtuald. penduulf. uilfrith. cuthfrið. liodberct. cyniberct. 115
alduulf. hildiberct. eanlac. friðuuini. eanberct. plegbrect.

cuthgils. bercht. leofuini. bedhaeth. tobeas. tiluini. ualchstod.
tilberct. cyniberct. dreamuulf. haðuulf. forthuald. hroðuald.
eaduini. bynni. uigbald. tunna. uigbald. hyguini. eada. bercht-
120 helm. tungils. theodric. aluchsig. maegenric. tydi. uighaeð.
helmuald. tiduini. eðilric. uerberct. hygbald. ealac. ceolmund.
eaduini. saeuini. balðhelm. tiduulf. aldhaeth. piuda. geruald.
burgfrið. cynifrið. hildiuald. garfrið. torchthelm. heaðuric.
hygberct. burgfrið. uilberct. hunuulf. eanbercht. gyðhelm.
125 ceoluulf. eðiluini. cyniðegn. uilberct. forðhere. uernberct.
tilfrið. alchmund. tilfrið. hyglac. uulfheard. uilðegn. uigberct.
berctuini. titfrith. tathaed *lect'*. friðhelm. berctgils. hygberct.
cynibald. alberct. berctuini. dycgfrith. sigberct. uulflaf. cynhelm. friouini. eadberct. huaetgils. alduulf. cyniuulf. lagudi
130 *lect'*. uuulfheard. eanfrith. abniar *lect'*. uulfsig. uilðegn. ecg-
mund. torctuulf. cynigils. eadberct. eanuini. eanuulf *lect'*.
maegenuald. ecguulf. cyniberct. ceoluini. bedhelm. heardred.
eanuulf. hygberct. eadbald. uulfheard *lect'*. hunberct. heaðured.
eatdegn. cyna. uulfsig. ceolred. londfrið. osberct. uilðegn.
135 berctred. ebbi. eðiluulf *lect'*. cuthberct. eðilmund. cynheard.
alduulf. tilberct. cuthbald. hroeðlac. eaduini. eatfrith. siguulf.
alduulf. eanfrith. tatuini. reachchcriðe *l'*. hygberct. atere.
heaðuuald. headured. frioðuulf. beornred. hysiuulf. hygbald.
cuðgar. eadberct. alduulf. guðmund. cynifrith. siguulf. eanred.
140 eada. alduulf. tatuini. bercthun *lect'*. eadmer. baduulf. eanred.
tidhaeth. ecgberct. cuthuulf. alberct. tidberct. eanuini. alduulf.
eanbald *lect'*. haðuuini. hunfrith. uilgils. baduulf. beornred.
beornuulf. uulfhaeth. heaðufrith. eaduulf. cyniuulf. cynibald.
eadmer. alberct. aella. aluuini *lect'*. heaðuulf. cynigils. badu-
145 uald. tilberct. eanberct. eaduulf. eaduini. haðuuini. eaduald.
beornuini. earduulf. heaðuulf. berctmund. eaduald. eanred.
berctuald. cyniuulf. uilmund. tiduini. beornuulf. ingeld.
botuulf. hunbald. tiduini. beornuulf. ingild. botuulf. aldred.
eadred. aelfuini. eadred. eaduulf. uchtred. saeuini. uulfheard

suiðred. hildigils. beornuulf. cuðred. uilðegn. aluðegn. 150
headuulf. cynigils. uinibald. helpric. eanbald. bercht. osbald.
berhtuulf. torhtmund. uiluulf. uigbercht. eanred. aldred.
alduini. uilðegn. berhtuulf. eaduulf. berhtuulf. eadred. eaduulf.
berhtuulf. uigmund. beornuini. alduulf.

Nomina diaconorum 155

Haðuuald. daeghelm. daeghelm. daegmund. ecca. eanuini.
eanmund. iohannes. tidberct. aeostoruini. eaduulf. torchtuini.
eðiluini. eðilmund. uulfheard. ebbi. hunfrið. cuthberct. aelberct. bercthaeð. cuthred. bota. alchmund. sigsceat. tidbald.
cynired. hygfrith. uulfsig. uilberct. cuthred. leofðegn. ald- 160
uulf. eadred. cuthgar. alduulf. eadmaer. cuðhelm. *tonberct.
eadmer. beornred.

V

LORICA PRAYER

(*Cambridge Univ. Lib. MS. Ll. 1. 10, fol. 2. 9th century. Mercian.*)

7 ðe georne gebide gece 7 miltse fore alra his haligra[1]
gewyrhtum 7 geearningum 7 boenum on[2] .. g . num, ða ðe
domino deo gelicedon from fruman middangeardes; ðonne
gehereð he ðec ðorh hiora ðingunge. Do ðonne fiorðan siðe
5 ðin hleor ðriga to iorðan fore alle Godes cirican, 7 sing ðas
fers: *domini est salus, salvum fac populum tuum, domine
praetende misericordiam tuam.* Sing ðonne *pater noster.* Gebide
ðonne fore alle geleaffullę menn *in mundo.* Ðonne bistu ðone
deg daelniomende ðorh Dryhtnes gefe alra ðeara goda ðe ænig
10 monn for his noman gedoeð, 7 ðec alle soðfestę fore ðingiað
in caelo et in terra, amen.

---

[1] ha- *now partly covered.*   [2] on[d]? (*no trace of a third letter*
visible).

VI

CODEX AUREUS INSCRIPTION

*(Stockholm, Kungl. Bibliotek, 'Codex Aureus', fol. 11.
Mid-9th century. Surrey dialect?[1])*

+*In nomine Domini nostri Ihesu Christi.* Ic Aelfred aldormon
7 Wérburg mín gefera begetan ðas béc æt haeðnum herge mid
uncre claene feo; ðæt ðonne wæs mid clæne golde. 7 ðæt wit
deodan for Godes lufan 7 for uncre saule ðearf[e][2], ond for ðon
ðe wit noldan ðæt ðas halgan beoc lencg in ðære haeðenesse 5
wunaden, 7 nu willað heo gesellan inn to Cristes circan Gode
to lofe 7 to wuldre 7 to weorðunga, 7 his ðrowunga to ðoncunga,
7 ðæm godcundan geferscipe to brucen[ne][3] ðe ín Cristes circan
dæghwæmlice Godes lof ræराð, to ðæm gerade ðæt heo mon
árede eghwelce monaðe for Aelfred 7 for Werburge 7 for 10
Alhðryðe, heora saulum tó ecum lecedome, ða hwile ðe God
gesegen haebbe ðæt fulwiht æt ðeosse stowe beon mote. Ec
swelce ic Aelfred dux 7 Werburg biddað 7 halsiað ón Godes
almaehtiges noman 7 on allra his haligra ðæt nænig mon seo to
ðon gedyrstig ðætte ðas halgan beoc áselle oððe áðeode from 15
Cristes circan ða hwile ðe fulwiht [s]t[on]da[n mote][4].

Aelfre[d]. Werbur[g]. Alhðryð *eorum* [*filia*][5].

---

[1] *the donors are testator and beneficiary of the will printed on
pp. 216 ff., below; on fol. 1 of the 'Codex Aureus' is the following invo-
cation, in an apparently tenth-century hand:* +Orate pro Ceolheard pr'
Niclas 7 Ealhhun 7 Wulfhelm aurifex.   [2] *final e cut off by binder.*
[3] *final ne cut off by binder.*   [4] *the lower half of the last four words
has been cut away, and the letters in brackets can no longer be identified.*
[5] *these names in the right-hand margin; letters in brackets have been cut
off by binder.*

VII

HYMNS FROM THE VESPASIAN PSALTER

(Cotton MS. Vespasian A. i, fols. 141 ff. 9th century. Mercian.)

1

HIC PSALMUS PROPRIE SCRIBTUS DAVID EXTRA NUMERUM CUM PUGNAVIT CUM GOLIA

lytel[1] ic wes betwih broður[2] mine 7   *iugra   in
*Pusillus   eram   inter   *frater meos,   et   adolescentior   in*

huse feadur mines ic foedde scep feadur mines honda mine
domo patris   mei . pascebam oves patris   mei . manus meae

dydun   organan   fingras mine wysctun   hearpan   7
fecerunt   organum ; digiti   mei aptaverunt   psalterium . et

hwelc   segde   dryhtne   minum   he   dryhten he
quis   adnuntiavit Domino   meo ? ipse   Dominus, ipse

5 allra   geherde mec   he sende engel   his   7 nom mec
omnium exaudivit me ; ipse misit angelum suum , et tulit me

of scepum feadur mines 7 smirede mec in mildheartnisse
de ovibus patris   mei , et unxit   me in   misericordia

smirenisse his broður mine gode 7 micle 7 ne wes
unctionis suae . fratres   mei   boni et magni , et non fuit

welgelicad in him dryhtne ic uteode ongegn[3] fremðes
beneplacitum in eis Domino .   exivi obviam   alieni-

cynnes men 7 wergcweodelade mec in hergum heara ic
genae , et   maledixit   me in simulacris suis ; ego

---

[1] *prec. by* ic wes, *er.*   [2] b::::roður.   [3] gn *from* m.

soðlice gebrogdnum from him his agnum sweorde ic acearf 10
autem evaginato ab eo ipsius gladio amputavi

heafud his 7 onweg afirde edwit of bearnum Israela
caput ejus, et abstuli obprobrium de filiis Israhel.

2

CANTICUM ESAIAE PROFETAE. II. FERIA

ic ondettu ðe dryhten fordon eorre ðu earð me ge-
Confitebor tibi Domine , quoniam iratus es mihi . con-

cerred is hatheortnis ðin 7 *frofrende earð mec sehðe god
versus est furor tuus , et consolatus es me . ecce Deus

hęlend min getreowlice ic dom 7 ne ondredu forðon
salvator meus ; fiducialiter agam , et non timebo . quia

strengu min 7 herenis min dryhten 7 geworden is me
fortitudo mea et laudatio mea Dominus , et factus est mihi

in haelu gehleadað weter in gefian of *wellu haelendes 5
*in salutem . *aurietis aquas in gaudio de fontibus salvatoris,*

7 cweoðað in ðæm dege ondettað dryhtne 7 gecegað
et dicitis in illa die : confitemini Domino ; et invocate

noman his *cyðe doð in folcum gemoetinge his ge-
nomen ejus . notas facite in populis adinventiones ejus ; me-

munað forðon heh is noma his singad dryhtne
mentote quoniam excelsum est nomen ejus . cantate Domino

forðon micellice dyde seggað ðis in alre eorðan
quoniam magnifice fecit ; adnuntiate hoc in universa terra .

gefeh 7 here eardung Sione forðon micel in midum 10
exulta et lauda habitatio Sion , quia magnus in medio

ðin halig Israel
tui sanctus Israhel .

3

CANTICUM EZECHIAE. III. FERIA

ic cweð in midum daega minra ic fearu to gete
Ego dixi in dimedio dierum meorum : vadam ad portas

helle ic sohte lafe gera minra ic cweð ic ne
inferi . quaesivi residuum annorum meorum ; dixi : non

gesio dryhten god in eorðan lifgendra ne gelociu ic
videbo Dominum Deum in terra viventium . non aspiciam

mon mae 7 eardiend gestilde cneoris min wið-
hominem ultra et habitatorem . quievit generatio mea ; ab-

5 laeded is 7 befalden is from me swe swe geteld
lata est , et convoluta est a me quasi tabernaculum

heorda forcorfen is swe swe from ðæm weofendan lif
pastorum . praecisa est velut a texente vita

min mit te nuget gehefeldad acearf mec of marne
mea ; dum adhuc ordirer succidit me . de mane

oð efen geendas mec from efenne oð
usque ad vesperam finies me ; a vespere usque ad

margen swe swe lea swe fordręste all ban min of
mane quasi leo sic contrivit omnia ossa mea ; de

10 marne ot efen geendas mec swe swe brid
mane usque ad vesperam finies me . sicut pullus

swalwan swe ic cleopiu ic smegu swe swe culfre
hirundinis sic clamabo ; meditabor ut columba .

geðynnade sind egan min gelocende in heanis dryhten
adtenuati sunt oculi mei aspicientes in excelso . Domine ,

ned ic ðrowiu ondsweora fore me hwet ic cweðe oððe
vim patior ; responde pro me , quid dicam , aut

hwet ondsweorað me ðæt ic[1] *seofa doa ic ðencu all
quid respondebit mihi quod ipse fecerim . recogitabo omnes

15 ger min in bitternisse sawle minre dryhten gif swe
annos meos in amaritudine animae meae . Domine , si sic

[1] *prec. by* he, er.

bið lifd oððe in weolerum lif gastes mines geðreas
vivitur , aut in talibus vita spiritus mei , corripies
mec 7 geliffestes mec sehðe in sibbe bitternis min sie
me , et vivificabis me . ecce in pace amaritudo mea a-
bittreste ðu soðlice generedes sawle mine ðet ic ne
marissima ; tu autem eruisti animam meam , ut non
forwurde 7 awurpe on bec ðinne alle synne mine
perirem . et projecisti post tergum tuum omnia peccata mea ,
forðon nales hel ondetteð ðe ne deað hereð 20
quia non infernus confitebitur tibi , neque mors laudabit
ðec ne bidað ða ofdune steogun in seað soð-
te . non expectabunt qui descendunt in lacum veri-
festnisse ðine lifgende lifgende he *onddetteð ðe swe
tatem tuam ; vivens vivens ipse confitebitur tibi , sicut
7 ic to dege feder bearnum cuðe *doð soðfestnisse
et ego hodie . pater filiis notam faciet veritatem
ðine dryhten hale us doa 7 salmas ure we sin-
*tuam . Domine , salvos nos fac ; et *psalmus nostros cantabi-*
gað allum degum lifes ures in huse dryhtnes 25
mus cunctis diebus vitae nostrae in domo Domini .

4

CANTICUM ANNAE VIDUAE. IIII. FERIA

gefaeh heorte min in dryhtne 7 upahefen is horn
Exultavit cor meum in Domino , et exaltatum est cornu
min in gode mine¹ gebraeded is muð min ofer
meum in Deo meo . dilatatum est os meum super
feond mine forðon geblissad ic eam in haelu dinre
inimicos meos , quia laetata sum in salutari tuo .
nis halig swe swe is dryhten ne soðlice is oðer
non est sanctus ut est Dominus , neque enim est alius

¹ e *at edge of page.*

5 butan ðe 7 nis strong swe swe god ur nyllað
extra te , et non est fortis sicut Deus noster . nolite

gemonigfaldian spreocan ða hean wuldrende gewiten ða
multiplicare loqui sublimia gloriantes ; recedant ve-

aldan of muðe eowrum forðon god wisdoma dryhten
tera de ore vestro ; quia Deus scientiarum Dominus

is 7 him earun gegearwad geðohtas boga strongra
est , et ipsi praeparantur cogitationes . arcus fortium

oferswiðed is 7 untrume bigyrde sind strengu gefylde
superatus est , et infirmi accincti sunt robore . repleti

10 ær fore hlafum *he bihyrdun 7 ðiowincelu werun
prius pro panibus se locaverunt , et familici saturati

gefylde oð ðæt unbeorendu cende monge 7 sie
sunt , donec sterelis peperit plurimos , et quae

monge hefde bearn geuntrumad wes dryhten cwælmeð
multos habebat filios infirmata est . Dominus mortificat

geliffesteð gelaedeð to helwearum 7 eft alaedeð dryh-
et vivificat , deducit ad inferos et reducit . Domi-

ten ðearfan doeð 7 geweolegað geeaðmodað 7 geheð
nus pauperem facit , et ditat ; humiliat et sublimat ;

15 *awecende of duste weðlan 7 of scearne uprærende
suscitans de pulvere egenum , et de stercore eregens

ðearfan ðæt he sitte mid aldermonnum 7 sundurseld
pauperem ; ut sedeat cum principibus , et solium

wuldres nimeð dryhten soðlice sind heorras eorðan 7
*gloriae teneat . Domini enim sunt *cardinis terrae , et*

sette ofer hie ymbhwyrft foet¹ haligra his heold
posuit super eos orbem . pedes sanctorum suorum servabit,

7 arlease² in ðeostrum geswigiað forðon nales in strengu
et impii in tenebris conticiscent ; quia non in fortitudine

20 his bið gestrongad wer dryhten forhtiað wiðerbrocan
sua roborabitur vir . Dominum formidabunt adversarii

---

¹ et on er., indistinct.   ² prec. by er.

his 7 ofer him in heofenum hleoðrað dryhten doemed
ejus , et super ipsis in caelis tonabit . Dominus judicabit

endas eorðan 7 seleð cynedom cyninge his 7 geheð
fines terrae ; et dabit imperium regi suo , et sublimabit

horn Cristes his
cornu Christi sui .

5

CANTICUM EXODII. QUINTA FERIA

singen we dryhtne wuldurlice soðlice gearad is
Cantemus Domino ; gloriose enim honorificatus est .

hors 7 onstigend awearp in sae fultum 7 gescildend
equum et ascensorem projecit in mare ; adjutor et protector

geworden is me in haelu ðes god min 7 ariu
factus est mihi in salutem . hic Deus meus , et honorabo

hine god feadur mines 7 ic *uphebu hine dryhten
eum ; Deus patris mei , et exaltabo eum . Dominus

forðræstende gefeht dryhten noma is him scrid Pha- 5
conterens bella ; Dominus nomen est ei . currus Pha-

raones 7 weoreda his awearp in sae gecorene upstigende
raonis et exercitum ejus projecit in mare ; electos ascensores

ðreo foeðan besencte in ðere readan sae widsae ofer-
ternos statores demersit in Rubro Mare ; pelago coope-

wrah hie bicwomun in grund *wwe swe stan swiðre
ruit eos ; devenerunt in profundum tamquam lapis . dextera

ðin dryhten gewuldrad is in megne sie swiðre honda
tua Domine glorificata est in virtute ; dextera manus

ðine dryhten gebrec feond 7 ðorh mengu me- 10
tua , Domine , confregit inimicos ; et per multitudinem

genðrymmes ðines ðu fordrestes wiðerbrocan ðu sendes
majestatis tuae conteruisti adversarios . misisti

eorre ðin 7 et hie swe swe halm 7 ðorh gast
iram tuam ; et comedit eos tamquam stipulam ; et per spiritum

eorsunge ðinre todaeled is weter   heardadun swe swe
*iraecundiae tuae   divisa   est   aqua .   gelaverunt   tamquam

wall   weter   heardadon   yde   in midre sae   cweð
muros   aquae ;   gelaverunt   fluctus   in   medio mare .   dixit

15 *feon   oehtende   ic befoo   daellu herereaf gefyllu
inimicus : persequens conpraehendam ; partibo spolia ; replebo

sawle   mine   ic ofslea   sweorde[1]   minum   waldeð
animam   meam ; interficiam   gladio   meo ;   dominabitur

hond   min   ðu sendes   gast   ðinne   7 oferwrah hie
manus   mea .   misisti   spiritum   tuum ; et   operuit   eos

sæ[2]   bisenctun   swe swe   lead   in   wetre ðæm stren-
mare ; merserunt   tamquam   plumbum   in   aqua   validis-

gestan   hwelc gelic ðe in godum dryhten   hwelc   gelic
sima .   quis similis tibi in   diis , Domine?   quis   similis

20 ðe   wuldurfest in halgum   wundurlic in megenðrymmum
tibi , gloriosus   in sanctis ,   mirabilis   in   majestatibus ,

donde   forebecen   ðu aðenedes   ða swiðran   ðine   7 for-
faciens   prodigia ?   extendisti   dexteram   tuam , et de-

swalg   hie eorðe steordes mid *rehtwinisse   dinre folc
voravit eos   terra . gubernasti   justitia   tua populum

ðin   ðis   ðæt   ðu gefreades   *ypped earð   in   *gne
tuum hunc quem   liberasti .   exortatus   es   in virtute

ðinum   7 in gereordnisse   ðere halgan   ðinre geherdun
tua , et in   refectione   sancta   tua . audierunt

25 ðiode   7 eorre werun   sar   befengun ineardiende
gentes , et iratae sunt ; dolores conpraehenderunt inhabitantes

Filisteos   ða   oefestun ladtowas   Edomes   7 alder-
Philistim . tunc festinaverunt   duces   Edom , et   prin-

men   Moab   gegrap   hie cwaecung aswundun
cipes Mohabitarum adpraehendit eos   tremor ; tabuerunt

alle   ineardiende   gefalle ofer[3] hie   ege 7 cwae-
omnes inhabitantes Chanaan . decidat super eos timor et tre-

---

[1] prec. by er. of three (?) letters, the first of which is m.   [2] sæ
from m.   [3] o from beginning of another letter.

cung   micelnisse   earmes   ðines   sien   swe swe stan
mor   *magnitudinis*   *brachii*   *tui ; fiant   tamquam lapis ,*

oð ðæt leoreð   folc   ðin   dryht*en* oð ðæt ðonne geond- 30
donec transeat populus tuus , Domine ; usque   dum pertrans-

fereð   folc   ðin   ðis   ðæt   ðu bigete   ingelaedes plantas
eat   populus tuus hunc quem adquisisti ,   induces ,   plantas

hie   in   munt   erfes   ðines   gegearwadu*m* eardung-
eos   in   montem hereditatis tuae ,   in praeparato   habita-

huse ðinu*m* ðæt gegearwades dryht*en*   halignisse   ðine
culo   tuo   quod praeparasti ,   Domine ; sanctimonium tuum ,

dryht*en*   ðæt   gegearwadun   honda   ðine   dryht*en*   ðu
Domine , quod praeparaverunt manus   tuae , Domine , qui

ricsas in   ecnisse 7 in weoruld 7 nuget forðon ineode 35
regnas in aeternum et in saeculum et adhuc . quia   introivit

eorud   Faraones[1] mid feoðurtemum 7   upstigendu*m*   in
equitatus   Farao   cum   quadrigis   et   ascensoribus   in

sae   7 ingelaedde ofer   hie   dryht*en*   weter   sae   bearn
mare ,   et   induxit   super   eos   Dominus aquas maris ; filii

soðlice   eodun   ðorh dryge ðorh midne[2]   se͜
autem Israhel ambulaverunt per siccum per medium mare .

6

CANTICUM ABACCU PROFETAE. SEXTA FERIA

dryht*en*   ic geherde gehernisse ðine 7 ondreord ic
Domine ,   audivi   auditum tuum , et   timui ; con-

sceawade werc ðin   7 ic forhtade in midle twoega
sideravi   opera tua ,   et   expavi . in medio duorum ani-

netna   cuðas   ðonne   toniolaecað   ger   ðu on-
malium innotesceris ; dum   adpropiaverint anni   cogno-

cnawes ðonne tocymeð   tid   odeawes in ðon   ðonne
sceris ; dum   advenerit tempus ostenderis in   eo . dum

---

[1] *second* a *from* o.   [2] m:idne; ne *on er.*

5 gedroefed bið sawul min in eorre mildheortnisse
conturbata fuerit anima mea in ira misericordiae ,

gemyndig¹ ðu bist god from Libano cymeð 7 halig of
memor eris Deus a Libano . *veniet et sanctus de*

munte scedehtum 7 ðiccum oferwrah heofenas megenðrym
monte umbroso et condenso ; operuit caelos majestas

his 7 lofe his ful is eorðe birhtu his swe
ejus , et laude ejus plena est terra . *splendor ejus sicut*

leht bið hornas sind in hondum his ðer getrymed is
lumen erit ; cornua sunt in manibus ejus . *ibi confirmata est*

10 megen wuldres his 7 sette birhtu trume strengu
virtus gloriae ejus , et posuit claritatem firmam fortitudinis

his biforan onsiene his gæð word² 7 utgaeð in feldum
suae . *ante faciem ejus ibit verbum ; et exibit in campis*

foet his stodun 7 onstyred wes eorðe gelocade 7
pedes ejus ; steterunt et mota est terra . *aspexit , et*

tofleowun ðeode tobrocene sind muntas swiðlice 7
defluxerunt gentes ; confracti sunt montes vehementer , et

tofleowun hyllas ecelice siðfetas ecnisse his fore
defluxerunt colles aeternales . *itinera aeternitatis ejus prae*

15 gewinnum weres geteld Sigelhearwena⁴ forhtiað
laboribus viri³ . *tabernacula Aethiopum expavescent* ,

geteld eorðan ah in flodum *ðines
tabernacula terrae Madian . *numquid in fluminibus ira⁵*

*earres dryhten oððe in flodum hatheortnis ðin
tua⁶ , Domine , aut in fluminibus furor tuus ,

oððe in sae onræs ðin forðon astigende astiges
aut in mare impetus tuus ? quoniam ascendens ascendes

ofer hors ðin 7 eored ðin haelu ðennende ðu
super equos tuos , et equitatus tuus sanitas . *tendens ex-*

20 aðenes bogan ðinne ofer cyneðrym cweð dryhten
tendes arcum tuum super sceptra . *dicit Dominus :*

¹ d *from* t *or unfinished* g. ² d *from* ð. ³ d *written above* r.
⁴ w *from* f. ⁵ *from* irae? ⁶ *foll. by* er., *apparently* e.

mid flodum bið tosliten eorðe geseað ðec 7 sargiað
fluminibus scinditur terra ; videbunt te et dolebunt

folc stregdende weter in siðfetum his salde niolnis
*populi . *aspargens aquas in itineribus suis dedit abyssus*

stefne his from heanisse scinhiowes his upahefen is
vocem suam ab altitudine fantasiae suae . elevatus est

sunne 7 mona stod in endebyrdnisse his in lehte sco-
sol , et luna stetit in ordine suo . in lumine ja-

tunge ðine gað in birhtu legite wepna ðinra in 25
cula tua ibunt in splendore fulgoris armorum tuorum . in

neoweste ðinre gewonas eorðan 7 in *hatheortniss
comminatione tua minorabis terram , et in furore

ðinre teles ðiode ðu gestode in haelu folces ðines
tuo detrahes gentes . existi in salutem populi tui ,

ðæt hale gedoe cristas ðine sendes in heafudu un-
ut salvos facias christos tuos . misisti in capita ini-

rehtra deað ðu awaehtes bende oð swirban
quorum mortem ; excitasti vincula usque ad cervices ;

forcurfe in afremðunge heafud maehtigra bioð onstyred 30
praecidisti in alienatione capita potentium . movebuntur

in ðon ðiode ontynað muðas heara swe ðearfa eo-
in ea gentes ; adaperient ora sua sicut pauper e-

tende in degulnisse sendes in sae hors ðin gedroefende
dens in occulto . misisti in mare equos[1] tuos turbantes

weter micelu heold 7 forhtade womb min from stefne
aquas multas . custodivit et expavit venter meus a voce

gebedes *beolera minra 7 ineode cwaecung in ban
orationis labiorum meorum , et introivit tremor in ossa

min 7 under me gedroefed[2] is megen min gerestu in 35
mea , et subtus me turbata est virtus mea . requiescam in

dege geswencednisse minre ðæt ic astige to folce
die tribulationis meae , ut ascendam ad populum

---

[1] *from* aequos, a *er.*   [2] o *from beginning of another letter.*

leornisse minre forðon fictreo no tobringeð
transmigrationis [m]eae[1] . *quoniam* *ficus* *non* *adferet*

westem 7 ne bið cneoris in wingeardum legað
fructum , *et* *non erit generatio in* *vineis* . *mentientur*

werc eletres 7 feldas ne doð mettas asprungun from
opus *olivae* , *et campi non facient escas* . *defecerunt* *ab*

40 mete scep 7 ne bioð in binne oexen[2] ic soðlice in
   esca *oves* , *et non erunt in praesepio boves* . *ego autem* *in*

dryhtne wuldriu gefio in gode haelende minum dryhten
Domino gloriebor ; *gaudebo in Deo Ihesu meo* . *Domine* ,

god megen min gesete foet mine in geendunge
Deus virtus mea , *constitue pedes meos in consummatione* ;

7 ofer ða hean geseteð mec ðæt ic oferswiðe in birhtu
et super excelsa statuit me , *ut* *vincam* *in claritate*

his
ipsius .

7

CANTICUM DEUTERONOMII IN DIE SABBA[TI][3]

bihald heofen 7 spreocu[4] 7 gehere eorðe word of
Adtende caelum , *et loquar* , *et audiat terra verba ex*

muðe minum sie abiden swe *sw regn gesprec min
ore *meo* . *expectetur* *sicut* *pluvia eloquium meum* ,

7 astigen swe swe deaw word min swe swe scur
et descendant *sicut* *ros verba mea* , *sicut* *imber*

ofer gred 7 swe swe snaw ofer heg forðon noma
super gramen , *et sicut* *nix super faenum* , *quia* *nomen*

5 dryhtnes ic gecegu sellað micelnisse gode urum
  Domini *invocabo* . *date* *magnitudinem* *Deo* *nostro* ;

god soðe werc his 7 alle wegas his domas
Deus , *vera opera ejus* , *et omnes viae ejus judicia* .

---

[1] transmigrations̄eę.   [2] *first e from unfinished* x.   [3] *last
two letters cut off.* [4] p *from* w.

god getreowe 7 nis unrehtwisnis in him rehtwis
Deus fidelis , et non est iniquitas in eo ; justus

7 halig dryhten syngadun nales him bearn unwemme
et sanctus Dominus . peccaverunt non ei filii inmaculati ,

cneoris ðweoru 7 forcerredu ðas dryhtne geedleanades
natio prava et perversa ; haec Domino retribuisti .

swe folc dysig 7 nales snottur ahne ðes illce ðu *ear 10
sic plebs fatua et non sapiens . nonne hic ipse tuus

feder gesiteð ðec dyde ðec 7 gescop ðec in mode
pater possedit te ; fecit te , et creavit te . in mente

habbað dægas weorulde ongeotað ger cneorisse cneo-
habete dies saeculi ; intellegite annos nationis natio-

rissa frign feder ðinne 7 segeð ðe ældran
num . interroga patrem tuum ; et adnuntiabit tibi seniores

ðine 7 cweoðað ðe ðonne todaeleð se hea ðiode to
tuos et dicent tibi , cum dividerit excelsus gentes ,

ðæm gemete tostrigdeð bearn Adames sette endas 15
quemadmodum dispersit filios Adae . statuit terminos

ðieda efter rime *enga godes 7 geworden
gentium secundum numerum angelorum Dei . et facta

wes dael dryhtnes folc his rap erfeword-
est pars Domini populus ejus , Jacob funiculum heredi-

nisse his genyhtsumiendne hine him dyde in
tatis ejus Israhel . sufficientem eum sibi fecit in

woestenne in *ðurs haetu ðer ne wes weter ymb-
heremo in sitim caloris ubi non erat aqua . circum-

laedde hine 7 gelærde hine 7 heold hine swe swe 20
duxit eum , et erudivit eum , et custodivit eum sicut

sian egan swe swe earn ðeceð nest his 7
pupillam oculi . sicut aquila tegit nidum suum , et

ofer briddas his geset aðenede fiðru his 7 onfeng
super pullos suos consedit . expandit alas suas , et accepit

hie 7 onfeng hie ofer gescyldru his dryhten ana
eos , et suscepit eos super scapulas suas . Dominus solus

lærde hie   7 ne wes mid him god fremðe   togelaedde[1]
docebat eos , et non erat cum eis deus alienus .   adduxit

25 hie in   strengu eordan   foedde hie cennende   londa[2]
eos in fortitudine terrae , cibavit eos *nascentias agrorum .

sucun hunig of stane   7   ele of trumum stane   ge-
suxerunt mel de petra , et oleum de firma petra , bo-

clystre[3] oxna   7 milc scepa mid smeorwe   *lobra   7
tyrum boum , et lac ovium cum   adipe   agnorum et

romma bearna   fearra   7 buccena mid smeorwe eðra[4]
arietum , filiorum taurorum et hircorum cum   adipe   renium

hwaetes 7   blod   winbergan   drinceð   win 7   et
tritici et sanguinem   uvae .   bibit   vinum , et mandu-

30   Iacob 7 gefylled wes 7   sporetteð   se liofa   faet
cavit Jacob , et satiatus est , et recalcitravit dilectus . pinguis

geworden wes   7 faettade   7 *gebreded wes   7   for-
factus   est , et incrassavit , et   dilatatus   est , et *dere-

leort god se   dyde hine   7 gewat from gode   ðæm
liquid Deum qui fecit   eum , et recessit   a   Deo   sa-

halwyndan his   onscunedun   mec in fremðum   in on-
lutari   suo . exacerbaverunt   me in alienis , in ab-

scuningum   heara   awehtun   mec   onsegdun   deo-
ominationibus suis   concitaverunt me . sacrificaverunt dae-

35 flum   7 nales gode   godas ða hie   ne   cuðun   nio-
moniis , et non   Deo ; deos   quos   non noverunt novi

winga cwomun[5] to ðæm ða nystun feddras heara   god
recentes venerunt , quos   nesciebant   patres eorum . Deum

se ðec cende ðu forleorte   7 ofergeotul earð god foedendne
qui te genuit dereliquisti , et   oblitus   es Deum alentem

ðec gesæh   dryhten 7   wreocende   wes 7   onscunad
te . vidit   Dominus , et   zelatus   est , et exacervatus

wes   fore   eorre   bearna   his 7   dohtra 7   cweð
est propter   iram   filiorum suorum et filiarum . et   dixit :

---

[1] letter (prob. e) er. between the two d's.   [2] a from e.   [3] t indistinct.   [4] prec. by er. (ed or eð).   [5] w from o?

ic acerru onsiene mine from him 7 oteawu hwet bið 40
avertam faciem meam ab eis , et ostendam quid erit

him ot nestan forðon cneoris ðweoru 7 forcerredu
eis in novissimo ; quia generatio prava et perversa

bearn in ðæm nis geleafa in him hie in hatheort-
filii in quibus non est fides in ipsis . ipsi in zelo

nisse neddun mec 7 nales in gode in eorre aweh-
conpulerunt me , et non in Deo ; in ira concitave-

tun mec in deofulgeldum hea[ra]¹ 7 ic in hatheortnisse
runt me in idolis suis . et ego in zelo

onweg adrifu hie 7 nales in ðiode in ðiode unwise 45
expellam eos , et non in gentem , in gentem insipientem

bismeriu hie forþon fyr born from eorre minum 7
inritabo eos . quia ignis exarsit ab ira mea , et

born oð helwearan ofdune et eorðe cennende
ardebit usque ad inferos deorsum . comedit terra nascentias

heara bernde steaðelas munta ic gesomniu in
eorum , concremavit fundamenta montium . congeram in

him yfel 7 strelas mine gefyllu in him aswin-
ipsis mala , et sagittas meas consummabo in eis ; tabe-

dende hungre 7 mete werun fugla 7 aðenenes beces 50
scentes fame et esca erunt avium , et extensio dorsi

ungehaelendlic toeð wildeora insendu in him mid hat-
insanabilis . Dentes bestiarum inmittam in eis cum

heortnisse telendra ofer eorðan utan butan bear-
furore trahentium super terram . a foris sine fi-

num bis25ereð hie sweord 7 in² hordernum ege gunge
liis privavit eos gladius , et in prumptuariis timor juvenis

mid fæmnan mid steaðulfestum aldum cweð ic to-
cum virgine³ , cum stabilito sene . dixit : di-

stregde hie biscergu soðlice of monnum gemynd heara 55
spergam eos ; privabo autem ex hominibus memoriam eorum .

---

¹ *last two letters cut off.*   ² *prec. by er.*   ³ *foll. by* [la]ctans
(*beginning now cut off*) *in left-hand margin of following line, by a corrector.*

nybðe[1]   fore   eorre   fionda   ðy læs   longe   tid   sien
nisi   propter   iram   inimicorum   ne   longo tempore sint

ofer eorðan   ðæt hie ne gedeafien   wiðerbrocum 7 cweðen
super terram . ne   consentiant   adversariis   et dicant :

honda   ure   hea   7 nales god dyde ðas all   forðon
manus   nostra   excelsa , et   non Deus fecit haec omnia . quia

ðiod   forlorenum   geðehte is   7   nis   in him   ðiodscipe
gens   perdito   consilio est , et non est in   eis   disciplina .

60 ne   hogedon   ongeatan   ðas   onfoð   in   towordre
non   sapuerunt   intellegere   haec ; percipient   in   futuro

tide   *h swe   efterfylgeð   an   ðusend   7   twegen on-
tempore , quomodo persequitur unus   mille , et   duo trans-

wendað   ten ðusendu   nemðe forðon dryhten underðiodde
movebunt dena   milia .   nisi   quia Dominus   subdidit

hie 7   god salde   hie   forðon   nis   god   ur   swe
eos , et   Deus tradidit illos .   quia   non est Deus noster sic-

swe   godas   heara   fiond   soðlice   ure   unondgetfulle
ut   dii   illorum ; inimici autem   nostri   insensati .

65 of wingearde *soðli[2] Sodomwearena wintreo heara   7 owe-
ex   vinea   enim   Sodomorum   vitis   eorum , et pro-

stem heara of Gomorra   winbergan   winbergan gallan[3]
pago eorum ex Gomorra .   uva   eorum   uva   fellis[4]

hatheortnis   draecena   win   heara
amaritudinis ipsis ;   furor   draconum vinum eorum ,

7 hatheortnis   nedrena   ungehaeledlic   ahne   ðas   gesom-
et   furor   aspidum   insanabilis .   nonne haec   congre-

nade sind mid mec 7 getacnad in goldhordum minum
gata sunt apud me , et   signata   in   thesauris   meis ?

70 in   dege   wrece   ic geldu   him   in   tid   on ða   asliden
in   die   ultionis reddam   illis   in tempore quo   lapsus

---

[1] b *from beginning of another letter; cross-stroke of* ð *uncertain.*
[2] *traces of two letters (apparently* ce) *er* (?) *after* i.   [3] *misplaced*
above ipsis (67).   [4] *foll. by* botrus *in left-hand margin of following*
line, by a corrector.

bið fot heara forðon neh is deg forlorenisse heara
fuerit pes eorum . quia prope est dies perditionis eorum ,

7 ðas sind gearu eow forðon doemeð dryhten folc
et haec sunt parata vobis . quia judicabit Dominus populum

his 7 in ðiowum his bið froefred gesaeh soðlice hie
suum , et in servis suis consolabitur . vidit enim eos

geswencte 7 asprungne in wiðlaednisse 7 tolesde[1] 7
fatigatos et defectos in abductione et dissolutos . et

cweð hwer sind godas heara in ðæm ge getreowdun 75
dixit : ubi sunt dii illorum in quibus confidebatis

in him ðeara smeoru onsegdnissa ge eton[2] 7 drun-
in ipsis , quorum adipem sacrificiorum edebatis , et bibe-

cun win onsegdnisse heara arisen nu gefultumen
batis vinum libationis eorum? exurgant nunc ; adjuvent

eowic 7 sien eow gescildend gesiað gesiað forðon ic
vos et fiant vobis protectores . videte videte quoniam ego

eam god 7 nis oðer butan me ic ofslea 7
sum Deus , et non est alius praeter me . ego occidam , et

lifgan gedom slea 7 ic gehaelu 7 nis se ðe 80
vivere faciam ; percutiam , et ego sanabo ; et non est qui

generge of hondum minum forðon ic afirru in heofen
eripiat de manibus meis . quia tollam in caelum

hond mine 7 swergu ðorh ða swiðran mine 7 cweo-
manum meam , et jurabo per dexteram meam , et di-

ðu ic lifgu in ecnisse forðon ic ascerpu swe swe
cam : vivo ego in aeternum . quia exacuam velut

legitu sweord min 7 doeð dom hond min 7
fulgur gladium meum , et aget judicium manus mea . et

geedleaniu dom feondum 7 ðissum ða fiodun mec 85
retribuam judicium inimicis , et his qui oderunt me

ic *gildu indrencu strelas mine in blode 7 sweord
reddam . inebriabo sagittas meas in sanguine , et gladius

---

[1] o *from beginning of another letter?*   [2] t *from* d.

min   iteð   flᶒsc from blode   gewundedra   7
meus   manducabit   carnes . *a sanguine   vulneratorum   et*

heftnede from heafde aldermonna   feonda   blissiað
captivitate   a   *capita   principum   inimicorum . *laetamini*

heofenas somud mid hine 7 weorðien hine alle englas
caeli   simul   cum   eo , *et   adorent   eum omnes angeli*

90 godes blissiað ðiode somud mid folce his 7 getry-
Dei . *laetamini gentes   simul   cum   populo ejus* , *et confir-*

men hine all bearn godes forðon blod bearna his
ment   eum omnes   filii   Dei . *quia   sanguis filiorum ejus*

bið gescilded 7   he gescildeð 7 geedleanað dom fi-
defendetur ; *et   defendet* , *et   retribuet   judicium ini-*

ondum 7   ðissum   ða fiodun hine gildeð 7 geclasnað
micis , *et   his   qui oderunt eum   reddet* , *et emundabit*

dryhten eorðan folces his
Dominus terram populi sui .

8

HYMNUM TRIUM PUERORUM

bledsiað   all   werc dryhtnes dryhten   bledsiað heo-
Benedicite omnia opera Domini Dominum . *benedicite cae-*

fenas dryhten   bledsiað englas dryhtnes dryhten bled-
li   Dominum , *benedicite angeli   Domini   Dominum* . *bene-*

siað weter ða ofer heofenas sind dryhten bledsiað
dicite aquae quae super   caelos   sunt Dominum , *benedicite*

all megen dryhtnes dryhten bledsiað sunne[1] 7 mona[2]
omnes virtutes Domini Dominum . *benedicite sol   et luna*

5 dryhten bledsiað steorran heofenes dryhten   bledsiað
Dominum , *benedicite stellae   caeli   Dominum* . *benedicite*

scur 7 deaw dryhten bledsiað alle gastas dryhten
imber et   ros Dominum , *benedicite omnes spiritus Dominum* .

    [1] *e on er. of two or three letters?*   [2] *foll. by er.?*

bledsiað fyr 7 sumur dryhten   bledsiað naeht 7 deg
benedicite ignis et   aestus Dominum , benedicite noctes et dies

dryhten   bledsiað deostru   7 leht dryhten   bledsiað
Dominum . benedicite tenebrae et lumen Dominum , benedicite

cele   7   haetu   dryhten   bledsiað forstas   7 snaw
frigus et caumas Dominum . benedicite pruina et nives

dryhten   bledsiað legite   7 wolcen dryhten   bledsie[1]   10
Dominum , benedicite fulgura et nubes Dominum . benedicat

eorðe dryhten   bledsiað muntas 7 hyllas dryhten   bled-
terra Dominum , benedicite montes et colles Dominum . bene-

siað   all   acennende eorðan dryhten   bledsiað   sae   7
dicite omnia nascentia terrae Dominum , benedicite maria et

flodas   dryhten   bledsiað wællan dryhten   bledsiað
flumina Dominum . benedicite fontes Dominum , benedicite

hwalas 7   all   ða bioð onstyred in wetrum dryhten
ceti   et omnia quae moventur   in aquis Dominum .

bledsiað fuglas heofenes dryhten   bledsiað wilddeor 7   15
benedicite volucres caeli Dominum , benedicite bestiae   et

all   netenu dryhten   bledsiað bearn monna   dryh-
universa pecora Dominum . benedicite filii hominum Domi-

ten   bledsie   Israel   dryhten   bledsiað biscopas
num , benedicat Israhel Dominum . benedicite sacerdotes

dryhtnes dryhten   bledsiað ðiowas dryhtnes   dryhten
Domini Dominum , benedicite servi Domini   Dominum .

bledsiað gastas 7 *sawe rehtwisre dryhten   bledsiað
benedicite spiritus et animae justorum Dominum , benedicite

halge 7   eaðmode on heortan dryhten   bledsiað   20
sancti et   humiles corde Dominum . benedicite Ananias

7   dryhten   bledsien we feder 7 su-
Azarias et Misahel Dominum ; benedicamus Patrem et Fi-

nu 7 ðone halgan   gast   hergen we 7   up hebben
lium et Sanctum Spiritum ; laudaemus et superexaltae-

---

[1] *last* e *on er. of two letters, the second of which is apparently* ð.

we   hine   in weorulde   gebledsad earð in   trymenisse
mus   eum   in   saecula . *benedictus   es   in   firmamento*
heofenes 7 hergendlic 7   up ahefen   in weorulde
caeli   , et laudabilis et superexaltatus in   saecula .

9

CANTICUM ZACHARIAE SACERDOTIS

gebledsad   dryht*en*   god   Israel forðon neasede   7
Benedictus   Dominus   Deus   Israhel , quia   visitavit , et

dyde   alesnisse   folces his   7 arehte horn hælu   us
fecit   redemptionem   plebis suae , et erexit cornu salutis nobis

in huse Dauiðes cnehtes his   swe spreocende wes ðorh
in domo   David   pueri   sui ; sicut   locutus   est   per

muð   haligra   his[1]   witgena   ða   from   weorulde
os   sanctorum   suorum prophetarum qui   a   saeculo

5 sind   7 gefreade[2] usic from fiondum uru*m*   7 of honda
sunt . et   liberavit   nos   ab   inimicis nostris , et   de manu

alra   da usic fiodun   to   donne   mildheortnisse mid
omnium   qui nos   oderunt ; ad faciendam misericordiam cum

fedru*m*   urum   7 gemunan cyðnisse   his haligre ðone
patribus   nostris , et   memorari   testamenti sui sancti : jus-

swergendan að ðone he swor to Abrahame feder   urum
jurandum   , quod   juravit ad   Abraham patrem nostrum ,

sellende hine   us   ðet butan   ege   of   hondum
daturum   se   nobis ; ut   sine   timore   de   manibus ini-

10 fionda   ura   gefreade we ðiwgen him in halignisse
micorum   nostrorum   liberati · serviamus illi   in   sanctitate

7 rehtwisnisse[3] biforan him allu*m* dægum uru*m*   7 ðu
et   justitia   coram   ipso omnibus diebus nostris . et tu

cneht   witga   ðes hestan   ðu bist geced   foregæst soð-
puer , propheta   Altissimi   vocaveris   ; preibis

---

¹ *prec. by* h, er.   ² d *from* ð.   ³ sn *from one or two other*
letters.

lice biforan onsiene dryht*nes* gearwian wegas his to
enim ante faciem Domini parare vias ejus , ad

sellenne wisdom hælu folce his in forletnisse synna
dandam scientiam salutis plebi ejus in remissione peccatorum

*minra ðorh innoðas mildheortnisse godes ures in ðæm 15
eorum per viscera misericordiae Dei nostri , in quibus

neasade usic ufancumende of heanisse inlihtan ðissum
visitavit nos oriens ex alto , inluminare his

ða in ðeostru*m* 7 in *deaðes deaðes[1] sittað to gerec-
qui in tenebris et in umbra mortis sedent , ad diri-

cenne foet ure in weg sibbe[2]
gendos pedes nostros in viam pacis .

10

CANTICUM SANCTAE MARIAE

miclað sawul min dryht*en* 7 gefaeh gast
Magnificat anima mea Dominum , et exultavit spiritus

min in gode halwyndum *minnu*m* forðon gelocade
meus in Deo salutari meo . quia respexit

eaðmodnisse menenes his sehðe soðlice of ðissu*m* eadge
humilitatem ancillae suae : ecce enim ex hoc beatam

mic cweoðað alle cneorisse forðon dyde me ða mi-
me dicent omnes generationes . quia fecit mihi ma-

clan se maehtig is 7 halig noma his 7 mildheortnis 5
gna qui potens est ; et sanctum nomen ejus ; et misericordia

his from cynne in cyn ondredendum[3] hine dyde
ejus a progenie in progenie timentibus eum . fecit

maehte in earme his tostregd oferhogan on mode
potentiam in brachio suo : dispersit superbos mente

---

[1] d from ð.   [2] first b from beginning of another letter.   [3] or
ondrẹd-?

heortan his   ofdune sette maehtge of selde   7 upahof[1]
cordis   sui ;   deposuit   potentes de sede ; et exaltavit

eaðmode hyngrende gefylde godum 7 weolie[2] forleort
humiles . esurientes implevit bonis ; et divites   dimisit

10 idelhende onfoeð   cneht his   gemyndig mild-
    inanes . *suscipit Israhel puerum suum recordatus mise-*

heortnisse his   swe spreocende wes to feadrum urum
ricordiae suae ; sicut   locutus   est ad   patres   nostros

Abram   7 sede his oð in weoruld
Abraham , et semini ejus usque in saeculum .

11

HYMNUM AD MATUTINOS

birhtu federlices wuldres of lehte leht forðbringende
Splendor paternae gloriae , de luce lucem   praeferens ,

leht lehtes   7 waelle lehtes   deg   dæga   inlihtende
lux lucis , et fons luminis , dies dierum inluminans ,

7 soð sunne inwege scinende mid sciman *ðrowian
verusque sol   inlabere , micans   nitore   perpeti ,

7 lioma halges gastes ingeot urum gehygdum willum
jubarque Sancti Spiritus infunde nostris   sensibus .   votis

5 cegen we to   feder   feder   eces   wuldres   feder
vocemus ad Patrem , Patrem perennis gloriae , Patrem

mehtigre gefe   scyld gebegeð glidder gehiowað
potentis gratiae , culpam redegit lubricam , informet

dede strece   toð gebegeð efe[stigne][3] fael gewyn-
actus strenuos , dentem retundat inv[idum][3] , casus secun-

sumie roeðe selle to donne gefe   mod steoreð 7
det   asperos , donet gerendi gratiam . mentem gubernet et

---

[1] *prec. by er. (traces of ge . . . h visible, and what otherwise remains
is consistent with a reading gefaeh [= exultavit]).*   [2] *last e from g.*
[3] inu[idum] *in right-hand margin, by a corrector; end of this word and
of gloss cut off.*

receð clęne getreowwum lichoman se rehta geleafa mid
regat castos fideli corpore . fides ca-
haetu walle facnes atur nyte 7 Crist us sie 10
lore ferveat . fraudis venena nesciat . Christusque nobis sit
mete 7 drync ur sie geleafa bliðe *dricen we ge-
cibus , potusque noster sit fides . laeti bibamus so-
ðungenlice[1] *drincennisse gastes bliðe deg ðes leore
brie ebrietatem spiritus . laetus dies hic transeat ,
clęnnes sie ðæt on ærmargen se rehta geleafa swe swe
pudor sit ut deluculo , fides velut
midne deg degred mod nyte degred ryne
meridies , crepusculum mens nesciat . aurora cursus
forðwegeð degred all forðypeð in feder all sunu 15
provehit , aurora totus prodeat . in Patre totus Filius ,
7 all in worde feder wuldur ðe feder wuldur ðæm
et totus in verbo Pater . gloria tibi Pater , gloria uni-
ancendan somud[2] mid ðy halgan gaste in ðere ecan
genito una cum Sancto Spiritu in sempiterna
weorulde[3]
saecula .

12

HYMNUM VESPERTINUM

god sceppend alra 7 heofenes reccere gerwende
Deus creator omnium , polique rector , vestiens
deg mid wlitige lehte naeht slepes gefe liomu
diem decoro lumine , noctem soporis gratia . artus
tolesde ðæt sie rest agefe gewinnes gewunan 7 mod
solutos ut quies reddat laboris usui , mentesque
woerigu gelihte 7 wopas onlese generwde ðoncas *ge-
fessas allevet , luctusque solvat ancxios . grates per-

---

[1] *er. below* l; *another letter begun in error?* [2] o *from beginning
of another letter.* [3] *last* e *apparently from* u (*or* r); *word might be
read* weoruldie.

5 doenu nu ða dege 7 naehte upcyme boene gehatum
  acto jam die et noctis exortu preces votis

scyldge ðæt ðu gefultume *humen¹ singende we onlesað
reos ut adjubes hymnum canentes solvimus .

ðæc heortan ða niðerlican hleoðriað ðec stefn smoeðu
*te cordis ima *concinat . te vox canora*

hlydeð ðec lufað clęne lufe ðec mod weorðað ge-
concrepet . *te diligat castus amor . te mens adoret*

ðungen 7 mit te grund biluceð deg dimnes naehta
sobria . et cum profunda clauserit diem caligo noctium ,

10 se rehta geleafa ðeostru nyte 7 naeht getreowum lihteð
  fides tenebras nesciat , et nox fidelis luceat ,

slepan mod ne let ðu slepan scyld cunne clæne
dormire mentem ne sinas . dormire culpa noverit ; castus

geleafa coelende slepes smec gemetgie ongered gehyg-
fides refrigerans somni vaporem temperet . exuta sen-

de glidderre ðec heortan ða hean slepað. ðylæs fiondes
su lubrico te cordis alta somnient . ne hostis

ðes efestgan² facne fyrhtu stille awecce Crist bidden
invidi dolo pavor quietos suscitet . Christum roge-

15 we 7 feder Cristes 7 feadur gast an maehtig
  mus et Patrem Christi , Patrisque Spiritum unum potens

ðorh all hirt biddende ðrines wuldur ðe feder
per omnia , fove precantes trinitas . gloria tibi Pater .

13

HYMNUM DIEBUS DOMINICIS

cyning ece dryhten wisena sceppend alra ðu
Rex aeterne , Domine rerum creator omnium , qui

were ær weorulde aa mid feder sunu ðu middan-
eras ante saecula semper cum Patre Filius ; qui mun-

---

¹ u (*uncertain*) *er. or on er.*   ² *second* e *from one or two other*
etters.

geardes in fruman   *gehiowadas mon   ðæm
di   *in primordio Adam*   *plasmasti hominem , cui*

ðinre onlicnisse ondwliotan saldes gelicne ðone dioful
tuae imaginis vultum dedisti similem , quem diabolus

biswac[1] fiond mennesces cynnes ðes ðu hiow lic- 5
deceperat hostis humani generis , cujus tu formam cor-

homan genioman *gemeode ðu were ðæt mon ðu ales-
poris adsumere dignatus es ut hominem rede-

des ðone ær soðlice gehiowades 7 usic to gode
meris , quem ante jam plasmaveras ; et nos Deo

gegadrades *ðoh flæsces gemænnisse ðone acennedne of
conjungeres per carnis contubernium , quem editum ex

fæmnan forhtað ylc[2] sawul ðorh ðone usic arisan
virgine pavescit omnis anima , per quem nos resurgere

holde mode we gelefað se us ðorh fulwiht forgefe 10
devota mente credimus , qui nobis per baptismum donasti

forgefenisse we earun numene mid bendum gebundne
indulgentiam , qui tenebamur vinculis ligati

mid ingehygde ðu fore men onfon ge-
conscientia ; qui crucem propter hominem suscipere

meodemad were saldes ðin blod ure haelu
dignatus es , dedisti tuum sanguinem nostrae salutis

weorð weotudlice[3] wagrift ðes temples tosliten is 7
pretium . nam velum templi scissum est , et

all eorðe cwaecade du monge slependra awehtes 15
omnis terra tremuit . tu multos dormientium resuscitasti ,

dryhten ðu fiondes ðes aldan megen ðorh rode deaðes
Domine . tu hostis antiqui vires per crucem mortis

fordrestende mid ðere usic gesegnade on foranheafdum
conterens , qua nos signati frontibus ,

guðfonan *gelean we beorað ðu hine from us aa
vexillum fidei ferimus . tu illum a nobis semper

---

[1] a *from beginning of* u.   [2] *foll. by* er. *of four* (?) *letters, the first*
of which is apparently s.   [3] t *from* d.

onweg adrifan ðu were gemeodemad ne æfre mege
repellere dignaveris , ne umquam possit

20 gedergan alesde mid ðine blode ðu fore us to
ledere redemptos tuo sanguine . qui propter nos ad

helwearum[1] astigan gemeodemad ðu were ðæt deaðes
inferos descendere dignatus es , ut mortis

borggeldum lifes forgefe gefe ðe on margentid
debitoribus vitae donaris munera , tibi matutino tempore

*hymen woepende we singað forgef[2] us dryhten
hymnum deflentes canimus . ignosce nobis Domine ;

forgef ondettendum forðon ðu geweota 7 doema earð[3]
ignosce confitentibus , quia tu testis et judex es ,

25 ðone nænig meg biwægan ða deglan ingehygde ure
quem nemo potest fallere . secreta conscientiae nostrae

gesionde sweðe ðu ura breosta ana[4] aspyrgend
videns vestigia , tu nostrorum pectorum solus investigator

earð ðu wunda lutiendra god ætstondes lece ðu
es . tu vulnerum latentium bonus adsistis medicus . tu

earð ðu on cuðe tid sellende ende weorulde ðu
es qui certo tempore daturus finem saeculi . tu cun-

alra geeorningum rehtwis geedleanend earð ðec soðlice
ctorum meritis justus remunerator es . te ergo

30 ðu halga we halsiað ðæt ure haele wunde ðu earð
sancte quaesumus ut nostra cures vulnera , qui es

mid feder sunu aa mid ðy halgan gaste wuldur ðe
cum Patre Filius semper cum Sancto Spiritu . gloria tibi

feder wuldur ancendum[5] somud mid halgum gaste in
Pater . gloria Unigenito una cum Sancto Spiritu in

ðere ecan weorulde
sempiterna saecula .

---

[1] *from* heol-, o *expuncted;* l *from beginning of some other letter.*
[2] e *from* i? [3] e *from beginning of some other letter.* [4] *final* a
from beginning of u? [5] *first* n *from beginning of some other letter.*

VIII

GLOSS TO THE LINDISFARNE
GOSPELS

(*Cotton MS. Nero D. iv, fols. 36v.ff. ?950–70. Northumbrian.*)

MATTH. Cap. VI

    behaldas *þæt* soðfæstnise iuerre gie doas before mon-
1. *Attendite ne justitiam vestram faciatis coram homi-*

nu*m þæt* gie se geseno fro*m* him eaðe mæg mearde nab-
nibus ut videamini ab eis ; alioquin mercedem non

bas ge mið fader iurre se ðe[1] in heafnas is   mið ðy
habebitis apud patrem vestrum qui in caelis est. 2. *cum*

ðonne ðu doas ælmessa nelle ðu bema *vel* stocc singa
  ergo facies elemosyna, noli   tuba   canere

before ðec suæ legeras gewyrcas in somnungum 7 in lon-
ante te, sicut hipocritae faciunt in synagogis et in

dum *vel* in gemærum *þæt* hia se *gearðad fro*m* monnu*m*
    vicis   ut honorificentur   ab hominibus.

soðlice *vel* soð is ic cueðo iuh to hie gefengon mearde hiora
    amen   dico   vobis, receperunt mercedem suam.

ðu *vel* ðeh uutedlice wyrcende ða ællmissa nyta winstra
3.   *te   autem   faciente aelemosyna nesciat sinistra*

ðin huæt wyrcas *vel* doas suiðra ðin   *þæt* sie ællmessa
tua quid   faciat   dextera tua; 4. *ut sit elemosyna*

ðin in degelnisse 7 fade[r] ðin se ðe gesiið in degelnisse
tua in abscondito; et pater tuus qui videt in abscondito

forgeldeð ðe   7 mið ðy gie gebiddas ne wosas ge suæ
  reddet tibi. 5. *et cum   oratis,   non   eritis sicut*

[1] ð:e.

GLOSS TO THE RUSHWORTH GOSPELS

(*Bodl. MS. Auct. D. ii. 19, fols. 8v. ff. 10th century.
Mercian. 'Ru¹'.*)

Matth. Cap. VI

1. behaldeþ *þæt* ge eowre soþfestnisse ne doan fore monnum *þæt* ge sie geseanę fro*m* heo*m*[1] elles *vel* elcur ge ne

habbaþ lean *vel* mearde mid eower fæder þæne þe in heofu-

nu*m* is 2. *forþon þonne* þu wirce ælmisse ne blau þu beman

for þe swa liceteras doan in heora somnungu*m* 7 in tunum

þæt hie sie weorþade fro*m* monnum soþ ic sæcge eow hie

onfengun heora lean 3. ðe þonne wircendum ælmesse nyte

se winstrae hónd þin[2] hwat þin sio swiþre dóa 4. þæt þin

ælmes sie in degulnisse 7 þin fæder se þe gesið in degul-

nisse geldeþ ðe 5. 7 þonne ge bidde eow ne beoþ ge swa

---

[1] from him *written after* from heom, *above* alio(quin).   [2] *Lat. omits* tua.

legeras ða ðe lufas in somnungum 7 huommum ðara
hypocritae qui amant in synagogis et in angulis

plæcena *vel* worðum stondes *vel* stondende gebiddas[1] *vel* to
platearum   stantes   orare

gebiddanne þæt hia gesene sie from monnum soðlic[2]
ut   videantur   ab   hominibus. amen

ic cueð iuch[3] to onfengon mearde heara   ðu uutedlice
dico vobis, receperunt mercedem suam. 6. tu   autem

við ðy gie gebiddes *vel* ingeong *vel* inga[4] in   cotte   ðinum
cum   orabis,   intra   in cubiculum tuum,

7 gesparrado dure ðin gbidd[5] fæder ðinne in degolnis
et clauso ostio tuo ora patrem tuum in abscondito;

7 fader ðin se ðe gesiið *vel* locas in degelnisse forgeldes ðe
et pater tuus qui   videt   in abscondito reddet tibi.

hea gebiddas uutetlice *vel* ðonne gie gebiddas nallas ge
7.   *orantes   autem   nolite*

feolo *vel* monigfald gespreca suæ esuico doas hia woenas
multum   loqui sicut ethnici faciunt; putant

forðon ða ðe in monigfald spréc his bið[on] gehered
*enim   *qui in multiloquio   suo exaudiantur.*

nallas ge ðonne wosa gelíc him wat forðon fader iurre
8. *nolite   ergo assimilari eis; scit enim pater vester*

of ðæm ðearf sie *vel* is iuh aer ðon gie bidde hine   suæ
quibus opus   sit   vobis antequam petatis eum. 9. sic

ðonne iuih gie bidde fader *urer ðu arð *vel* ðu bist in
ergo vos orabitis: Pater noster qui   es   in

heofnum *vel* in heofnas sie gehalgad noma ðin   tocymeð
caelis,   sanctificetur nomen tuum. 10. adveniat

ríc ðin sie willo ðin suæ is in heofne 7 in eorðo
regnum tuum. fiat voluntas tua sicut in caelo et in terra.

---

[1] *from* to gebiddas, to *expuncted.*   [2] c *from* s.   [3] c *uncertain.*
[4] intra *first glossed* betuih, *this then underlined and other glosse sadded in margin.*   [5] *from* gbidda, a *expuncted.*

liceteras þa þe lufigaþ stalle *vel* stonde[1] in gesomnungum

7 in hwommum worþana stondende him gebidde *þæt* hie

sie gesęnæ fro*m* monnum soþ ic sæcge eow hie onfengun

heora lean 6. ðu þonne þonne þu gebidde ga in þine cofan

7 *betun[2] þine dure bidde þin fæder 7 þin fæder se þe gesihð

in degulnisse[3] geldeþ ðe 7. 7 þonne gebiddendae ne scule

ge feola spreocan swa hæðene doan *for* þon þe hiae woenaþ

þæt[4] him sie in heora feolasprece gehéred 8. ne scule for-

þon gelice[5] beon him . . . for þon þe eower fæder hwæs

eow ðærf sie ær þon ge hine biddan 9. þus ge þonne eow

gebiddað fæder ure þu þe in heofunum earð beo gehalgad

þin noma 10. cume to þin rice weorþe þin willa swa swa[6]

---

[1] *Lat. adds* stare.   [2] *Lat.* clause *from* cluso.   [3] *Lat.* ora patrem tuum in absconso, *with* et pater tuus qui uidet *and gloss added in margin by glossator.*   [4] *Lat.* quod.   [5] l *from unfinished* g.   [6] sw *on* er.

hlaf   userne   oferwistlic   sel   ús   to dæg   7
11. *panem nostrum supersubstantiale da   nobis   hodie.   12. et*

forgef us scylda usra suæ u°e forgefon scyldgum
demitte nobis debita nostra sicut   nos dimittimus debitoribus

usum   7 ne inlæd usih in   costunge   ah gefrig usich
nostris. 13. et ne inducas nos   in temtationem; sed libera nos

from yfle   gif forðon gie forgeafas monnum synna
a   malo.   14. si   enim   dimiseritis   hominibus peccata

hiara forgefes 7^ec iuh fader iuer heofonlic synna iuerra
eorum, dimittet   et vobis pater vester caelestis   delicta vestra;

gif soðlice gie nalles forgeafa monnum ne fader iuerre
15. *si   autem   non dimiseritis   hominibus, nec pater   vester*

forgefes synna iuerre   mið ðy uutetlice gie gefæstas[1]
dimittet peccata vestra. 16.   cum   autem   jejunatis,

nællæs ge wosa sua legeras *vel* godes esuicæ unrótæ
nolite   fieri sicut   hypocritae   tristes;

misbegaas forðon onsione hiora *þæt* hia se gesene monnum
exterminant enim   facies suas ut   pareant   hominibus

fæstende soð ic cueðo iuh to forðon onfengon mearde
jejunantes. amen   dico   vobis,   quia   receperunt mercedem

hiora   ðu uutedlice mið ðy ðu fæstas ðuah heafud ðin
suam.   17. tu autem   cum   jejunas, unge caput tuum

7 onsione ðin ðuah   forðon *þæt* ðu ne se gesene
et   faciem   tuam lava; 18.   ne videaris

monnum fæstende ah federe ðinu*m* se ðe is in degolnisse
hominibus jejunans sed patri   tuo   qui est in abscondito.

7 fader ðin se ðe gesiið in degolnise forgeldeð ðe
et pater tuus   qui   videt   in abscondito   reddet   tibi.

nællas gie gestrionaige iuh gestriono[2] in eorðo
19.   *nolite   thesaurizare vobis thesauros   in   terra,*

ðer *vel* huer rust 7 mohða gfreten[3] bið *vel* gspilled[4] bið
ubi   aerugo et tinea   demolitur,

---

[1] a *above er.*   [2] *from* gestriona, *second o above expuncted* a.
[3] *from* gfreaten, a *expuncted.*   [4] *from* gespilled, *first* e *expuncted.*

on heofune swilce on eorþe 11. hlaf userne *vel* ure dæg-
hwæmlicu[1] *vel* instondenlice sel us to dæge 12. 7 forlet[2]
us ure scylde swa swa we éc forleten[3] þæm þe scyldigat
wið us 13. 7 ne gelaet us gelaede[4] in *constungae ah gelese
us of yfle 14. for þon þy gif ge forleteð monnum heora[5]
synna heow swilce fo[r]leteþ[6] eower fæder se heofunlica
eowre scyldæ 15. gif ge þonne ne forleteþ monnum eora
synne ne eower fæder se þe in heofunum is[7] forleteð eow[8]
eowra synne 16. þonne ge þon*n*e faesten ne beoþ ge swa
swa licetteras unrote for þon þe hię weorfaþ[9] heora and-
wliotu *þæt* hie sie geséanae monnu*m* fæstende soþ ic eow
sæcge for þæt[10] hiæ onfengun heora lean 17. þu þonne
þonne þu fæste smere þin heafod 7 þine andwlitu þwah
18. þyles þu sie gesene monnum fæstende ah þinu*m* fæder
ðæ*m* þe in degulnisse[11] is 7 þin fæder se þe geseoþ in degulnisse[11] geldeþ ðe 19. ne hydeþ eow hord in eorþe þær[12]
om 7 mohþa[13] gewyrfeþ *vel* etaþ 7 þær ðiofes adelfaþ 7

ðer ðeafas ofdelfes *vel* hrypes 7 forstealas   strionas gie
ubi   fures   effodiunt   et furentur.   20. thesaurizate

soðlice iuh striona in heofnum ðer ne[1] ʰrust ne ec
autem vobis thesauros in   caelo,   ubi neque erugo neque

mohðe gespilles 7 ðer ðeafas ne ofdelfes ne forstelað
tinea demolitur, et ubi fures non effodiunt nec furantur.

ðer *vel* huer forðon is   strion   ðin   ðer is 7 hearta ðin
21.   *ubi   enim est thesaurus tuus, *ubi est et cor tuum*

læhtfæt lichomæs is ego gife bið   ego   ðin bliðe
22. *lucerna   corporis est oculus. si fuerit oculus tuus simplex,*

leht   bið all lichoma ðin   gif uut*edlice* ego
lucidum erit totum corpus tuum. 23. si   autem   oculus

ðin unbliðe *vel* yfelwyrcende se *vel* bið   all   lichoma ðin
tuus   nequam   fuerit, totum corpus tuum

ðiostrig bið gif ðon*ne* leht *þæt* in ðec is ðiostro[2]
tenebrosum erit. si   ergo lumen quod in te est tenebrae

sint ða ðiostro sua miclo biðon   ænig monn ne mæg
sunt tenebrae quante erunt? 24.   nemo   potest

tuæm hlaferdum   hera   *vel* forðon an *vel* enne mid læððo
duobus dominis   servire: aut enim   unum   odio

he hæfeð *vel* he scile habba 7 oðerne lufað *vel* enne
           habebit   *et alterum diliget, aut unum*

hræfneð 7 oðerne geteleð *vel* forogas ne maga gie gode
sustinebit et alterum   contemnet.   non potestis Deo

gehera 7 dioble[3]   forðon ic cueðo to iuh ne gemende
servire et Mamonae. 25. ideo   dico   vobis, ne   solliciti

gie sie saules iurres huæt ge gebrucca scile ne lichoma
 sitis animae vestrae quid   manducetis   neque corpori

iuer huæt ge gearuiga iuⁱh ah ne sauel forðor is
vestro quid   induamini.   nonne anima plus est

---

[1] *foll. by* ec, er.   [2] *from* ðiostræ, *second* o *above expuncted* æ.
[3] mamoñ. *þæt* is gidsunges hlaferd ðe diowl. he is sua genemned.
mammonis (*margin*).

forstelaþ 20. hydeþ eow þonne hord in heofunum þær[1]

ne om ne mohþa[2] gewyrfeð 7 þær þeof ne adelfaþ

ne forstelaþ 21. forþon þær þin hord is þær is[3] þin

*eorta 22. lichoma blæcern is þin ege gif þin ege biþ[4] anfald

all þin lichoma biþ liht 23. gif þin ege þonne ne bið

nan[5] eall þin lichoma beoþ ðeostru forþon gif þæt leht

þætte in ðe is þeostru sint þæt þeostre hu micel biþ 24. ne

mæg ænig twæm godum ðeowigan for þon þe he þa

oþerne fiað *vel* hateþ 7 oþerne lufað eþa oþerne hræf-

neð 7 oþerne herweþ ne magun ge gode ðeowige 7

dwale 25. forþon ic cweþe to eow *þæt* ge sorgige . . .

eowru*m* fere hwæt ge etan ne eowrum lichoma hu ge

eowic gearwige ah nis mare *þæt* ferh þonne se mete

---

[1] þæ7, *with* 7 *for* r?　　　[2] *Lat.* neque tinea neque erugo.
[3] *Lat.* ibi erit et.　　[4] *Lat.* est.　　[5] ne bið nan *glosses* nequam
est.

ðon   mett   7   lichoma   forðor   is   ðon   wede
quam esca   et   corpus   plus   est quam vestimentum?

    behaldas *vel* locas   ða flegendo fuglas   heofnes   forðon
26.   *respicite   volatilia   caeli   quoniam*

ne   settas   *vel* saue/ᵃs ne   rioppas   7   ne   somnigas   in
non   serunt   neque metunt   neque congregant in

berern 7 fader iuer heofonlic foedæs ða ilco *vel* hia ahne
horrea, et pater vester caelestis pascit   illa.   nonne

iuih suiðor *vel* mare mone/ⁱgeⁱ aro² ge bi him *vel* from him
vos   magis   plures   estis   illis?

    huælc uutetlice iurre geðences mæge æt *vel* to ece
27.   *quis   autem vestrum cogitans   potest   adicere*

to   licnesse *vel* to lengo   his   elne   an *vel* enne   7 of
ad   staturam   suam cubitum   unum?   28. et de

gewedo huæt gemende aro ge sceauiges *vel* locas *vel* behaues
vestimento quid solliciti estis?   considerate

ðæt wyrt londes   huᵘ   wæxas   ne wynnes 7   ne nestas
lilia   agri quomodo crescunt: non laborant neque   nent.

   ic cueðo soðlice iuh forðon ne Salamon in   all
29.   *dico   autem vobis quoniam nec Salomon   in   omni*

wuldre his efnebeðeht *vel* gegearued wæs sua enne *vel* an
gloria sua   coopertus   est sicut   unum

of ðisum   gif uutedlice gers *vel* heg londes þæt to dæg
ex istis.   30.   si   autem   faenum   agri   quod hodie

is   7   to morgen   in *heofone   bið gesended   god   suæ
est et   cras   in   clibanum   mittitur   Deus sic

geuedes³ *vel* gegearuas sua forðor *vel* sua mara iuih⁴
    vestit,   quanto magis   vos

lytles geleafes   nælleð gie ðonne gemende ge sie
minimae fidei?   31.   nolite   ergo   solliciti   esse,

---

¹ *prec. by* suiðe, *underlined.*   ² *from* ari, o *above expuncted* i.
³ *from* geuoedes, o *expuncted.*   ⁴ gegerues god suiðor. alle ðingo
hæfeð us gesald monnum bi allum wihtum (*margin*).

7 se lichoma þonne[1] þæt hrægl 26. geseoþ *vel* behaldeþ

heofunfuglas þæt hię ne sawed ne ripath ne somniaþ in

berern 7 eower fæder[2] se heofunlica foedeþ þa ah ge ne

sindun diorre þonne þa 27. hwilc eower[3] mæg þonne

þencende ætece to his lengo ane elne 28. 7 be hræglę for-

hwon sorgiaþ ge sceawigaþ lilia londes hu hie waexaþ ne

winnaþ ne spinnaþ 29. soþ ic eow þonne sæcge þæt[4] ne

Salomon in allum his wuldre węs beþæht swa swa an þara

30. nunu þonne þæt londes hóeg þæt to dæge is 7 to mær-

gen *vel* marne bið in ofne[5] sended god swa gearwæþ hu

miccle mae eowic þæs medmasta[6] geleafe menn 31. for-

þon ne sorgigaeþ ge cweþende hwæt geetaþ wæ oþþe hwæt

[1] *Lat. omits* plus est.   [2] fæ : der   [3] eow *on er.* (mæg ?).
[4] *verse begins in Lat.* amen dico autem uobis quoniam.   [5] *er.*
between ofne *and* sended.   [6] *Lat.* modice.

gecueðas huæt walla ue eatta *vel* huæt we gedrince
dicentes quid manducabimus aut quid bibemus
vel of huon we biðon wrigen ðas forðon alle
aut quo operiemur? 32. *haec enim omnia*
cynna *vel* hædno insoecas *vel* befraignes wat forðon fader
gentes inquirunt. scit enim pater
iuer forðon of ðæm allum ge behofes *vel* iuh behofes
vester quia his omnibus indigetis.
soecas *vel* biddas ge uutedlice ærist ric godes 7
33. *quaerite autem primum regnum Dei et*
soðfæstnisse his 7 ðas alle tógeéced biðon iuh
justitiam ejus, et haec omnia adicientur vobis.
nælleð ge ðonne sie gemendo[1] in merne morgen
34. *nolite ergo esse solliciti in crastinum. crastinus*
forðon dæg gemende bið him seolfum wel mæg *vel* wel lícas
enim dies sollicitus erit sibi ipse: sufficit
ðæm dæg werignise his.
diei malitia sua.

MATTH. Cap. VII

nellað ge doeme ꝥæt ge ne se gedoemed in ðæm
1. *Nolite judicare, ut non judicemini.* 2. *in quo*
forðon dome gie doemes ge biðon gedo^emed 7 in
enim judicio judicaberitis, judicabimini; et in
sua huelc wo^egas hripes ge biðon gewegen bið iuh
qua mensura mensi fueritis, metietur vobis.
huæt ðonne gesiistu stré *vel* mot in ego broðres ðines
3. *quid autem vides festucam in oculo fratris tui,*
7 ðone beam in ego ðin ne gesiistu *vel* hu
et trabem in oculo tuo non vides? 4. *aut quomodo*
cueðestu broeðer[2] ðinum buta ic worpe mot *vel* stre of ego
dicis fratri tuo, sine eiciam festucam de oculo

---

[1] *from* gemende, o *above expuncted final* e. [2] b *from* d.

drincaþ wæ oþþe hv[1] beoþ we gewrigene 32. for þon þe

þas þeode all soeceþ for þon þe eower fæder wat *þæt* ge

þissa alra[2] ðurfun 33. soecaþ þonne[3] ærest godes rice 7

his soþfæstnisse 7 all þas bioð[4] geeced eow 34. ne forþon

sorgigaþ ge in morgen se morgen forþon dæg *sorgaþ beoþ[5]

selfa him genoh weotudlice[6] dæge wea his

Matth. Cap. VII

1. ne doemeþ ge þyles ge siẹn doemed 2. in ðæm[7]

wiotudlice[8] dome þe ge doemeþ ge beoþ doemde 7 in

ðæm gemete þe ge metaþ bið eow meten[9] 3. forhwon

þonne gesihstu streu in ege broþer þine 7 beam in ege

þinum ne geseẹs *vel* sis 4. oþþa hu cweþestu broþer

þinum broþer[10] abíd *þæt* ic ofdo *þæt* streu of ege þinum

---

[1] v *from another letter* (y?).   [2] *Lat.* quid horum omnium.
[3] *Lat.* ergo.   [4] *prec. by er.* (g?).   [5] beo *on er.*   [6] *Lat. adds* enim.
[7] *rewritten above blurred in* ðæm.   [8] *first* i *from another letter.*
[9] *Lat.* remittietur.   [10] *Lat. adds* frater.

ðin 7 heonu beam is in ego ðin   ðu esuica worp[1]
tuo; et   ecce   trabes est in oculo tuo? 5. *hypocrita, eice*

ærest ðone beam of ego ðin 7 ðon*ne* ðu gesiist geworpe
primum   trabem   de oculo tuo; et tunc   videbis   eicere

ðone mot of ego broðres ðines   nellas ge se[a]lla[2]
festucam de oculo fratris tui.   6. *nolite   dare*

halig[3] hundu*m* ne sendas ge meregrotta[4] iurre before
sanctum canibus, neque mittatis   margaritas vestras ante

berg ðy læs hia getrede ða ilco mið fotu*m* hiora 7
porcos; ne forte conculcent   eas   pedibus   suis, et

gewoendo *vel* gecerdo toslitas iuh giw[i]as *vel* gebiddas ge
    conversi   disrumpant vos. 7.   *petite,*

7 gesald bið iuh soecað ge 7 ge infindes *vel* ge begeattas
et   dabitur vobis; quaerite, et   invenietis;

cnysað *vel* cnyllas ge 7 untyned bið iuh   eghwelc forðon
   pulsate,   et aperietur vobis. 8. *omnis enim*

se ðe giuæð *vel* biddes onfoeð 7 se ðe soecas infindes 7
 qui   petit,   accipit; et qui quaerit, invenit; et

ðæm cnysende *vel* cnyllende *untuned bið   *vel* hua is
     pulsanti   aperietur.   9. *aut quis est*

from iuh monn ðene gif he giuias sunu his hlaf cuidestu
 ex vobis homo quem si petierit filius suus panem numquid

done stán ráeceð *vel* seles him   *vel* gif ðone fisc
 lapidem   porriget   ei? 10. *aut si   piscem*

wilniað *vel* giuias cuiðestu ða nedræ ræces him   gif
 petet   numquid serpentem porriget ei? 11. *si*

ðon*ne* iuh mið ðy ge aron yflo wutas ge godo gesealla sunu*m*
ergo vos cum   sitis mali nostis bona dare   filiis

---

[1] *from* aworp, a *expuncted and er.*   [2] *from* se[a]lle, *second* a *above
expuncted second* e.   [3] *sanctum* cueð halig þæt is ðy halga
gesaegdnisse æt hundu*m* nere gesald þæt is unwyrðu*m* 7 unclænu*m*
monnu*m* (*margin*).   [4] *precepta euangelii þæt* aron ða meregrotta
þæt sindon godspelles bebodo. *ante porcos* before bergum ðæt sindon
ða mæstelbergas þæt aron ða gehadade menn 7 ða gode menn 7 ða
wlonce men forhogas godes behod 7 godspelles (*margin*).

7 sihþe beam in ege þinum is 5. þu licettere *geþo æræst

þone beam of ege þinum 7 þonne gesihst þu awearpe[1]

þæt streu of þines broþer ege   6. ne sellað ge halig

hundum ne gewearpaþ ercnanstanas eowre beforan swinum

þyles hiæ tredan ða heora fotum 7 gehwerfæþ toslite

eowic 7. biddaþ 7 eow biþ sald soecaþ 7 ge gemoetaþ

cnyssaþ 7 eow biþ ontyned 8. æghwilc wiotudlice se þe

bit he onfoeþ 7 se þe soeceþ he findeð 7 cnyssande him

bið ontyned 9. oþþa hwælc is eower monn þe hine

bidde sunu his hlaf ah he stan ræceþ thæm 10. oþþe

gif he fiscæs biddeth[2] ah he nedra ræceþ him 11. nunu

þonne ge þe ge sindun yfle cunneþ gód sellan beaearnum

[1] r *from* p?   [2] *Lat.* petierit.

iurum   mara woen is fader iuer se ðe in heofnum is geselleð
vestris, quanto magis pater vester qui in   caelis   est dabit

godo biddendum *vel* giuiendum hine   alle ðonne *vel* forðon
bona   petentibus   se! 12. *Omnia   ergo*

sua huæt gie welle *þæt* hea gedoe iuh ða menn 7 gee
quaecumque vultis   ut   faciant   vobis homines, et vos

doeð *vel* wyrcas him ðius is forðon æ 7 witgas *vel* witgo
facite   eis; haec est enim lex et   prophetae.

inngeonges ðerh neªrᵘo   port *vel* dure *vel* gæt forðon
13. *intrate   per angustam   portam;   quia*

ðiu wide geat 7 rumwelle weg ðiu lædas to lose *vel* losing
lata   porta et spatiosa via quae ducit ad perditionem,

7 monigo¹ sint ða ðe inngeongas ðerh ða ilco   suiðe
et multi sunt qui   intrant   per eam.   14. quam

naruᵘ port *vel* gaet 7 bogehte woeg ðiu lædes to life 7
angusta   porta   et   arta   via quae ducit ad vitam, et

huon aron ða ðe onfindes ða ilco   behaldas ge from
pauci sunt qui inveniunt eam. 15. attendite   a

leasum witgum ða ðe cymes to iuh in   wedum scipa
falsis prophetis qui veniunt ad vos in vestimentis ovium;

innaueard uutedlice sint uulfes férende   from uæstmum
intrinsecus autem sunt lupi rapaces. 16. a   fructibus

hiora ongeatas ge *vel* oncnauæs hia *vel* ða ilco cuiðestu *vel*
eorum   cognoscetis   eos.   num-

hueðer somnigas of hryum *vel* of ðornum scearpum   *vel* of
quid   colligunt   de spinis   uvas aut de

hagaðornum ficbeamas suæ eghwelc treeº god wæstmas goda
tribolis   ficos? 17. *sic omnis arbor bona fructos bonos*

doæð [*vel*] gewyrces ðe yfle uutedlice treo wæstmas yfle doas
facit;   mala   autem arbor fructus malos facit.

ne mæg treᵘo god wæstmas yfle gewyrca ne tre yfle
18. *non potest arbor bona fructus malos facere, neque arbor mala*

¹ *from* monige, *second* o *above expuncted* e.

eowrum hu miccle mae fæder ewer se þe in heofunum

is selleþ gód þæm þe[1] biddaþ hine 12. all forþon swa

hwęt[2] swa ge willað þæt dóa eow menn gód swa[3] 7 ge

doaþ heom þis is wiotudlice áe 7 witgu 13. gaþ inn

þurh naarwe[4] geate forþon wíd geate 7 rúm weg þe lǽdeþ

to forwyrde *vel* forlore 7 monige sindun[5] þa þe ingan þurh

þære *vel* þæne 14. hu[6] naru *vel* wiðerdune geate 7 eorfeþe

is[7] se wég þe lædeþ to life 7 feawe sindun þa þe gemoetaþ

þane[8] *vel* cymeð in þara 15. behaldeþ eow[9] wið lyge *vel*

lease witgu þa þe cumaþ to eow[10] in gewedum scépa[11] ininnan

þonne sindun wulfas risænde *vel* woedende 16. from

wæstmum eora ge ongetaþ heo ah he somnigaþ of þornum

winbegęr oþþe of gorstum[12] ficos *vel* *nyte 17. swa ægwilc

treow gód *godne węstmas bereþ *vel* wyrceþ yfel þonne

treow yfle westmas *vel* blęd bereþ 18. ne mæg treow

---

[1] *foll. by* hine, *er.*   [2] t *on er.* l.   [3] *Lat. adds* bona ita.
[4] *second* a *may be* u, *perhaps altered to* a.   [5] d *from* t.   [6] *foll.*
by nearu, *er.*   [7] *Lat. adds* est.   [8] þa:ne.   [9] *Lat.* adten-
dite uobis.   [10] o *from* w?   [11] scé:pa.   [12] g:orstum.

wæstma godo gewyrce   eghuelc tre ðy/[iu] *vel* ne doeð
fructus bonos facere. 19. *omnis arbor   quae   non facit*

wæstm   god   gecorfen bið *vel* gecearfas 7 in fyr
fructum bonum   exciditur   et in ignem

bið gesended *vel* gesendes   ðonne from wæstmum hiora
          mittitur.   20. *igitur ex fructibus eorum*

ongeatas ge *vel* oncnaues ða *vel* hia   ne eghuelc se ðe
      cognoscetis   eos.   21. *non omnis   qui*

cueðæs to me drihten drihten inngaas in   ric   heofna
   dicit mihi Domine Domine intrabit in   regnum caelorum,

ah se ðe doeð   willo   faderes mines se ðe in heofnum is
sed qui facit voluntatem patris   mei   qui in   caelis   est

ðe ingeonges in   ric   heofna   monig wælle gcueada
ipse intrabit in regnum caelorum. 22. *multi   dicent*

to me in ðæm dæg drihten drihten ah ne in noma ðinne *vel*
mihi in illa die, Domine Domine, nonne in nomine   tuo

ðinum we gewitgedon 7 in noma ðinne *vel* ðinum dioblæs
      prophetavimus et in nomine   tuo   daemonia

we fordrifon *vel* forworpon 7 in noma ðinum mæhto monigo
      ejecimus   et in nomine tuo virtutes multas

we dydon   7 ða *vel* ðonne ic ondeto him *vel* ðæm forðon
fecimus?   23. *et   tunc   confitebor   illis   quia*

næfra ic cuðe *vel* oncneawu[1] iuih afirres from me ða ðe
numquam   novi   vos; discedite a   me   qui

ge worhton unrehtuisnisse   eghuelc ðonne se ðe geheres
operamini iniquitatem.   24. *omnis   ergo qui   audit*

uorda mina ðas 7 *ðoes[2] ða ilco geefned bið *vel* gelic[ed] bið *vel*
verba mea haec et facit   ea   assimilabitur

geteled bið wer snotre se ðe getimbres   hus   his ofer *vel* on
          viro sapienti qui aedificavit domum suam   supra

carr *vel* stan   7 ofdune astag *vel* gefeall regn 7 cuomon
   petram.   25. *et   descendit   pluvia et venerunt*

---

[1] u *written small as in alternative spellings, but not above the line.*
[2] *cross-bar of* ð *er.*?

þæt góde yfle westmas beoran *vel* wyrcende ne *þæt* treow

yfle góde wæstmas *vel* blędd beoran 19. æghwilc þara

treow[1] þe ne bereþ westęm[2] gódne bið acorfen 7 in fyre

sended 20. forþon *vel* cuþlice of wæstmum eora ge

ongetaþ heo *vel* hię 21. ne *vel* nallæs æghwilc þara þe

cweþ to me dryhten drihten gæþ in rice heofuna ah se

þe wyrceþ wille fæder mines þæs þe in heofunum is se

vel he gáeþ in heofuna rice 22. monige cweþað to me

on ðæm dæge dryht*en* dryhten ah ne in þinu*m* noma

witgadun we 7 in þinu*m* noma deoful ut wyrpon 7 in

þinu*m* noman mægen monige worhton 23. 7 ic þonne

ondetu heom þæt ic næfræ cuþe eow gewitaþ fro*m* me

ge þe wyrcaþ unrihtnisse 24. æghwilc þara þe gehéreð word

min þas 7 fremmað hie he bið lic were þæ*m* snottra þe

getimbrade hus is on[3] stane 25. 7 astág niþer rægn 7

---

[1] *verse begins in Lat.* omnis ergo arbor.   [2] *er. between* s *and* t; m *begun?*   [3] *Lat.* super.

ea *vel* streamas 7 geblewun windas 7 inræsdon in hus
   flumina   *et flaverunt*   *venti* *et inruerunt in domum*
ðæm 7 ne gefeall *gewru/ynded *vel* geseted forðon wæs ofer
illam, et non cecidit;   *fundata*   *enim erat supra*
stane   7 eghuelc se ðe geheres worda mina ðas 7 ne
petram. 26. *et omnis qui audit verba mea haec et non*
doeð ða ilco gelíc bið were dysge se ðe getimberde hus
facit ea similis erit viro stulto qui aedificavit domum
his ofer *vel* on sonde   7 ofdune astag regn 7
suam supra harenam. 27. *et descendit pluvia et*
cuomon streamas 7 gebleuun windas 7 inræsdon in huse
venerunt flumina et flaverunt venti et inruerunt in domum
ða ilco 7 gefeall 7 wæs fæll his micel   7 geworden
illam, et cecidit, et fuit ruina ejus magna. 28. *et factum*
is *vel* uæs mið ðy geendade   ðe hælend worda ðas
est cum consummasset Jesus verba haec
geuundrade weron ða ðreatas ofer lár his   wæs
  ammirabantur turbae super doctrinam ejus; 29. *erat*
forðon lærde hia suæ mæht hæfde ne suæ *vel* nalles suæ
  enim docens eos sicut potestatem habens,   *non sicut*
vel suelce uðuta hiora 7
     scribae eorum et pharisaei.

Matth. Cap. VIII

mið ðy uutedlice of gestag of mor fylgende weron *vel*
1. *Cum autem discendisset de monte,*   *secutae*
sint *vel* gefylgdon hine ðreata menigo   7 heonu lícðrouer
sunt eum turbae multae. 2. *et ecce leprosus*
cuom[1] he worðade hine cueð drihten gif ðu wilt ðu mæht
veniens adorabat eum dicens, Domine, si vis, potes
mec geclænsige   7 aðenede *vel* gespræde hond geʰran
  me mundare. 3. *et extendens manum tetigit*
him hælend ðus cueð ic uillo geclænsia 7 sona geclænsad
eum Jesus dicens, volo mundare. et confestim mundata

---

    [1] *from* ða cuom, ða *underlined for deletion.*

cuomun eáé 7 blewan windas 7 fellun on hus þæt 7 hit
no gefeoll gestaþulad soþlice hit wæs on[1] stáne   26. 7
æghwilc þe gehéreþ word min þas 7 ne fremmaþ þa[2] gelic
bið were dysig *vel* dolum þæ*m* þe timbrade hus his on[1]
sónde   27. 7 astag rægn niþer 7 cuomon eae 7 bleowen
windas 7 feollun in hus þæt 7 hit gefeoll 7 wæs hryre
his micel   28. 7 gewarð þa[3] hæfde geendad hælend word
þas þæt wundradun[4] þa mengu be láre his   29. he wæs
forþon hie[5] lǽrde swa swa mæht hæbbende nallas swa
swa bocera heora 7 fariseas

MATTH. Cap. VIII

1. þa he þa wæs astigen of dune folgedun him menga
monige.   2. 7 henu hreof *sumne[6] cumende togebędd him
cweþende driht*en* gif þu wilt þu mæht mec geclęnsige
3. 7 aþenende hælend honda his 7 æthrán him[7] cwæþende
ic wille geclænsige 7 hrǽþe geclensad wæs hreoful his

---

[1] *Lat.* super.   [2] þ *and some other letters er. before* þa.   [3] *prec.*
by þa, *er.*   [4] *Lat.* admirantur.   [5] *from* he, i *above the line*;
Lat. omits eos.   [6] *Lat. adds* quidam.   [7] *verse begins in Lat.*
et extendiens Iesus manum suam et tetegit eum.

wæs hriofol his 7 cueð him hælend loca *vel* geseh þæt ðu
est lepra ejus. 4. *et ait illi Jesus,* *vide*

ænigum menn ðu gecuoeða *vel* gesæcga ah gaa ædeau ðec
  nemini *dixeris;* *sed vade ostende te*

ðæm meassepreost 7 breng *vel* gef ðing þæt bebead *vel*
  sacerdoti, *et offer munus quod prae-*

geheht Moyses in cyðnisse *vel* witnesa him mið ðy
cepit Moses in testimonium illis. 5. *cum*

uutetlice inneade *vel* innfoerde ða burug geneolecade *vel*
autem introisset Capharnaum, acces-

tocuom to him ðe centur þæt is hundraðes monna hlaferd
sit ad eum centurio

gebæd hine 7 cuoeð ðus drihten cnaeht min liges
rogans eum 6. *et dicens, domine, puer meus jacet*

in hus eorðcryppel 7 mið yfle is gecunned *vel* gecosted
in domo paralyticus et male torquetur.

   cueð to him se hælend ic cymo 7 gemo hine
7. *ait illi Jesus, ego veniam et curabo eum.*

   7 geonduearde ðæm aldormenn cueð *drihter nam ic
8. *et respondens centurio ait, domine, non sum*

wyrðe þæt ðu inngae under rof min ah an cuoeð
dignus ut intres sub tectum meum; sed tantum dic

mið word 7 gehaeled bið cnæht min forðon 7 *vel* ec
verbo, et sanabitur puer meus. 9. *nam et*

ic monn amm under mæht hæfis *vel* hæfo under mec
ego homo sum sub potestate habens sub me

ðeignas *vel* innheardmenn 7 ic cueðo ðissum *vel* ðæm gaæ 7
  milites, et dico huic vade, et

gaes *vel* geongas *vel* faeres 7 to oðrum cymm 7 cu/ymeð 7
  vadit, et alio veni, et venit, et

ðeᵘa minum do ðis 7 does mið ðy geherde soðlice
servo meo fac hoc, et facit. 10. *audiens autem*

ðe haelend gewundrad wæs *vel* geuundrade 7 ðæm fylgendum
  Jesus miratus est et sequen-

vel fylgdon hine cuoeð soð is ic cueðo iuh ne fand ic
tibus se dixit, amen dico vobis, non inveni

4. 7 cweþ to him hælend gesech þæt þu nængum sæcge

ah gá 7 æteaw þe messepreoste 7 breng þæt lác þætte

bebead Moyses in cyþnisse heora 5. æfter þas þa he

þa éode¹ Cafarnaum cuom to him . . . biddende hine 6. 7

cweþende drihten cneht min ligeþ in huse loma 7 is yfle

wælid 7. 7 cweþ to him se hælend ic cume 7 gehæle

hine 8. 7 ondswarande centurio cweþ to him² drihten

nam ic wyrðe þæt ðu gá under þacu minne ah efne

gecweþ word 7 bið gehæled cneht min 9. wiotudlice

7 ic monn eam under mæhti geseted³ hæbbende under

me cempa 7 ic cweðe þissum gá 7 he gæþ 7 to oþrum

cvm   he cymeþ 7 to esne vel ðeow minum 7 ic cweþe⁴

do þis 7 he doeþ 10. geherende he þa hælend wundriende⁵

wæs 7 fylgendun him to þæm cwæþ soþ ic sæcge eow

---

¹ *verse begins in Lat.* post haec cum autem introisset.   ² *Lat.*
adds illi.   ³ *Lat. adds* constitutus.   ⁴ *Lat. repeats* dico.
⁵ *from* wundrade, ien *above er.* a.

suæ miclo[1] leafa *vel* lufa in Isr*ahel*   ic cueðo soðlice iuh to
tantam   fidem   in Israhel. 11. *dico   autem   vobis*

þætte monige from eastdael *vel* easta 7 woesta cymas 7
quod   multi   ab   oriente   et occidente venient et

ge[h]restas mið Abraham 7 Isaac 7 Iacob in ríc heofna
recumbent cum Abraham et Isaac et Jacob in regno caelorum,

     suna uutedlice rices biðon gedrifen in ðyostrum
12. *filii   autem   regni   eicientur   in   tenebras*

wytmesto ðer bið wop 7 gristbiottung to[e]ða 7
exteriores ibi erit fletus et stridor dentium. 13. *et*

cuoeð ðe hælend ðæm haldormenn gaa 7 suæ ðu gelefdest
dixit   Jesus   centurioni,   vade, et sicut credidisti

sie ðe 7 gehæled wæs cnæht in *ðit ðæm 7 mið ðy
fiat tibi; et sanatus est puer in hora illa. 14. *et   cum*

gecuom ðe hælend in hus Petres gesaeh suer his *vel* his
venisset   Jesus   in domum Petri,   vidit   socrum

wifes moder liccende 7 cuacende *vel* bifigende[2] 7
ejus   jacentem et   febricitantem. 15. *et*

gehran hond his 7 forleort ða *vel* hia of feberadlu*m* 7
tetigit   manum ejus, et dimisit   eam   febris,   et

arrás 7 embehtade *vel* geherde him mið ðy eferntíd *vel*
surrexit et   ministrabat   eis. 16.   *ve-*

in eferntid uutedlice geworden wæs gebrohton him menigo
spere   autem   facto   optulerunt ei multos

     diobles hæfdon 7 forwearp *vel* fordráf gaastas mið word
daemonia habentes;   et   eiciebat   spiritus   verbo

7 alle yfle hæfdon *vel* mishæbbende *vel* unhale
et omnes   male habentes   curavit;

     þæt were gefylled *vel* geendad þæt gecueden wæs ðerh
17. *ut   adimpleretur   quod dictum est per*

Esaiam ðone witgo ðus cuoeðende ðe ilca untrymmnise
Esaiam   prophetam   dicentem,   ipse   infirmi-

vel unhælo[3] usra onfoeng *vel* genom *vel* underhof 7
tates   nostras   accepit   et

---

[1] l *expuncted and er. between* i *and* c.   [2] bififigende.   [3] æ(?)
er. between n *and* h.

swa micel geleafa ne *gemotte ic in Israhęle 11. sæcge

þonne eow þæt monige from eastan 7 wéstan cumaþ 7

hleonigaþ mid Abraham 7 Isaac 7 Iacob in heofuna rice

12. bearn þonne rice þeos[1] bioþ aworpenne in þiostre þa

ytmæste þær bið wóp 7 gristbatung tóþa 13. 7 cwæþ

ða se hælend to þæm centurione gang 7 swa þu gelefdest

geweorðe ðe 7 gehǽled wæs se cneht on þære hwile

vel tide 14. 7 þa cuom se hælend in huse Petrus gesæh

swægre his licgende[2] 7 bifgende 15. 7 æthrán honda his

7 forlet hiae sio drif 7 hiu áras 7 ðægnade heom 16. efen

þonne[3] hit þa wæs þa brohtun[4] him monige deofulseoke

hæbbende 7 ut awearp þurh his[5] worde þa gastas únklene[6]

7 alle yfle hæbbende gehælde 17. þætte gefylled węre

þæt gecwæden wæs þurh Esaiam þe witgu cweþende he

wiotudlice untrymnissum urum onfeng 7 metrymnisse[7] ure[8]

---

[1] *Lat. adds* huius.   [2] i *on er., prob. of* e. *other letters er. before* þonne.   [4] r *from* o. *after glossing?*   [6] *Lat. adds* inmundos.   [8] *Lat. repeats* nostras.   [3] þ *and some five* *other letters er. before* þonne.   [5] þurh his *added*   [7] *Lat.* egritudines.

untrymnise *vel* hefignise gebær   ða gesæh uutedlice
  aegrotationes   *portavit.* 18. *videns   autem*

ðe hælend threatta *vel* hergas menigo uta ymb hine geheht
  Jesus   turbas   multas circum se jussit

fara *vel* gaa ofer luh *vel* stream   7 to cuom *vel* genealacde
  ire   trans   fretum.   19. *et   accedens*

án uðuutta coeð to him ðu larua ic fylgo ðe¹ *vel* ic ðeh sohte
  unus scriba ait illi, magister,   sequar te

sua huider ðu færes *vel* gaes   7 cuoeð to him hælend
  quocumque   ieris.   20. *et dicit   ei   Jesus,*

  foxas holas habbas 7 flegende heofnes nestas *vel* nesto
  vulpes foveas habent et volucres caeli   nidos,

sunu soðlice monnes ne hæfis huer heafud gehlutes *vel* gebeges
  filius autem hominis non habet ubi caput   reclinet.

  oðer *vel* sum oðer uutedlice from ðegnum his cueð to him
21.   *alius   autem   de discipulis ejus ait illi,*

drihten ðerhsend *vel* forlet *vel* forgef *vel* lef meh   ærest
  domine,   permitte   me   primum

fara *vel* gæ 7 bebyrge faeder min   hælend soðlice
  ire   et sepelire patrem meum.   22. *Jesus autem*

cuoeð to him soec meh *vel* fylge meh 7 forlet ða deado
  ait illi,   sequere me,   *et dimitte mortuos*

to bebyrgenne ða deado hiora   7 ofstigende hine *vel*
  sepelire   mortuos suos.   23. *et   ascendente*

ða he ofstag in lytlum scipe *vel* in cuople gefylgdon
eo   *in navicula*   *secuti sunt*

hine *vel* him ðegnas his   7 heonu styrnise *vel* hroernis
  eum   discipuli ejus. 24. *et ecce   motus*

michelo geworden wæs in sae suæ *þæt* scipp oferwrigen wæs
  magnus factus est in mari ita ut navicula operiretur

mið yðum he soðlice geslepde *vel* slepende wæs   7
  fluctibus; ipse vero   dormiebat.   25. *et*

to geneolecdon *vel* tocuomon 7 awehton hine   ðus cuedon
  accesserunt,   *et suscitaverunt eum dicentes,*

¹ *from* ðec, c *expuncted.*

he bær 18. geseonde þa hælend mengu monige ymb

hine heht feran ofer sáé *vel* bry*m*stream[1] 19. 7 cumende

an bokera cweþ to him laruw ic wille folgian þe hwider

swa þu ganges *vel* gæst 20. 7 cwæþ to him hælend

foxes hole habbaþ 7 fuglas heofunas selescota þer hie

restaþ[2] bearn *vel* sunu þonne monnes næfð wær he heafud

ahélde 21. oþer þa of[3] leornere his cwæþ to him drihten

læt me ærest gangan 7 bebyrgen fæder minu*m* 22. hælend

þanne cweþ to þ<u>e</u>m fylge me 7 forlet deaða bebyrgen

deada heora 23. 7 þa stag[4] he on scipe folgadun him

leorneras his 24. 7 henu hreornis micel geworden[5] wæs

on þæ*m* sǽ wæs þonne heom wind wiðerweard[6] swa *þætte*

þe scip wæs urnen yðum he wiotudlice *vel* he[7] soþ *vel*

þonne[7] slepte 25. 7 eodun to him discipulas his[8] 7 wehton

---

[1] *first* r *from* y.   [2] *Lat.* et uolucres caeli tabernacula ubi requiescant.
[3] *on* er.   [4] g *on beginning of* er. *before next word*; g *on* er. l?
[5] o (*and* d?) *from another letter.*   [6] *verse begins in Lat.* et ecce
tempestas magna facta est in mari, erat autem illis uentus contrarius.
[7] he *is alternative to* he wiotudlice, *for* ipse; þonne *to* soþ, *for* uero.
[8] *verse begins in Lat.* et accesserunt ad eum discipuli eius.

drih*ten* hæl usic we deade biðon *vel* we aron *vel* biðon gelosad
domine, salva nos;   *perimus.*

7 cueð to him huæt frohtende aron gie lytle/⁰   geleafa
26. *et dicit   eis,   quid   timidi   estis   modicae   fidei*[1]*?*

ða   aras *geðreadade to wind 7 to sae 7 geworden
tunc surgens increpavit   vento   et mari,   et   facta

wæs smyltnisse miclo   soðlice *vel* uuted*lice*   menn*[2]*
est   tranquillitas magna. 27.   porro   homines

gewundrade weron ðus cueðende *vel* cuedon huᵘlig   is
mirati   sunt   dicentes,   qualis   est

ðes forðon 7 uindas 7 saes geheras *vel* eðmodas him
hic quia et venti et mare   oboediunt   ei?

7 mið ðy gecuom ofer luh in lond ðara ðeade
28. *et cum   venisset trans fretum in regione Gerasenorum*

geuᵘrnon him tuoege haebbende *vel* hæfdon diobles of
occurrerunt ei   duo   habentes   daemonia de

byrgennum ut *vel* of geeadon hroeðo suiðe suæ *vel* ðus
monumentis   exeuntes   saevi nimis   ita ut

ænig*[3]* monn mæhte oferfara *vel* gae *vel* geonge ðerh woeg
nemo   posset   transire   per viam

ða ilco   7 heonu geceigdon ðus cueðende huætd
illam.   29. et ecce clamaverunt   dicentes,   quid

betuih us*[4]* *vel* us*[4]* 7 ðe sunu godes ðu cuome hider ær   tíd
nobis   et tibi fili Dei? venisti huc ante tempus

to pinenne usih   wæs uutedlice nehuarne long from
torquere nos? 30. erat autem   non   longe ab

him *vel* ðæm suner berga monigra gefoede*[5]*   diowles
illis   grex porcorum multorum pascens.   31. daemones

uutedlice gebedon hine cueðende gif ðu worpes usig send
autem   rogabant eum dicentes, si   eicis   nos, mitte

usig in suner   berga   7 cueð to him gaeð *vel*
nos in gr[e]gem porcorum 32. et ait illis,   ite.

---

[1] ðæm ðe tuas ymb godes mæht him forstondes mæht 7 geleafa fore
is ungelefnise (*margin*).   [2] *from* ða menn, ða *underlined for deletion.*
[3] *from* nænig, *first* n *expuncted.*   [4] *prec. by* h, er.   [5] *from*
gefoeded, *second* d *expuncted.*

hine cweþende dryhten hǽl usic we forweorðað   26. 7

cweþ to heom se hǽlend[1] for hwon[2] *vel* hwæt gefrohte

sindun medmiccles geleafa 7 þa arisende bebead wínd[3] 7

sáé 7 geworden wæs smyltnisse micel   27. þa menn

wundradun cwæþende hulic is þes þe wind 7 sáé gehęraþ[4]

him 28. 7 þa he cuom ofer sáé in lond Gerasinga urnon

ongægn him twegen menn[5] deofulseoka hæbbende of

byrgennum utgangende grimme swiðe swa þætte nænig

mæhte faran þurh[6] wæge þæm 29. 7 henu cegende

cwæþende hwæt is us 7 ðe hælend[7] sunu godes cwome

hider ær tide tinterga usic   30. wæs þa unfeor suner

swina[8] from heom monegra etende 31. þa deoful þonne

bedun[9] hinae cweþende gif ðu ut awearpa usic send usic

in þas sunrae swina 32. 7 cweþ to heom gaeð 7 hię[10]

utgangende eodun in swinum *vel* in þassum 7 henu ungerece

vel ræsed eode all siu suner *vel* wræð niðerweardes in

---

[1] *Lat. adds* Iesus.   [2] n *now scarcely visible.*   [3] *Lat.* imperauit
uentis.   [4] *from* gehęreþ, a *above expuncted third* e.   [5] *Lat.*
adds homines.   [6] u *from* y.   [7] *Lat. adds* Iesu.   [8] i *on*
er., *prob. of* n.   [9] *Lat.* rogauerunt.   [10] 7 hię *on er.*

faereð soð ða *vel* hia eadon *vel* gefoerdon geeadon in bergum
      at   illi   exeuntes   abierunt in porcos;

7 heonu mið ʰræs geeade   all   suner *vel* édo ðerh
et ecce   impetu   abiit   totus   grex   per

hrædlice *vel* oefestlice in sæ 7 deade weron *vel* deadedon
      praeceps   in mare et   mortui sunt

in wætrum   ða hiorda uutedlice geflugun 7 cuomon
in   aquis.   33. pastores   autem   fugerunt et venientes

in   byrig   gesaegdon[1] alle   7 of ðæm ða ðe ða diobles
in civitatem nuntiaverunt omnia et de his   qui   daemonia

 hæfdon   7 heonu all ceastra geeade togægnas hælende
habuerunt. 34. et ecce tota civitas   exiit   obviam   Jesu

7 gesene hine *vel* ða hine gesegon gebedon þæt ofereade *vel*
et   viso eo   rogabant ut   trans-

ofergefoerde from gemærum hiora.
iret   a   finibus   eorum.

    [1] *from* gesaehgdon, h *expuncted.*

sáé 7 deade¹ wurdon in wættrum 33. hiordes þonne flugon 7 cumende in cæstræ sægdun *vel* cyðdon all 7 be þæm þe deofulseoke werun ær *vel* æfdon² 34. 7 henu all cæstra uteode ongægn hælend 7 geseende hine bedun hine³ *þæt* he ferde *vel* liorde fro*m* gemeru*m* eora.

¹ *prec. by er.* ² *Lat.* [h]abebant. ³ *Lat. adds* eum.

X

KENTISH GLOSSES

(Cotton MS. Vespasian D. vi, fols. 2v.ff.[1] Late 10th century.)

(Cotton MS. Vespasian D. vi, fols. 2v.ff.[1] Late 10th century.)

PROVERBS

I

jacitur: is worpen.
pennatorum: gefiðeradra.
moliuntur (fraudes): be-
reafiað.
sic rapiunt: swa reafiað.
5 *praedicat*: bodað.
clamitat: hi clepað.
cupiunt: gewilniað.
odibunt: hatiað.
en proferam: efne nu ic
forð brenge.
10 *quia vocavi*: for ðam ic
geceide.
ego ridebo: ic hlihe.
cum insonuerit: ðonne
swęið.
ingruerit: onbricð.
exosam: onscunede.
15 *detraxerunt*: hio teldan.
perfruetur: he brecð.

timore sublato: atogenum
ege.

II

penes te: nih ðe.
gradientes: farende.
20 *omnem semitam bonam*:
ealne godne siðfet.
per vias tenebrosas: ðurh
*ðriostrie weogas.
qui letantur: ða geblissiað.
in rebus pessimis: on wer-
stum ðingum.
infames: unhlisie.
25 *qui mollit*: sio hnescað.
pupertatis suae: hire meið-
hades.
calles: siðfata.

III

non deserant: ne forleton.
gutturi tuo: ðinre hraca.
30 *ne innitaris*: ne getrua ðu.
recede: gewit.

---

[1] *some glosses on fol. 2 are no longer legible.*

umbil[ic]o tuo: þinum nafe-
lan.

inrigatio: leccinc.

saturitate: of gesundful-
nesse.

35 *torcularia tua*: þine win-
wringan.

redundabunt: genihsumiað.

ne abicias: ne awearp ðu.

nec defi[ci]as: ne ðu ne
atiara.

cum cor[r]iperis: þonne ðu
bist ðread.

40 *complacet*: gelicað.

affluit: swelhð.

non valent comparari: ne
magon bion wiðmetene.

qui tenuerit: þe hefð.

stabilivit: gestaðelade.

45 *erumperunt*: up abrycan.

rore: of deauwe.

ne affluant: ne aflowan.

non impinget: ne etspernð.

ne paveas repentino terrore:
ne *forta ðu of ferlican
ógan.

50 *ne capiaris*: ðet ðu ne sio
gripen.

prohibere: forbiodon.

si vales et ipse benefac: gif
ðu meht 7 ðu self tela
do.

ne dicas: ne sege ðu.

cras: to morgen.

55 *ne moliaris*: ne þen ðu.

ne contendas: ne flit ðu.

frustra: on idel.

ne aemuleris: ne ðu ne on-
here.

ne immiteris: ne ðu ne ge-
efenlęc.

60 *omnis inlusor*: ęl bismeriend.

sermocinatio ejus: his[1]
wordlunc.

IV

tenellus: myra.

adquire: gestrion.

arripe: gegrip.

65 *glorificaberis*: ðu bist gewuldrad.

au[g]menta: eacan.

corona inclita: myrlic cynehelm.

ne delecteris: ne gelustfulla
ðu.

desere: forlet.

70 *dormiunt*: h . . .

non rapitur: ne bið ge-
gripen.

nisi supplantaverint: buton
hi beswican.

[1] *from* hiora; *ora* er. *and* s *added above.*

comedunt: hi etað.

ausculta: hlest.

75 *ne recedant*: ne gewitan.

vita: líf.

quia ex ipso procedit: ðara
for ðam forð gewit.

remove: fram astere.

palpebre tue: ðinum bre-
wum.

80 *stabilientur*: sin gestaðelade.

novit: wát.

perverse: forhwerfede.

faciet: he deð.

V

ut custodias: þet ðu . . .

85 *conservent*: ge . . .

nitidius: scinendre.

(*gladius*) *biceps*: twiicce.

descendunt: niðer . . .

penetrant: farað.

90 *vagi*: woriende.

in[inve]stigabiles: una-
speriendlic.

ne recedas: ne gewit ðu.

ne des: ne sele ðu.

gemas: ðu giomras.

95 *cur detestatus sum*: for
hwe onscunede ic.

non adquievit: ne geða-
fede.

audivi: ic . . .

docentium: . . . ra.

magistris: . . . m.

100 *paene*: fornion.

sinagoge: werede.

de cisterna tua: of ðinum
seaðe.

diri[g]entur: sint ge-
reahte.

divide: todel.

105 *habeto*: . . . ðu.

solus: ane.

vena tua: ðin edra.

letare: geblissa.

adulescentiae tuae: ðinre
giogeðe.

110 *cerva carissima et gratissi-
mus hinnulus*: eala ðu
liofestæ hind 7 ge-
cwemest hindcealf.

inebriant: ginddrencað.

delectare: gelustfulla.

quare seduceris: for hwi
eart ðu beswicen.

foveris: ðu bist gestrangad.

115 *considerat*: he besceawað.

capiunt: gegripað.

const[r]ingitur: he við ge-
wriðen.

multitudine: of . . .

decipietur: he við be-
swicen.

VI

120 *si spoponderis*: gif ðu be-
hete.
defixisti: ðu afesnadest.
inlaqueatus es: ðu eart ge-
grinad.
captus: geheft.
incidisti: hrure.
125 *discurre*: irnn.
nec dormitent: ne hnep-
pian.
eruere: ðu[1] ut *alened.
dammula: hind.
aucupis: *hireres.
130 *ad formicam*: to emet.n[2].
ducem: lateau.
nec praeceptorem: ne bodiend.
parat: hio[3] gerewað.
estate: on sumere.
135 *paululum dormitabis*: ge-
hwede hneppast.
conseres: ðu on *arets.
quasi viator: swa wi-
ferend.
pauperies: ermð.
quasi vir armatus: swa
gewepned wer.
140 *impiger*: *nusleac.

homo apostata: afliged
mon *id retrogradiens*.
perverso: ðweran.
annuit: he beacnað.
terit: he trepeð.
145 *jurgia*: tionan.
extimplo (*e*): feringa.
conteretur: he bið for-
bret.
medicinam: lecedom[4].
detestatur: onscunoð.
150 *sublimes*: up ahafene.
machinans: *saarwiende[5].
proferentem: forð breng-
ende.
testem fallacem: *leasec-
gewitnesse.
eum: ðane.
155 *discordias*: unðwernesse.
liga: gewrið.
circumda gutturi tuo: uton
ymbsele ðinre hraca.
gradiantur: hi faran.
a blanda lingua extraneae:
fram swesere tungan
utoncumenre.
160 *concupiscat*: . . . ge.
ne capiaris nutibus illius:
ðeles ðu sio gegripen
hiora ónwaldum.

---

[1] *prec. by* si, *er.*   [2] *fifth letter prob.* e.   [3] *from* hit, o *written*
below t; *refers to* emet.n (130).   [4] *cross-stroke of second* e *missing.*
[5] *foll. by* er. (*two letters*?).

scorti: forlegese.

vix: uneaðe.

ut non ardeant: ðet ne
   byrnan.

165 *plante ejus*: his fotwelme.

sic non erit: swa ne bið.

cum tetigerit: ðonne et-
   hrinð.

deprehensus: anfunden.

adulter: unrihthemere.

170 *inopiam*: ermðe.

turpitudinem: *fólnesse.

non delebitur: ne bið adil-
   egad.

quia non parcet: for ðam
   ne arað.

*nec adquiescet cujusquam
   precibus*: ne hio ne ge-
   þafoð eniges benum.

175 *dona plurima*: manega
   giofa.

VII

reconde: behéd.

quasi pupillam: swa sion.

custodiat: ðu . . .

dulcia: werede.

180 *per cancellos*: ðurh cre-
   pelas.

prospexi: ic . . .

video: . . . ge.

vecordem juvenem: gionne
   dysine.

transit: fęrð.

185 *in obscuro*: on forswor-
   cenan.

advesperescente diae: ge-
   ęfenedan deige.

occurrit: ongen arn.

garrula et vaga: hlud 7
   widscriðel.

nec valens: ná megende.

190 *consistere*: wunian.

insidiatur: hio searwað.

*adprehensumque deoscu-
   latur*: gegripen 7 hio
   cyst.

procaci vultu: gemagnum
   andwlitan.

blanditur: hio sweslecð.

195 *victimas*: onsegednesse.

debui: ic scolde.

reddidi: ic ageald.

repperi: ic gemete.

intexui: ic wef.

200 *tapetibus pictis*: gemetum
   tepedum.

aspersi: ic giondstreide.

veni: cum.

uberibus: of udrum.

fruamur: wuton brucon.

205 *cupitis amplexibus*: ge-
   . . . . . d. y.clepp.[1].

[1] *only* ge *certain; some letters may be cut off at end.*

donec inlucescat: oð ðet
onliohte.
via longissima: ðam leng-
estan wige.
sacculum: sęc.
tulit: he nam.
210 *plene lunae*: . . . les
monan.
inretivit: hio refte[1].
blanditiis: swesendum.
protraxit: hio teah.
quasi agnus lasciviens:
swa plegende lamp.
215 *ignorans*: nat.
quod trahatur: þet to-
gen . . .
donec transfigat: oð ðet
afestnige.
jecor ejus: his lifere.
vel ut si avis festinet: oððe
swa . . f efst fugel.
220 *de periculo*: be freced-
nesse.
quia agitur: þet hit . . s
don.
ne abstrahatur: ne sio
atogen.
neque decipiaris: ne þu ne
sio beswicen.
fortissimi quique: gehwilce
*stongeste[2].
225 (*ab*) *ea*: hire.

[1] f *uncertain.*   [2] o *uncertain.*

penetrantes: farende.
in interiora: on ða ínran.

VIII

in ipsis foribus: on ðam
forðtege.
clamito: ic . . .
230 *animadvertite*: ongiotað.
de rebus magnis: be mes-,
tum ðingum.
aperientur: siont onte . .
ut praedicent: ð . . hio
bodian.
guttur meum: min hraca.
235 *detestabuntur*: onsc . . . að.
neque perversum: ne forhwerfed.
*cunctis opibus pretiosis-
simis*: eallum dior . . . . .
omne desiderabile: all[3] ge-
wilnienlic.
comparari: bion wiðme-
ten.
240 *eruditis cogitationibus*:
*gelereddum geðan-
cum.
intersum: ic betwi. eam.
arrogantiam:
u . a . . . e . esse.
os bilingue: twispecne
muð.

[3] *traces of another letter before* a?

detestor: ic onscunige.

245 *legum conditores*: *scept-
tenras.

decernunt: gescadað[1].

imperant: bebiodað.

potentes: rica.

superbe[2]: ofermode[3],
prede[4].

250 *lapide presiosa*: dior-
weorðum stane.

genimina mea: mine ciðas.

ut ditem: ðet ic geweole-
gie.

repleam: ic gefelle.

possedit: ahte.

255 *initium*: on fruman.

quicquam: enig ðinc.

antequam faceret: er ðon
ðe he dede.

eterno: . . . m.

ordinata sum: ic eam ge-
endebyrd.

260 *ex antiquis*: of ealdum.

antequam fieret: er ðan ðe
gewurde.

necdum erant abysi: ne
ða get weron grundas.

concepta: geeacnad[5].

necdum erumperant: ne
ða get up brecon.

265 *gravi mole*: ahefegum hefe.

necdum constiterant: ne
ða get asette weron.

ego parturiebar: ic wes
geeacnad.

cardines: hearran.

quando praeparabat: ða
he gegearwade.

270 *aderam*: ic et wes.

gyro: *emhferte.

quando vallabat: ða he
gestrangade.

aethera: roderas.

librabat: wẹi.

275 *ne transirent*: þet hi ne
oferferdan.

appendebat: wei.

cuncta conponens: ealle
*a geglengende.

delectabar: ic wes gelus-
fullad.

ludens: plegende.

280 *ad fores meas*: et minum
gatum.

observat *potest[6] *ostii mei*:
begemð stoðe minre
dure.

hauriet: he hlet.

ledet: dereð.

283a *oderunt*: . . . dan.

---

[1] ge *and* ð *indistinct.*   [2] *subpuncted.*   [3] f *uncertain.*
[4] pr *uncertain.*   [5] *from* geeacnan, d *above expuncted final* n.
[6] *read* postes.

IX

excidit: hio forcearf.

285 immolavit victimas suas:
hio offrede hiore anse-
gednesse.

miscuit: hio gemende.

ad arcem et ad maenia: to
burge 7 to wealle.

relinquite: forletað.

derisorem: telend.

290 qui arguit: se ðe ðreað.

generat: cynð.

maculam: wam.

diliget: . . . ð.

da: sele.

295 occasionem: intigan.

addetur: si *geaht.

multiplicabuntur: bioð . . .

inlusor: bismeriend.

portabis: ðu byrst.

300 clamosa: hlúd.

inlecebris: on *forspane-
gum.

omnino: eallunga.

cedet: hio sit.

super sellam: ofer setol.

305 vocaret: . . . ge.

pergentes: ferende.

itinere suo: *hio siðfate[1].

vecordi: gedwolenum.

aque furtive: ðiofende
weteru.

310 suavior: *wensure.

ignoravit: hio nat.

convivie ejus: hiora ge-
biorscipes.

X

non proderunt: ne fro-
miað.

non affliget: ne geswenð.

315 subvertit: he *gehwerf.

*egestastem: wedle.

operata est: worhte.

manus remissa: aslacad
hand.

fortium: . . . ra.

320 divitias: weolan.

parat: gegearwað.

qui stertit: se ðe hret.

operit: oferwrihið.

putrescet: forrotað.

325 ceditur: bið swungen.

*confidentur: getrioulice.

qui depravat: se ðe ge-
sweotelað.

qui annuit: se ðe gebeac-
nað.

verberabitur: bið swun-
gen.

330 vena: edra.

aperit: ontenð.

invenietur: bið . . .

qui indiget: se *ð wedlat.

---

[1] e uncertain.

custodienti: to geheal-
dene.
335 *non deerit*: na wana bið.
egestate: of . . .
nec sociabitur: ne gefer-
lecð.
dabitur: bið sald.
acetum: eced.
340 *non commovebitur*: ne bið
astered.
parturiet: eacnað.
peribit: forweorð.

XI

*stetera (*stat*-): anmitta.
pondus: wiht.
345 *contumelia*: tiona.
diriget: gerecð.
supplantatio: biswic.
vastabit: berefat.
corruit: hreosþ.
350 *capientur*: bioð *gribene.
mortuo: . . . dum.
sollicitorum: ymbhedi-
gra.
simulator: lecetere.
decipit: beswicð.
355 *liberabuntur*: biodh ale-
sede of.
in perditione: on forspil-
lednesse.

tacebit: swigað.
fraudulenter: facenlice.
archana: diohla.
360 *fidelis*: getriowe.
celat: bediolað.
commissum: gelt.
affligitur: bit geswenced.
cavet: warat.
365 *securus*: orsorh.
mulier *gratioso: gefol
wif.
crudelis: welhriou.
propinquos abicit: magos
aweorpð.
opus *instabili: unstaðol-
fest weorc[1].
370 *seminanti*: sawondum.
sectatio: *efterfelgnic[2].
voluntas: g . . .
circulus aureus: gelden
trendel.
373a *pulcra*: *fege[3].
prestolatio: anbidinc.
375 *dividunt*: todeleð.
propria: agene.
ditiores: *weliogarn.
fiunt: bioð.
qui inebriat: se ðe drin . . .
380 *inebriabitur*: bit drucen.
frumenta: hwetes.
maledicitur: bið wereged.

---

[1] *only* we *now legible.*   [2] c *uncertain; might be* s.   [3] ge
above er.

vendentium: cypendra.

investigator: speriend.

385 *obprimetur*: bið . . .

corruet: ahriosð.

virens folium: growende
leaf.

possidebit: ah.

ventos: . . . s.

390 *serviet*: ðiowað.

sapienti: . . . m.

XII

impie: . . . ce.

non roborabitur: ne bið
gestrangad.

non commovebitur: ne bið
astered.

395 *putredo*: forrotadnes.

res dignas: medeme ðinc.

qui gerit: se ðe det.

verte: *acyrað.

doctrina sua noscitur: of
his lare bit *ancwawen.

400 *excors*: modleas.

patebit: openað.

novit: wát.

jumentorum suorum: his
netena.

qui operatur: se ðe *werð.

405 *munumentum*: getrem-
minc.

proficiet: fremet.

malo: . . . m.

effugiet: forflioh.

replebitur: bið . . .

410 *retribuetur*: bið golden.

dissimulat: forberet.

callidus: leti.

novit: wat.

mentitur: wegð.

415 *testis fraudulentus*: facenful gewita.

qui promittit: se behęt.

pungitur: bið witnod.

labium: . . . ra.

concinnat: geþiod.

420 *qui ineunt*: ðe onginnað.

consilia: geðeaht.

acciderit: *belipmð.

malo: of . . .

homo versutus: leti mon.

425 *celat*: bediolað.

tributis: trifetum, gafel.

letificabitur: he bið . . .

iter: siðfet.

decipiet: beswicð.

430 *fraudulentus*: facenful.

lucrum: gestrion.

devium: welise.

XIII

inconsideratus: unbescea-
wad.

operantium: wercendra.

435 *detestabitur*: onscunoð.

confunditur: he biÐ ge-
  scend.
est: he is.
consilio: . . . s.
reguntur: bioÐ gereahte.
440 *substantia festinata*: geo-
  net sped.
minuetur: biÐ gewanad.
paulatim: litlum 7 litlum.
qui differtur: þe biÐ geeld.
affligit: geswenÐ.
445 *desiderium veniens*: cu-
  mede gewilnug.
alicui rei: enigum Ðince.
obligat: gewriÐ.
versabitur: drohnat.
vorago: swelgend.
450 *astutus*: letig.
agit: deÐ.
aperiet: ántenÐ.
nuntius: boda.
ignominia ei qui deserit:
  netenes Ðam se Ðe for-
  let.
455 *qui adquiescit*: se Ðe ge-
  ÐafeÐ.
arguenti: . . . m.
si complebitur: gif hio biÐ
  gefelled.
delectat: gelusfullaÐ.
detestantur: onscuniaÐ.
460 *qui fugiunt*: Ðe flioÐ.

efficietur: he biÐ geworden.
persequitur: felÐ.
retribuentur: biÐ golden.
nepotes: neofan.
465 *custoditur*: biÐ gehealden.
in novalibus: on dengum.
congregabuntur: bioÐ ge-
  samnode.
qui parcit: se Ðe areÐ.
instanter: anredlice.
470 *erudit*: lerÐ.
insaturabilis: unaseÐend-
  lic.

XIV

(*domum*) *exstructam*: tim-
  brunga.
despicitur: b . . .
ab eo: fram Ðam.
475 *infami via*: on unhlisum
  wige.
labia: . . . s.
plurime segetes: manega
  ecyras.
dolosus testis: facynful cy-
  Ðere.
prudentium: . . . ra.
480 *facili[u]s*[1]: eÐre.
inludit: bepęcÐ.
morabitur: wunaÐ.
germinabunt: growaÐ.

[1] *from* facilius, u *er.*

extrema: endas.

485 replebitur: bið . . .

astutus: letig.

operabitur: *werð.

vir versutus: letig węr.

odiosus: hatol.

490 divitum: . . . n.

qui despicit: se ðe for-
siohð.

errant: dwoliað.

praeparant: gegearwiað.

versipellis: ficol id
pretti.

495 in paucitate: on gehwed-
nese.

gubernatur: is begemed.

ossuum: bana[1].

qui calumniatur: se ðe
hespð.

exprobat: hespð.

500 factori ejus: his wertan.

eum: hine.

elevat: up ahefð.

XV

responsio mollis: hnesce
andswore.

sermo durus: heard spec.

505 fatuorum: stunra.

ebullit: wapolað.

*contepplantur: bescea-
wiað[2].

inmoderata: ungemete-
gad[3].

inridet: tirhð.

510 astutior fiet: węrra bið.

conturbatio: gedrefednes.

disseminabunt: tosawað.

dissimile: ungelic.

deserenti: forletendum.

515 qui corripit: ðe ðreað.

nec graditur: ne he ne
geð.

exiraret (exhilarat): ge-
gladað.

in merore animi: on gror-
nunga modes.

deicitur: bið aworpen.

520 pascitur: bið féd.

imperitia: of ungleau-
nesse.

quasi juge convivium: swa
singal gebiorscipe.

insatiabiles: unaseðenlic.

vocari: b . . .

525 ad olera: to wertum.

quam ad vitulum sagina-
tum: ðonne to fettum
stiorce.

suscitatas: awehte.

---

[1] faint and indistinct. [2] c closed, indistinguishable from o.
[3] from ungemeteged, a above fourth e.

(quasi) sepis (-es): .. g .[1].

absque offendiculo: *buto otspernince.

530 despicit: forsioð.

dissipantur: sin tostente.

confirmantur: sint . . .

in sententia: on cwide.

optimus: selest.

535 super eruditum: ofer ge-
leredne.

pulcherrimus: fegerest.

qui sectatur: se ðe felð.

fama bona: god hlisa.

impinguat: amest.

540 sapientium: . . . ra.

commorabitur: wunað[2].

despicit: forsioð.

qui adquiescit: se ðe geða-
feð.

possessor: agend.

545 praecedit: forð gewit.

XVI

ponderator: *pundern-
gen[3].

dirigentur: b . . .

omnis arrogans: elc upa-
hafenes.

redimitur: is alesed.

550 declinatur: he bið aheld.

cum placuerint: þonne
liciað.

disponit: gedihnað.

pondus: pund.

iudicia: . . . mas.

555 divinatio: wilung.

non errabit: ne dwolað.

impie: . . . c.

solium: cynesetl.

dirigetur (dil.): bið . . .

560 placabit: gegladað.

imber serotinus: smelt ha-
gol.

semita: . . . ta.

declinat: . . . ð.

humiliari: b . . .

565 aeruditus: gelered.

repperiet: gemet.

appellabitur: bit genem-
ned.

majora: mare.

percipiet: onfehð.

570 addet: to geecð.

composita: geglengede.

ossuum: bana.

compulit: genet.

ardescit: *birð.

575 perversus: forhwerfed.

---

[1] Zupitza read haga, only g being clear; the letter before g, although the clearest of the others, is not much like a; there appear to be traces of a gloss above quasi, the first letter being perhaps s.   [2] from wanað, u above expuncted first a.   [3] punderngeo, apparently altered by addition of third n above o.

lites: saca.
verbosus: werdi.
separat: toscereð.
lactat: secet.
580 *attonitis*: areahtum.
mordens: slitende.
perficit: fulfremet.
dignitatis: werðnes.
repperietur: bit gemet.
585 *animo suo*: is mode.
urbium: burga.
set temperantur: ac hio
bioð gemetgode.

XVII

bucella sicca: drege bite.
victimis: onsegednessum.
590 *obedit*: hersumað.
optemperat: hersumað.
exprobrat: hespð.
letatur: b . . .
senum: eldra[1].
595 *non decet*: ne glenget.
composita: glengede.
labium mentiens: wegende
welere.
gemma: gim.
gratissima: gecwemest.
600 *prestolantis*: anþidincges.
celat: bediolað.

amicitias: freondscipas.
repetit: *gehyðlęct.
separat: toscereð.
605 *faederatos*: gesibbade.
expedit: fremet[2].
urse: byrene.
raptis fetibus: oðbrode-
num hwelpum.
confidenti: getriowende.
610 *deserit*: forlet.
comprobatur: bið *afan-
dan.
plaudet: hafet.
perversi cordis: ðwerre
hiortan.
qui vertit: se *de[3] cyrð.
615 *incidet*: befelð.
in ignominia sua: on his
netenesse.
set nec letabitur: ac ne
blissað.
aetatem floridam: blow-
ende elde[4].
exsiccat: a . . .
620 *inferre*: on geledan.
ne percutere: ne slean.
qui moderatur: se ðe gemetegað.
doctus: gelered.
pretiosi: diores.

---

[1] foll. by er. of one or two letters.   [2] m *apparently from* c *or* o.
[3] e *from* i?   [4] l *of* blowende *has loop, as if a second* b; elde *from*
helde, h *expuncted.*

625 *spiritus* (gen.): gast.
　　reputabitur: bið geteald.
　　si conpresserit: gif he ge-
　　　　welt.

XVIII

　　occasiones: intigan.
　　reprobabilis: *afadodlic.
630 *dixeris*: ðu . . .
　　que versantur: ðe droh-
　　　　niað.
　　contempnit: forhegeð.
　　redundans: eðienðe.
　　torrens: burne.
635 *inmiscent*: on gemengað.
　　rixis[1]: of sacum.
　　bilinguis: twispeces.
　　interiora: inran.
　　dissolutus: toslacad.
640 *dissipantis*: tostencendes.
　　fortissima: strengest.
　　currit: irnð.
　　validus: *stran.
　　dignum: weorðne.
645 *sustentat inbecillitatem
　　　　suam*: *uðerwreoðað
　　　　his untrumnesse.
　　ad irascendum: to ior-
　　　　sienne.
　　sapientium: . . . ra.
　　donum: gefe.

　　dilatat: tobręt.
650 *spatium*: féc.
　　accussator sui: wrehten[2]
　　　　his selfes.
　　venit: . . . ð.
　　investigabit: smeað.
　　contradictiones: wiðer-
　　　　cwidas.
655 *conprimit*: ofðrect.
　　sors: hlet.
　　dijudicat: tosced.
　　qui adjuvatur: ðe is geful-
　　　　tumad.
　　vectes: scetelas.
660 *cum obsecrationibus*: mid
　　　　halsungum.
　　ri[gi]de: stiðlice.
　　vir amicabilis: lufwendlic
　　　　wer.

XIX

　　torquens: ðreagende.
　　festinus: hred.
665 *contra*: on.
　　fervaet: welð.
　　animo suo: his mod.
　　addunt: to geęcað.
　　quos habuit: ðæ habbað.
670 *separantur*: bioð tosce-
　　　　rede.
　　non effugiet: ne aflihð.

---

[1] *Lat.* labia stulti inmiscent (635) se rixis.　　[2] *from* wretten, h
above expuncted first t.

colunt: weorðiað.

dona: of . . .

distribuentis: todelendes.

675 hominis pauperis: earmne
monnon.

oderunt: . . . n.

insuper: ðertoeacan.

procul: fior.

recesserunt: gewiton.

680 qui sectatur: se ðe felð.

abebit: . . . ð.

non decent: ne riseð.

stultum: . . . ne.

deliciae: . . . s.

685 dominari: wealdan.

praetergredi: forgeman id
forbugon.

fremitus: gremetunc.

herbam: werta.

hiraritas (hil.) ejus: his
glednes.

690 *tacta (tecta) perstillantia: driopende hrof.

litig[i]osa mulier: sacful
wif.

dantur: sint sealde.

propriae: senderlice.

uxor prudens: glea wif.

695 pigredo: sleuþ oððe scle-
acnes.

soporem: mamor.

dissoluta: asclacad.

esuriet: hinrað.

mortificabitur: bið cwel-
med.

700 fenerator (-ur): lenð[1].

domino: . . . ne.

vicissitudinem suam: his
*gewricl.

ne desperis (-es): ne geór-
wen ðu.

ad interfectionem ejus: to
his cwale.

705 damnum: hénðo.

cum rapuerit: ðonne he
*gegrip.

apponet: to geset.

in novissimis tuis: on
ðinum endum.

homo indigens: beðear-
fende mon.

710 commorabitur: hio wunað.

absque visitatione: buton
niosunga.

pessimi: metestum.

nec applicat: ne he ne
geþiod.

flagellato: geswungen.

715 si corripueris: gif ðu
dreast.

ignominiosus: ungewis.

infelix: ungeselig.

non cesses: ne ablin ðu.

deridet: teld.

---

[1] er. (e and one other letter) between n and ð.

720	*devorat*: forswelð.
	parata sunt: gerewe sint.
	derisoribus: telerum.
	iudicia: . . . s.
	mallei percutientes:
		sleande slicc.
725	*corporibus*: . . . m.

XX

	tumultuosa: maðeli.
	sicut ru[g]itus: swa grime-
		tung.
	qui separat: se toscereð.
	a contentionibus: fram fli-
		tum.
730	*miscentur*: . . . d.
	arare: herian.
	mendicabit: he wedlat.
	exhauriet: a . . .
	vocantur: bioð . . .
735	*beatos*: . . . ge.
	pos[t] se: wiðeftan.
	intuitu suo: on his bege-
		mene.
	saturare: sio ðu . . .
	emptor: *beccen.
740	*cum recesserit*: ðonne he
		gewit.
	gloriabitur: hit . . .
	vas pretiosum: diorrest
		fet.
	fidejussor: borhhond.
	exstitit: wunade.

745	*alieni*: . . . s.
	calculo: of griosne.
	consiliis: . . . m.
	roborantur: sint gestran-
		gade.
	gubernaculis: . . . m.
750	*tractanda*: to smyagenne.
	ad quam festinatur: to
		ðam ðe hit *ests wes.
	carebit: ðolað.
	pondus: hefe.
	devorare: forswelgan.
755	*post vota*: efter behate.
	curvat: gebegð.
	eos: ða.
	spiraculum: orð.
	iuvestigat: asperet.
760	*roboratur*: bið . . .
	invenum: . . . ra.
	senum: . . . ra.
	canicies: harnes.
	livor: lela.
765	*abstergit*: adreið.
	in secretioribus: on deoh-
		lum.

XXI

	divisiones: todal.
	inclinabit: he . . .
	appendit: aweget.
770	*impingetur*: hio *oðsperð.
	detrahent: telað.
	noluerunt: . . . dan.

perversa via: ðuer[1] wig.

miserebitur: hi[2] . . .

775 *multato pestilente*: gewit-
nodum cwilde.

excogitat: ðenð.

ut detrahet (-at): þet he
ut atio.

qui opturat: se fordett.

ad: et.

780 *non exaudietur*: ne bið
gehered.

munus absconditum: be-
hed[3] lac.

indignationem maximam:
mestan ebylhð.

justo: . . . m.

pavor: ferht.

785 *qui erraverit*: se ðe ge-
dweleð.

in coetu: on weorede.

commorabitur: wunað[4].

epulos (-as): wiste.

pinguia: fetto.

790 *non ditabitur*: ne bið ge-
weolegad.

*quam *com muliere rixosa*:
ðonne mid secfullan
wife.

thesaurus desiderabilis:
gewilniendlic gold-
hord.

justi: . . . s.

dissipabit: *totercð.

795 *fortium*: strangere.

robur: strenð.

arrogans: up ahafen.

occidunt: ofsleað.

desiderat: gegernð.

800 *non cessabit*: ne ablinð.

que offeruntur: ðe bioð
brohte.

testis mendax: leas ge-
witnes.

obediens: . . . sum.

victoriam: sige.

805 *procaciter*: geaplice.

offirmat: afestnað.

corrigit: gerecð.

equus paratur: hors is gegearwad.

XXII

operator: werhta.

810 *callidus*: letig.

afflictus est: is geswenced.

damno: of henðe.

in via perversi: on *ðre-
orum wige.

proverbium: bicwide.

815 *adolescens*: iunges.

---

[1] *from* ðrer, u *above first* r.   [2] *foll. by* er.; i *from another letter?*
[3] h *from* b *or* l.   [4] n *closed at bottom*; u *or* a *begun in error?*

cum senuerit: ðonne he
ealdað.
imperat: bebiot.
mutuum: to borge.
fenerantis: lened.
820 virga: of ...
consummabitur: he bið
fornumen.
promptus: arod.
dedit: he ...
pauperi: ... n.
825 eice: ut aweorp *ð.
exibit: ut geð.
supplantantur: beoð be-
swicene.
verba: of ...
occidendus: to ofslanne.
830 fovea profunda: diop seað.
incidat (-et): on ahriasð[1].
colligata est: is gegederad.
fugabit: bið afligð[2].
ut augeat: þet he geęce.
835 ditiori: weolegrum[3].
egebit: he wedlað.
sapientium: ... ra.
appone: to gesete[4].
redundabit: hio ...
840 tripliciter: *ðriofeeald-
lice[5].

firmitatem: trumnesse.
illis: ðam.
violentiam: strenðe.
non conteras: ne forbrec[6]
ðu.
845 configet: ofsticoð.
viro furioso: *hathort
were.
ne discas: ðe les ðu liornie.
qui defigunt: ðe afestniað.
vades: borhhande.
850 pro debitis: for geltum.
unde restituas: hwonon
agelts ðu.
causae est: ðinga his.
tollas (-at): nime.
operimentum: oferbredels.
855 ne transgrediaris terminos
antiquos: ne oferstepe
ðu ealde gemero.
posuerunt: settan.
vidisti: ð ...
ante ignobiles: beforan
eðelborenum.

XXIII

cultrum: scęr.
860 ne desideres: ne gewilna
*di[7].

---

[1] from ahreasð, i above e.
(u begun in error?).   [2] aflig: ð.   [3] r from another letter
[4] gest- begun, then corrected to gese-.
[5] first e prob. repeated because spoiled by down-stroke from line of Latin
above.   [6] c indistinct.   [7] last letter is incomplete u.

de: of.

ut diteris: þet ðu sio ge-
weolugad.

modum: gemet.

ne erigas: ne ðu up[1] ne
arer.

865 *opes*: *werce[2].

facient: . . . ð.

non comedas: ne et ðu.

cibos: . . . s.

arioli: dreas.

870 *conjectoris*: wiccan.

quoniam estimat: for ðam
ðe he wenð.

quod ignorat: þet he[3] nat.

evomes: ðu . . .

pulchros sermones tuos:
ðine fegeran specce[4].

875 *nec adtingas*: ne ðu ne
ethrín.

introeas: in ga.

propinquus: mygð.

ingrediatur: iń ga.

aures tue: . . . n.

880 *subtrahere*: ation.

si percusseris: gif ðu
slehst.

virga: of . . .

morietur: he . . .

liberabis: ðu alest.

885 *renes*: edran.

non emuletur: ne onherie.

prestulatio tua: þin anbidinc.

via: . . . e.

comesationibus: oferętum.

890 *qui conferunt*: þa bregað.

vacantes: ge . . .[5].

cymbala: hearpan.

qui consummentur: ðe bioð
*fornume.

vestietur: bið . . .

895 *dormitatio*: rest.

eme: bege.

exultat: . . . nað.

genuit: *ceið.

gaudeat: . . . sie.

900 *exultet*: . . . nie.

genuit: . . . d.

puteus angustus: neare
pyt.

incautos: unuuere.

foveae: . . . s.

905 *suffusio*: agotenes.

nonne: w . . .

ṁs: ðam.

calicibus epotandis:
*drunendum calice.

flavescit: glitenat.

910 *splenduerit*: scinð.

---

[1] a *begun, then made into* u.   [2] *from* werte, t *altered to* c (?).

[3] e *indistinct*.   [4] *letter apparently added above* p; *read* sprecce?

[5] *or* . . . ge?

color: blio.
ingreditur: hit ...
blande: lufwedlice.
regulus: slawer*m*.
915 *diffundet*: togiot.
videbunt: ... þ.
loquetur: ... þ.
sopitus: swefed.
repperiam: ic gemete.

XXIV

920 *dispositione*: dehtnunge.
initur: bið ongunnen.
stulto: ... m.
aperiet: h ...
vocabitur: bið ...
925 *detractatur*: is teled.
si desperaveris: gif ðu
    georwenst.
lapsus: aslidenu*m*.
imminuetur: b ...
qui ducuntur: þe sion
    ledde.
930 *qui trahuntur*: þe sin to-
    gene.
vires: megene.
non suppetunt: ne gehel-
    paþ.
servatorem: weard.
fallit: wegð.
935 *quam*: þane.

insidieris: *searw þ[1].
vastes: reafa.
displiceat: ... ge.
cum detractoribus: mid
    telendu*m*.
940 *prepara*: gegearawa.
exerce: bega.
ut aedifices: þet ðu ge-
    timbrige.
lactes: gęl.
urtice: of netelan.
945 *parum*: litel.
inquam: witodlice.
modicum: gehwęde.
pauxillum: lithwon.
conseres: ðu on asets.
950 *quasi cursor*: swa renel.
mendicitas: þerflicnes.

XXV

quas transtulerunt: ða
    rehton.
celare: bedeahlian.
investigare: smegan[2].
955 *rubiginem*: hóm.
quam ut humilieris: þonne
    þet ðu sio geniðerad.
ne proferas: ne ep ðu.
emendare: gebetan.
ne non possis: ðe les ðu ne
    meige.

---

[1] *foll. by* er.?   [2] m *from beginning of another letter.*

960 *cum dehonestaveris*: ðonne
  ðu gearweorðas.
  ne reveles: ne onwrih
  ðu.
  non cesset: he ne ablinð.
  malum: eppel.
  inauris aurea: gylden ear-
  spinl.
965 *lenietur*: bið geliðgod.
  jaculum: gár.
  dens putridus: forrotad
  toð.
  amittit: forlet.
  pallium: wefels.
970 *carmina*: lioð.
  pruinas (prunas): gleda.
  domatis: huses.
  *quam cum muliere litig[i]o-
  sa*: ðanne mid flitgeor-
  nan wife.
  vena corrupta: gewem-
  med weteredre.
975 *opprimitur*: bið ofðreced.
  urbs patens: open burh.
  cohibere: geweldan.

XXVI

  indecens: ungerisenu.
  quo: hwider.
980 *prolatum*: forð broht.
  in quaempiam: on enine.

chamus: bridel.
pulchras tibias: fegere
  scacan.
quomodo: swa.
985 *nascatur*: sio ancenned.
  temulenti: windruncynes.
  terminat: endað.
  silentium: swigan.
  qui iterat: ðe geedlecð.
990 *leena*: wildior.
  sicut vertitur: swe forhwerfed bið.
  in cardine suo: on hiore
  hyrran.
  sub ascella sua: under his
  óxne.
  sententias: cwidas.
995 *deprehensus*: anfunden.
  ludens: plegende.
  sussurrone substracto:
  abrodenum gedwilde.
  conquiescunt: gerestað.
  susurronis: desiges.
1000 *ad intima*: to incundum.
  quomodo si [velis]: *swil
  gif ðu wille.
  vas fictile: lemen fet.
  labia tumentia: *ðinden-
  dende weleras.
  sociata: geferlehte.
1005 *quando summiserit*: ðonne
  he underðiod.
  qui operit: se ðe werð.

qui volvit: se ðe welt.
(*os*) *lubricum*: twisprece.

XXVII

pariat: atewð.
1010 *laudet*: herie.
   saxum: stan.
   honerosa: byrdenmete.
   gravior: hefegre.
   concitati: asterede.
1015 *ferre*: acuman.
   calcabit: tret.
   variis odoribus: misseli-
      cum sweccum.
   dulcoratur: bið *geweorð-
      leht.
   sustinere: forðelgiað.
1020 *dispendia*: leras.
   qui spopondit: þe behet.
   tecta perstillantia: drio-
      pende hrofas.
   litig[i]osa: *flitgeor.
   comparantur: sint wið-
      metene.
1025 *ventum*: wind.
   quasi qui teneat: swa se
      ðe helt.
   jacuitur (*exac.*): is scer-
      ped.
   exacuit: scerpð.
   qui servat: se ðe helt.
1030 *quomodo resp[l]endent*:
      swa swa scinað.

prospicientium: beheal-
   denra.
insatiabiles: unaseðenlic.
conflatur: is blawen.
in conflatorio: on smið-
   ðan.
1035 *si contuderis*: ðeh ðu
   þercce.
quasi tipsonas (*ptisanas*):
   swa berecorn.
feriente: ðerccedum.
diligenter: georlice.
sed tribuitur: ac is seald.
1040 *prata*: geheige.
collecta sunt: sint gega-
   derade.

XXVIII

nemine: nenegum.
persequente: ehtende.
paratur: is gegearwod.
1045 *commessatores*: id wesan
   oþþe eteras.
coacervat: geheapað.
fenore liberali: of frilicum
   gestrione.
fugerit: flio.
concidet: ahriosð.
1050 *deserit*: forlet.
invidet: angað.
jactat: gelpð.
concitat: awecþ.

indigebit: beðearf.
1055 *penuriam*: *erða.

XXIX

non sequetur: ne felhð.
sumpserint: nimþ.
perdet: forleose.
involvet: befelt.
1060 *in posterum*: forð on.
obviaverunt: ongen co-
man.
correptio: ðreal.
refrigerabit: he arᶒrð.
delicias: estas.
1065 *profetia*: witedom¹.
delicatae: estelice.
a pueritia: fram cniht-
hade.
nutrit: fet.
proclivior: forðloten.
1070 *sublevabitur*: bið up ahafen.

XXX

morante: wuniendum.
novi: ic cuðe.
si nosti: wastu ðe nasðu.
ignitus clipeus: feren-
targa².
1075 *ne addas*: ne geᶒc ðu.

arguaris: ðu sio ðread.
inveniaris: ðu sio gemet.
ne deneges: ne forwern ðu.
victui meo: minre anli-
fene.
1080 *ne inliciar*: ðe les ic sio
forspanen.
ad negandum: to wið-
sacenne.
furer: ic stele.
perjurem: ic swerige.
nec accuses: ne ðu ne
wrei.
1085 *molaribus suis*: of his cin-
toðum.
sanguissuge: lyces.
affer affer: bren bryn.
insaturabilia: unaseðen-
lice.
sufficit: genoh is³.
1090 *qui subsannat*: se ðe
hyspð.
qui despicit: se ðe forsiohð.
partum: eacnunga.
effodiant: up adelfað.
dificilia: earfoðu.
1095 *penitus*: eallunga.
colubri: nedran.
in adolescentia: on giohð-
hade.
tergens: dregende.

---

¹ *from* witedomeð, eð *er.*
and targa *in MS.*   ³ *er. before* is.

² *horizontal stroke between* feren

odiosam: hátol.

1100 *in matrimonium*: on ge-
    sinscipe.

minima: lyssan.

sapientiora: wisran.

formicae: emetan.

que parant: ða gearwiað.

1105 *lepusculi*: haran.

invalida: unstran.

qui collocat: se ðe gesta-
    ðelað.

cubile suum: his dén.

egreditur: ut geð.

1110 *per turmas*: ðurh heapas.

stelio: hryremus.

nititur: he geð.

in aedibus: on hofum.

gradiuntur: gað.

1115 *non incedit*: ne stepð.

aries: ram.

qui aparuit: se ðe ateauð.

postquam elevatus est:
    seoððan he hup
    ahafen bið.

in sublime: up id heah.

1120 *ad eliciendum*: ut to
    ationne.

expremit: ofðrecð, swete-
    lað.

qui emulgit: se ðe melcð.

elicit: ut atiohð.

producit: forð gelet.

1125 *discordias*: twirednesse.

XXXI

dilecte mi: eala ðu min
    gecorena.

nullum secretum: enig de-
    ahle.

mutent: hio wendan.

siceram: bior.

1130 *merentibus*: *grnornien-
    dum.

doloris: sares.

non recordentur: ne sint
    *gemunene.

causis: ðinc.

qui pertranseunt: ðe ge-
    witað.

1135 *decerne*: toscad.

lanam: *wullai.

institoris: cypan.

praedam: huðe.

domesticis suis: hiore ge-
    husan.

1140 *cybaria*: andlifene.

emit: hi bohte.

ad fortia: to strenran.

fussum: spinle.

duplicibus: of twifealdum.

1145 *stragulam vestem*: gebliod
    reaf.

byssum: of twine.

indumentum: reaf.

nobilis: eðelboren.

sindonem: scetan.

1150 *cingulum*: gerdels.

ridebit: hio hlihð.
tu supergressa *est: ðu
oferstope.

ALCUINI EXHORTATIO
AD GUIDONEM COMITEM
1152a *vetat*: forbiet[1].
explicare: onwrion.
constans: anred.
1155 *in ea intentione*: on ða
gerad.
valet: fremeð.
percutit: slęhð.
appetit: geornð.
proditor: lęwend.
1160 *praedicator*: bodiend.
non promittitur: nis be-
haten.
instantiss[i]me: geornli-
cost.
contendat: efstf.
principalia: heafodlicf.
1165 *originalia*: frfmðlice[2].
pullulant: wfacsað.
ratum: gescad.
extirpatis: arubfdxm.
praecidere: bprckpfbn.
1170 *ex contemptu*: of forhp-
gxngb.

per contumaciam: þurh
bþxndfnnfsf.
praesumptio: ðrksnfs.
pertinacia: bngknnb.
lascivia: wild.
1175 *enervatio*: awordenes.
1175a *jura*: gerihta.
pollicentur: sint behat . .[3].
condonavit: forgef.
sugestiones: lare.
tollerare: forberan.
1180 *constat*: wunað.
in quacumque causa: on
eihwilcum ðinge.
sapores: stencas.
sonos (suaves): sweigas.
transitorias: gewitenlice.
1185 *volatilis*: fugeles.
*pader: fe[der][4].
mater: modor.
frater: broðor.
soror: sweost[or].
1190 *filius*: [s]una.
filia: dohtor.
patruus: fędera.
amita mea: min fað[u].
matertera maea: min mo-
driæ.
1195 *avunculus meus*: min eam.

[1] e *indistinct.*   [2] *from* frfmeðlice, *first* e *expuncted.*   [3] *some
letters cut off?* at now v. *faint.*   [4] *the reading of most of the glosses
on fol. 77v, of which this is the first, is uncertain; letters here enclosed in
brackets are not now legible.*

victricius: ste[op]feder.

privig[n]us[1]: ste[o]psunu.

filiaster: steopdohter.

vir: ciorl.

1200 *virgo*: ides.

[*puell*]*a*: [mei]den.

mamilla: tit[t].

papilla: for[we]ard titt.

creverat: wfpx[2].

---

[1] *hole in MS. between* g *and* u.   [2] *from* wfpux, u *expuncted*;
some seven further glosses follow, none sufficiently clear to be intelligible.

XI
CHARTERS

7TH TO 8TH CENTURY, SAXON

1

Oeðelred. Cott. Aug. ii. 29

692–3 (*late copy*)

Barking (Essex) archives

ego ho.ilredus *parens* sebbi *provincia* eastsexanorum. *tibi* hedil[b]urge *abbatissae. monasterii quae dicitur* beddanhaam. *terram quae appellatur* ricingahaam, budinhaam, dęccanhaam, angenlabeshaam. *in silva quae dicitur* uuidmundesfelt—*termini sunt isti*: writolaburna, cęntinces triow *et* hanchemstede, 5 *flumen tamisa*—sebbi *rex* eastsax'. oedelraedus. ercnuualdus. uuilfridus. *ego* haedde. guda. egcbaldus. hagona. hooc. sebbi *regis.* sigiheardi *regis.* suebredi *regis.*—odilredus.

2

Waldhere (bp. of London). Cott. Aug. ii. 18

704–5 (*late copy*)

Brentford (Middlesex). Cant. arch.

berctualdo. ualdharius. uestsęxanorum. *in loco qui dicitur* breguntford. coenredi *regis. de reconciliatione* [aelfdrydę]—*a* ualdh . . .

3

Cynewulf. Cott. Ch. viii. 4

778 *(late copy)*

Bedwin (Wilts.). Abingdon (Berks.) archives

cynewulf *rex saxonum.* bican *comiti meo. in loco qui dicitur*
bedewinde. .. erratuun. *vallem vocatam* cymenes denu. .. nes
geat. *ad* peadan stigele. *in* filiðleage. *in quoddam vallu in* haran
dene. *agellum qui dicitur* tatan edisc. *in* bedewindan. *in* horsel-
5 get. .. brames dene geate. to holhrygcgete. to [h]adfeldgeate.
to baggan gete. to brad[an] leage. *illo septo* bradan leage. *in*
standene. *in* puttan .ealh. to bulcan pytte. *in quoddam petrosum
clivum et ex eo* baldwines healh *appellatur. austro* bulcan pyttes.
in illa antiqua monumenta in locum ubi a ruricolis dicitur æt ðam
10 holenstypbum, *sicque ad illos gabulos in longum* gemærweges
to wadbeorge. *sicque* of wadb[eorge] *in illum fontem qui dicitur*
forsca burna, *et ejus ex alveo intrat* bedewindan. *in* cymenes . . .
—æðelmodus. egcbaldus. sc[illi]nges. [ham] . . . æðelnoðes.
ceolbrehtes. æðelmundes. .. [ser]des. fad[ol].

4

Hloðhere. Cott. Aug. ii. 2

679

Cant. arch.

ego hlotharius *rex* cantuariorum. *terram in* tenid, *quae
appellatur* uuestanae. *tibi* *bercuald. *cum meriscis, silvis. cum
consensu theodori et* *ędrico, *filium fratris mei. in civitate* recuulf.
terram in sturia—hlothari *regis.* gumbercti. gębredi. osfridi.
5 irminredi. aedilmaeri. hagani. aeldredi. aldhodi. gudhardi.
bernhardi. uelhisci.

5

Wihtred. Stowe Ch. 1; Cott. Aug. ii. 88

697 or 712 (Stowe); 700 or 715 (Cott.)

Cott. from Cant. arch.

ego uihtredus[1] *rex* cantuariorum. *in loco qui dicitur* limingae. *terram quae dicitur* wieghelmes[2] tun. *terminos, id est,* bereueg *et* meguines paed[3] *et* stretleg[4]—berichtualdum[5]. berichtual-dus[6]. uihtredi[7] *regis.* aedilburgae[8] *reginae.* enfridi. botta. frodi. adda. aedilfridi. bernhaerdi. aehcha. egisberichti[9]. hagana. 5 theabul. aessica[10].

6

Æðelberht[1]. Cott. Aug. ii. 91

732

Cant. arch.

juxta liminaee. *ego* aethilberhtus *rex* cantuariorum. *ante-cessori tuo* hymbran. *tu* dun[11]—aethilberhtus. tatuuinus. aethilberhti *regis.* albinus. *rege* aethilberhto[12].

7

Æðelberht[2]. Cott. Aug. ii. 101

740

Cant. arch.

ego aethilberht *rex* cantuariorum. *fluminis cujus nomen* limi-naea. *juxta marisco qui dicitur* biscopes uuic, *usque ad silbam*

---

[1] uuihtredus *Cott.*   [2] wi *on er.* ((?p)l); pleghelmes *Cott.*
[3] meguuines paeð *Cott.*   [4] *Cott. adds after* stretleg: *terrulae par-tem cuius uocabulum est* ruminingseta. *fluminis quae appellatur* liminaea.
[5] berhtuualdum *Cott.*   [6] berhtuualdus *Cott.*   [7] uuihtredi
Cott.   [8] aethilburgae *Cott.*   [9] egisberhti *Cott.*   [10] aesica
Cott.   [11] (*in a later hand:*) *ego* aethilberhtus *rex. in loco qui dicitur* sandtun. *fluuius qui dicitur* limenaee. hudan fleot.   [12] (*in a later hand:*) balthhaeardi. bynnan. aeanberhti. aethiliaeardi.

qui apellatur ripp, *et ad terminos* suthsaxoniae. *in* liminiaeae.
cuthberhto. *in loco qui dicitur* liminiaee—aethilberhtus. cuth-
5 berhtus. balthhardi. aeðelhuni. dunuualhi. duunuuallan. ald-
berhti. aethelnothi.

8

Eardwulf. Stowe Ch. 3

c. 767

ego eardulfus *rex cantiae.* heaberhcto *abbate. in monasterio
quod nominatur* ricuulfi. *in loco qui dicitur* perhamstede. *in
regione*[1] caestruuara, *ubi nominatur* heahhaam. *patre meo*
*eadberhtuo[2]—*episcopi* earduulfi. eardulfus. earduulfus. *signum
5 manus* folcuuinis. byrnhames. *uuihtbrordis. uuealhhunes.
aethelnothes.

8TH CENTURY, MERCIAN

9

Æðelbald[1]. Cott. Aug. ii. 3

736

Worcester arch.

ego aethilbalt *rex marcersium et provinciarum quae* sutangli
dicuntur. comite meo cyniberhtte. *in provincia cui nomen inditum
est* husmerae, *juxta fluvium vocabulo* stur. *silvam quam nominant*
cynibre, *aliam cui nomen est* moerheb—aetdilbalt. uuor. uuil-
5 fridus. aethilbaldo *rege.* aethilric. *principis* ęthilbal[di][3]. *ego*
ibe. heardberht. ebbella. onoc. oba. sigibed. bercol. ealduuft.
cusa. pede—*agrum in silva* moreb, *cui vocabulum est* brochyl,
quem ego edilbalt, *rex* suutanglorum, *comite meo* cyniberhttę
donavi.

[1] *foll. by* er, *deleted.*   [2] *on er.?*   [3] *last two letters cut off.*

10

Eanberht. Add. Ch. 19,789

759

Worcester arch.

regis offan *merciorum*. eanberht. uhctred. aldréd. *tibi* h[e]adda *abbati* æt onnan forda. uuisleag. rindburna. meosgelegeo. onnan duun—offa. eanberht. uhctred. aldred. milred. tilhere. cusa. [acan]. [dil]ran. bobban. bynnan. berhtuuald. tilberhti.

11

Offa[1]. Cott. Aug. ii. 26

(764 for) 767

Cant. arch.

ego offa *rex mercior*. stidberhtae *venerabili viro terram in* middilsaexum bituih gumeninga hergae end liddinge *ab oriente torrentis* lidding *donabo*. stidberht. *in* ciltinne, *in loco ubi dicitur* wichama—offa. gengberht. eadberht. cuutfert.

12

Pilheard's Endorsement. Cott. Aug. ii. 27

801

Cant. arch.

reguum aethelbaldi *atque* offani. pilheardus *comis regis mercionum* coenuulfi. *locum qui dicitur* caelichyth—coenuulfus. æthelheardus. unuuona. aldulf. utol. eadulf. deneberht. haðoberht. cyneberht. uuigberht. alhheard. tiðferð. uuihthun. beonna. folðred. coenuulf. heaðoberht. æðelmund. esne. 5 heardberht. ceolmund. wigga. cydda. cuðred. osulf. beornnoð. cynhelm.

13

Uhtred. Worcester arch.

770

ego uhtredus *regulus* huiccioru*m meo ministro* æðelmundo,
filio ingeldi, *qui fuit dux et praefectus* æðelbaldi *regis merciorum
cum licentia* offani *regis merciorum.* [*j*]*uxta fluvium in orientale
parte qui dicitur* salu[uerpe]. æðelmundo—eadbald. cyneðryð
5 *regina.* ecgferð. ælfflæd *filia—hii sunt termini donationis istius*:
saluuerpæ. cymedes halh. huitan stan. readan solo.

14

Offa². Cott. Aug. ii. 4

779

Windrush (Glouc.), Widford (Glouc.), Turkdean (Glouc.). Evesham
(Worc.) arch.

offa *rex mercionum meo ministro* duddono. sulmonnes burg.
torrentis qui vocatur theodningc. *fluvii qui nuncupatur* uuenrisc
—uuithigford *usque in* wines burg. *vallis qui dicitur* turca denu.
slohtran ford. *fluvius* uuęnrisc—*regis* offan. æt iorotlaforda—
5 offa. eadberhtus. ceolulfus. tilherus. hygeberhtu[.]. aldberhtus.
botuuine. brordan¹. berhtuualdi. esne. eamberht. eadbaldi.
esn[e]. brordan. bryni. eadbal[di]²—godmundes leah.

15 (15, 16)

Offa⁴/⁵. Add. Ch. 19,790

793–6

Westbury (Glouc.). Worcester arch.

offa *rex. terram in provincia* huuiccioru*m ubi nominatur*
uuestburg, *prope flumen qui dicitur* aben. aeðelmundo. *in loco*

¹ *from* broddan, r *above first* d.   ² *in margin*; di *covered.*

qui nuncupatur clobes hoas—offa. ecgferð. hygeberhti. æðel-
heardi. ceolulfi. haðoredi. unuuona. [c]yneberhti¹. [d]eneferði¹.
ceolmundi. coenwalh. uuermundi. alhheardi. ælfhuni. uuioht- 5
uni. alhmund. beonnan. uuigmundi. utel. brorda. bynna.
alhmund. esne. æðelmund. uuigberht². heardberht. uuyn-
berht. ceolmund. ubba. lulling. eafing.

8TH CENTURY, MERCIAN-KENTISH

16 (17)

Æðelbald². Cant. arch. Chart. Ant. M. 363 (Red Book
No. 1)

742

æðelbaldi *regis merciorum. in loco ubi nominatur* clofes hos.
æðelbaldus *rex.* cutberh[tus]³. æðelberhti *regis cantiae.* wiht-
redi *regis.* æðelbald. æðelberhti *regis.* cutberhti *archiepiscopi—*
æðelbald. cuðberhtus. uuita. torhthelm. willfredi. cuðberht.
huetlac. eanfrið. ecglaf. aluuig. hunwald. daniel. aldwulf. 5
æðelfrið. herewald. sigcga. redwulf. ofa. aldwulf. æðelmod.
heardberht. eadbald. bercul. cyneberht. freoðorne. wermund.
cuðred. buna.

17 (18)

Offa³. Cant. arch. Chart. Ant. M. 340 (Red Book No. 2)

788

offa *rex merciorum tibi* osberhto *ministro meo trado terram in
provincia cantiae in regione* eastrgena *ubi nominatur* duningcland.
in loco u[bi no]minatur celchyð—offa. iaenberhtus. hygeberht.
. . . ulf. heardraed. aethilmod. cyneberht. unuuano. uuaerm . . .
haðor. . . ealgheard. ceolmund.   5

¹ *initial letter damaged by hole in MS.*   ² ig *indistinct.*   ³ *hole
in MS.; tops of* t *and* s *visible.*

18 (19)

Coenwulf[1]. Cott. Aug. ii. 97

798

Bobbing, Lyminge (Kent). Cant. arch.

ego coenuulfus *rector et imperator merciorum regni.* oswulfo
duci. in loco qui vocatur hrempingwíic *et alia nomine* hafingseota.
fluminis qui dicitur liminea. *terrae qui dicitur* bobingseata—
coenuulf. aeðelhard. hygeberht. haðored. unuuono. cyneberht.
5 haðoberht. eaduulf. utel. alhhard. wiohthun. tidfrið. alhmund.
beonna. uuigmund. forðred. brordan. heaberhti. esne. wig-
berhti. aeðelmundi. eadgari. uuicggan. ciolmundi. beornnoði.
heardberhti. cyddan—osuulf. *conjugis* beornðryðe. *monasterio
quod dicitur* aet liminge. æt limingge.—hafingseotan boec.

9TH CENTURY, SAXON

19 (20)

Æðelwulf[4]. Cott. Ch. viii. 36

847

South Hams (Devon), Dorchester (Dorset). Cant. arch.

ætheluulf *occidentalium saxonum rex. territoria ista sunt
cassatorum qui* ætheluulfe *regi* *om homme *senatores ejus con-
cedissent in illo loco qui nuncupater* dornuuarana ceaster. ærest
on merce cumb. ðonne on grenan pytt. ðonne on ðone torr æt
5 mercecumbes æwielme. ðonne on denewaldes stan. ðonne on
ðone díc, ðær esne ðone weg fordealf. ðonon ofdune on ðæs
wælles heafod. ðonne ðær ofdune on broc oð tiddes ford. ðonne
up on broc oð heottes dic to ðære flodan. from ðære flodan
ofdune ðær fyxan díc to broce gæð. 7 ðonne ofdune on broc

oð sǽ. ðonne from ðyrelan stane up on broc oð smalan cumb. 10
fram smalan cumbes heafde to grǽwanstane. ðonon wiðufan
ðæs wælles heafod on odencolc. ðonon on ðone healdan weg
wið huitan stanes. ðonon to ðæm beorge ðe mon hateð æt
ðæm holne. ðonon an haran stan. ðonon on secgwælles heafod.
ðonon on ða burg eastewearde. ðonon on ða lytlan burg weste- 15
wearde. ðonon to strǽte. ðonan benioðan wuda on geryhte ut
on hreodpól. ðonne up on afene, oð ðæt ðe se alda suínhaga
utscioteð to afene. ðonne be ðæm hagan on anne beorg. ðonne
on sueordleage wælle. ðonon on wulfwælles heafod. ðonon on
wealweg on ðone stan æt ðære flodan. from ðæm stane forð 20
on ðone herepað on ðone díc. ðonon ofdune oð wealdenes ford.
ðonon on ðone holan weg. ðonon ofdune on bróc on hun-
burge fleot 7 ðær to sǽ—ætheluulf. alhstan. æðelbaldi. osrici.
osmundi. ecgheard. lulling. uulflafi. ecguulfi. lulluc. ceorli.
uulfræd. alhstan. milræd.   25

9TH CENTURY, KENTISH

20 (34)

Cuðred. Stowe Ch. 8, Cott. Aug. ii. 100

805–7

Æðelnoð's endorsement only in Stowe

ego cuðredus *rex* cantwariorum[1] *cum consensu* coenuulfi *regis*
merciorum dabo æðelnoðo *praefecto meo in provincia cantiae*
terram in loco qui dicitur æt heagyðe[2] ðorne—coenuulf. cuðred.
uulfredus[3]. coenwald. osuulf. ealdberht. wealh. æðelieard[4].
berhtnoð. ceolnoð. wulfred. alduulf. uerenberht[5]. deneberht. 5
tidferð. alhheard. eaduulf. wulfheard. beornmod. wigberht.
alhmund. wiohthun. wigmund. beonna.

---

[1] cantuuariorum *Cott.*   [2] hegyðe *Cott.*   [3] wulfredus *Cott.*
[4] *so also Cott.*   [5] uuerenberht *Cott.*

Æðelnoð se *gerefa to Éastorege, 7 Gænburg his wif aræddan
hiora érfe beforan Wulfrede arcebiscope, 7 Æðelhune his
10 mæsseprioste, 7 Esne cyninges ðegne, suæ hueðer hiora[1] suæ
leng lifes were foe[2] to londe 7 to alre æhte. Gif hio bearn hæbbe,
ðonne foe ðæt ofer[3] hiora boega dagas to londe 7 to æhte. Gif
hio ðonne bearn næbbe, 7 Wulfred archibiscop lifes sie, þonne
foe he to ðæm londe, 7 hit forgelde, 7 ðæt wiorð gedæle fore
15 hiora gastas suæ ælmeslice 7 suæ rehtlice suæ he him seolfa
on his wisdome geleornie. 7 ðas *prece nænig mon uferran
dogor on nænge oðre halfe oncærrende sie, nymne suæ þis
gewrit hafað. wulfred. feologeld. æðelhun. cuðberht. æðelnoð.
gænburg. esne.
20 þisses londes earan ðrie sulong æt Hægyðe-ðorne. 7 gif
hiora oðrum oððe bæm suð forgelimpe, biscop ðæt lond
gebycge suæ hie ðonne geweorðe.

21 (37)
Oswulf. Cott. Aug. ii. 79
805–10
Cant. arch.

Ic Osuulf aldormonn mid Godes gæfe, ond Beornðryð min
gemecca sellað to Cantuarabyrg, to Cristes cirican, ðæt lond
æt Stanhamstede, xx swuluncga, Gode allmehtgum 7 ðere
halgon gesomnuncgæ, fore hyhte 7 fore aedleane ðæs aecan
5 7 ðaes towardon lifes, 7 fore uncerra saula hela 7 uncerra
bearna. Ond mid micelre eaðmodnisse biddað ðæt wit moten
bion on ðem gemanon ðe ðaer Godes ðiowas siondan, 7 ða
menn *ða ðaer hlafordas wæron, 7 ðara monna ðe hiora lond
to ðaere cirican saldon; ond ðættæ mon unce tide ymb tuælf
10 monað mon geuueorðiae on godcundum godum 7 æc on
aelmessan suæ mon hiora doeð.

¹ at end of line; ra er. and repeated at beginning of next line.
² on er.   ³ in margin.

Ic ðonne Uulfred mid Godes gaefe arc. epis. ðas forecuae-
denan uuord fulliae, 7 bebeode ðæt mon ymb tuælf monað
hiora tid boega ðus geuueorðiae to anes daeges to Osuulfes
tide ge mid godcundum godum ge mid aelmessan, ge aec mid   15
higna suesendum. Ðonne bebeode ic ðaet mon ðas ðing selle
ymb tuælf monað of Liminum, ðe ðis forecuaedene lond to
limpeð, of ðaem ilcan londe æt Stanhamstede: cxx huaetenra
hlafa 7 xxx clenra, 7 án hriðer dugunde, 7 iiii scæp, 7 tua flicca,
7 v goes, 7 x hennfuglas, 7 x pund caeses, gif hit fuguldaeg   20
sie. Gif hit ðonne festendæg sie, selle mon uuęge cæsa, 7 fisces,
7 butran, 7 aegera ðaet mon begeotan maege, 7 xxx ombra
godes uuelesces aloð ðet limpeð to xv mittum, 7 mittan fulne
huniges, oððа tuęgen uuines, suę hwaeder suae mon ðonne
begeotan maege. Ond of higna gemęnum godum ðaer aet ham   25
mon geselle cxx gesuflra hlafa to aelmessan for hiora saula,
suae mon aet hlaforda tidum doeð. Ond ðas forecuędenan
suęsenda all agefe mon ðęm reogolwarde, 7 he brytnię swæ
higum maest red sie 7 ðaem sawlum soelest. Aec mon ðaet
weax ágæfe to *ciricican, 7 hiora sawlum nytt gedoe ðe hit   30
man fore doeð. Aec ic bebeode minum aefterfylgendum ðe
ðaet lond hębben aet Burnan ðaet hiae simle ymb xii monað
foran to ðære tide gegeorwien ten hund hlafa 7 swae feola
sufla, 7 ðęt mon gedele to aelmessan aet ðere tide fore mine
sawle 7 Osuulfes 7 Beornðryðe aet Cristes cirican, 7 him se   35
reogolweord on byrg gebeode foran to hwonne sio tid sie. Aec
ic bidde higon ðette hie ðas godcundan god gedon aet ðere
tide fore hiora sawlum: ðaet ęghwilc messepriost gesinge fore
Osuulfes sawle twa messan, twa fore Beornðryðe sawle; 7
aeghwilc diacon arede twa passione fore his sawle, twa fore   40
hire; ond ęghwilc Godes ðiow gesinge twa fiftig fore his sawle,
twa fore hire, ðaette ge fore uueorolde sien geblitsade mid
ðem weoroldcundum godum 7 hiora saula mid ðem godcundum godum. Aec ic biddo higon ðaet ge me gemynen aet

45 ðere tide mid suilce godcunde gode suilce iow cynlic ðynce,
ic ðe ðas gesettnesse sette ge hueder ge for higna lufon ge
ðeara saula ðe haer beforan hiora namon auuritene siondon.
Valete in domino.—Ðis is gesetnes [O]sulf[es 7] Bearnðryðe.

22 (38)

Eadwald. Cott. Aug. ii. 19

859–70

Cant. arch.

Ðis is geðinge Eadwaldes, Osheringes, 7 Cyneðryðe, Eðel-
modes lafe aldormonnes, ymbe ðet lond et Cert ðe hire
Eðelmod hire hlabard salde. Wes hit becueden *Osbearte his
broðar suna, gif he Cyneðryðe oferlifde, 7 siððan *neniggra
5 meihanda ma ðes cynnes, ac hia hit atuge yfter hira dege swe
hit him boem rehtlicast 7 elmestlicast were.

Ðonne *hebfað Eadwald 7 *Cyne ðas wisan ðus fundene
mid hira friandum. Gib Eadweald leng lifige ðonne Cyneðryð,
geselle et ðem londe et Cert x ðusenda. Gif he gewite er
10 ðonne hia, his barna sue hwelc sue lifes sie agefe ðet feoh,
ond atee sue hit soelest sie for ða hit begetan. Nis Eðelmode
enig meghond neor ðes cynnes ðanne Eadwald, his modar,
his broðar dohtar: mest cyn ðet he det lond hebbe 7 his beorn
yfter him, 7 sue ateon sue him *nytlicas ðynce for ða ðe hit
15 mid reohte begetan.

Ego Ceolnoð mid Godes gefe ercebiscoƿ þis mid Xps'
rodetacne festnie 7 write. biarnhelm. eðelmund. osmund.
biarnheah. sefreð. *ðelwald. *whelm. eðelwald. eardulf.
biarnhelm. eadgar. elfstan. sigefreð. sigefreð. ealhstan.
20 biarnnoð[1]. cialbarht. wealdhelm. tirwald. oba. biarnhelm.
sigemund. herefreð. wynhelm. wunbeald. wermund.

[1] *much worn, but all except* bi *clear under ultra-violet light.*

23 (39)

Ealhburg. Cott. Aug. ii. 52

c. 850

Cant. arch.

Ðis sindan geðinga Ealhburge 7 Eadwealdes et ðem lande
et Burnan hwet man elce gere ob ðem lande to Cristes cirican
ðem hiwum agiaban scel for Ealhburge 7 for Ealdred 7 fore
Eadweald 7 Ealawynne: xl ambra mealtes, 7 xl 7 cc hlaba,
i wege cesa, i wege speces, i eald hriðer, iiii weðras, x goes,   5
xx henfugla, iiii foðra weada. 7 ic Ealhburg bebiade Eadwealde
minem mege an Godes naman 7 an ealra his haligra, ðet he
ðis wel healde his dei, 7 siððan forð bebeode his erbum to
healdenne, ða hwile ðe hit cristen se. 7 suelc mon se ðet lond
hebbe eghwylce sunnandege xx gesuflra hlafa to ðare[1] cirican   10
for Ealdredes saule 7 for Ealhburge.

Ðis is sia elmesse ðe Ealhhere bebead Ealawynne his doehter
et Ðenglesham, et iii sulungum: elce gere c pen' to Cristes
cirican ðem higum. 7 suelc man se ðisses landes bruce, agebe
ðis fiah an Godes gewitnesse 7 an ealra his haligra, 7 suilc man   15
sue hit awege, ðonne se hit on his sawale, nas on ðes ðe hit
don het.

24 (40)

Lufu. Cott. Aug. ii. 92

843–63

Cant. arch.

Ic Lufa mid Godes gefe *ancilla domini* wes soecende 7
smeagende ymb mine saulðearfe mid Ceolnoðes ærcebiscopes
geðeahte 7 ðara hiona et Cristes cirican. Willa ic gesellan

---

[1] *indistinct*; *may be* ðære.

of ðem ærfe ðe me God forgef 7 mine friond to gefultemedan
5 ęlce gere LX ambra maltes 7 CL hlafa, L hwitehlafa, cxx
*elmeshlafes, an hriðer, an suin, IIII weðras, II węga spices 7
ceses ðem higum to Cristes *circcan for mine saule 7 minra
frionda 7 mega ðe me to gode gefultemedan, 7 ðęt sie simle
to adsumsio Scæ¹ Marie ymb XII monað. End sue eihwelc
10 mon swe ðis lond hebbe minra ærbenumena ðis agefe 7 mittan
fulne huniges, X goes, XX henfuglas.

Ic Ceolnoð mid Godes gefe ercebisco*p* mid Cristes rodetacne
ðis festnie 7 write. Beagmund pr' geðafie 7 mid write. Beornfrið
pr' geðafie 7 mid write. wealhhere. osmund. deimund. æðel-
15 wald. werbald. sifreð. swiðberht. beornheah. æðelmund. wig-
helm. lubo.

Ic Luba eaðmod Godes ðiwen ðas forecwedenan god 7 ðas
elmessan gesette 7 gefestnie ob minem erfelande et Mundlingham ðem hiium to Cristes cirican. 7 ic bidde 7 an Godes
20 libgendes naman bebiade ðæm men ðe ðis land 7 ðis erbe
hebbe et Mundlingham ðet he ðas god forðleste oð wiaralde
ende. Se man se ðis healdan wille 7 lestan ðet ic beboden hebbe
an ðisem gewrite se him seald 7 gehealden sia hiabenlice
bledsung. Se his ferwerne oððe hit agele, se him seald 7 geheal-
25 den helle wite, bute he to fulre bote gecerran wille Gode 7
mannum. *Uene ualete.*—Lufe þincggewrit.

25 (41)

Abba. Cott. Aug. ii. 64

833–9

Cant. arch.

Ic Abba geroefa cyðe 7 writan hate hu min willa ís þæt mon
ymb min ærfe gedoe æfter minu*m* dæge.

---

¹ *no mark of contraction.*

Ærest ymb min lond þe ic hæbbe, 7 me God lah, 7 ic æt
minum hlafordum begæt, is min willa, gif me God bearnes
unnan wille, ðæt hit foe to londe æfter me, 7 his bruce mid 5
minum gemeccan, 7 sioððan swæ forð min cynn ða hwile
þe God wille ðæt ðeara ænig sie þe londes weorðe sie 7 land
gehaldan cunne. Gif me ðonne gifeðe sie ðæt ic bearn begeotan
ne mæge, þonne is min willa þæt hit hæbbe min wiif, ða hwile
ðe hia hit mid clennisse gehaldan wile, 7 min broðar Alchhere 10
hire fultume 7 þæt lond hire nytt gedoe. 7 him man sælle an
half swulung an Ciollan-dene to habbanne 7 to brucanne, wið
ðan ðe he ðy geornliocar hire ðearfa bega 7 bewiotige. 7 mon
selle him to ðem londe IIII oxan, 7 II cy, 7 L scæpa, 7 ænne
horn. Gif min wiif ðonne hia nylle mid clennisse swæ gehaldan, 15
7 hire liofre sie oðer hemed to niomanne, ðonne foen mine
megas to ðem londe, 7 hire agefen hire agen. Gif hire ðonne
liofre sie a. mynster to gánganne, oððа suð to faranne[1], ðonne
agefen hie twægen mine mægas, Alchhere 7 Aeðelwald hire
twa ðusenda 7 fon him to ðem londe. 7 ágefe mon to Liminge 20
L eawa 7 V cy fore hie, 7 mon selle to Folcanstane in mid minum
lice X oxan, 7 X cy, 7 C eawa, 7 C swina, 7 higum an sundran D
pend' wið ðan ðe min wiif þær benuge innganges swæ mid
minum lice swæ sioððan yferran dogre, swæ hwæder swæ hire
liofre sie. Gif higan ðonne oððe hlaford þæt nylle hire myn- 25
sterlifes geunnan, oðða hia siolf nylle, 7 hire oðer ðing liofre
sie, þonne agefe mon ten hund pend' inn mid minum lice me
wið legerstowe 7 higum an sundran fif hund pend' fore mine
sawle.

7 ic bidde 7 bebeode swælc monn se ðæt min lond hebbe 30
ðæt he ælce gere agefe ðem higum æt Folcanstane L ambra
maltes, 7 VI ambra gruta, 7 III wega spices 7 ceses, 7 CCCC
hlafa, 7 an hriðr, 7 VI scep. 7 swælc monn se ðe to minum
ærfe foe, ðonne gedele he ælcum messepreoste binnan Cent

[1] first a from o; the scribe probably meant to write foeranne.

35 mancus goldes, 7 ælcum Godes ðiowe pend', 7 to Sancte
Petre min wærgeld twa ðusenda. 7 Freoðomund foe to minum
sweorde, 7 agefe ðer æt feower ðusenda; 7 him mon forgefe
ðeran ðreotene hund pending¹. 7 gif mine broðar ærfeweard
gestrionen ðe londes weorðe sie, þonne ann ic ðem londes.
40 Gif hie ne gestrionen, oðða him sylfum ælles hwæt sęle, æfter
hiora dege ann ic his Freoðomunde, gif he ðonne lifes bið.
Gif him elles hwæt sæleð, ðonne ann ic his minra swæstar
suna, swælcum se hit geðian wile 7 him gifeðe bið. 7 gif þæt
gesele þæt min cynn to ðan clane gewite ðæt ðer ðeara nan ne
45 sie ðe londes weorðe sie, þonne foe se hlaford to 7 ða higon æt
Kristes cirican, 7 hit minum gaste nytt gedoen. An ðas redenne
ic hit ðider selle ðe se monn se ðe Kristes cirican hlaford sie,
se min 7 minra erfewearda forespreoca 7 mundbora, 7 an his
hlaforddome we bian moten.
50 Ic Ciolnoð mid Godes gefe ærcebiscop ðis write 7 ðeafie,
7 mid Cristes rodetacne hit festniæ. Ic Beagmund pr' ðis
ðeafie 7 write. Ic Wærhard pr' ab' ðis ðeafie 7 write. Ic Abba
geroefa ðis write 7 festnie mid Kristes rodetacne. Ic Aeðelhun
pr' ðis ðeafie 7 write. Ic Abba pr' ðis þeafie 7 write. Ic Wig-
55 mund pr' ðis write 7 ðeafie. Ic Iof pr' ðis ðeafie 7 write.
Ic Osmund pr' ðis ðeafie 7 write. Ic Wealhhere diac'
ðis write 7 ðeafie. Ic Badanoð diac' ðis write 7 ðeafie. Ic
Heaberht diac' ðis write 7 þeafie. Ic Noðwulf subdiac' ðis
write 7 ðeafie. Ic Wealhhere subdiac' ðis write 7 ðeafie. Ic
60 Ciolwulf subdiac' ðis write 7 ðeafie.
Heregyð hafað ðas wisan binemned ofer hire deg 7 ofer
Abban. Ðæm higum et Cristes cirican of ðæm londe et
Cealflocan: ðæt is ðonne ðritig ombra alað, 7 ðreo hund hlafa,
ðeara bið fiftig hwitehlafa, an weg spices 7 ceses, an ald hriðr,
65 feower weðras, an suin oððe sex weðras, sex gosfuglas, ten
hennfuglas, ðritig teapera, gif hit wintres deg sie, sester fulne

¹ end of line (but not at edge of page); for pendinga?

huniges, sester fulne butran, sester fulne saltes. 7 Heregyð
bibeadeð ðem mannum ðe efter hire to londe foen on Godes
noman ðæt hie fulgere witen ðæt hie ðiss gelęsten ðe on ðissem
gewrite binemned is dem higum to Cristes cirican, 7 ðæt sie 70
simle to higna blodlese ymb twelf monað agefen. 7 se mann
se to londe foe agefe hire erfehonda XIII pund pendinga; 7 hio
forgifeð fiftene pund for ðy ðe mon ðas feorme ðy soel gelæste.
—[Abban geroefan ærfegedal, his geðinga to Kristes cirican.]

26 (42)

Badanoð. Cott. Aug. ii. 42

845–53

Cant. arch.

Ic Badanoð Beotting cyðo 7 writan hato hu min willa is
ðet min ærfelond fere ðe ic et Aeðeluulfe cyninge begæt 7
gebohte mid fullum friodome on æce ærfe æfter minum dege
7 minra ærfewearda, ðet is, mines wifes 7 minra bearna. Ic
wille ærist me siolfne Gode allmehtgum forgeofan to ðere 5
stowe æt Cristes cirican, 7 min bearn ðęr liffest gedoan, 7
wiib 7 cild ðæm hlaforde 7 higum 7 ðære stowe befestan ober
minne dei, to friðe 7 to mundbyrde 7 to hlaforddome on
ðæm ðingum ðe him ðearf sie. 7 hie brucen londes hiora dei,
7 higon gefeormien to minre tide swæ hie soelest ðurhtion 10
megen; 7 higon us mid heora godcundum godum swę gemynen
swæ us arlic 7 him ælmeslic się.

7 ðonne ofer hiora dei, wifes 7 cilda, ic bebeode on Godes
noman ðæt mon agefe ðæt lond inn higum to heora beode
him to brucanne on ece ærfe, swæ him liofast sie. 7 ic biddo 15
higon for Godes lufe ðæt se monn se higon londes unnen to
brucanne ða ilcan wisan leste on swæsendum to minre tide,
7 ða godcundan lean minre saule mid gerece swę hit mine
ærfenuman ær onstellen.

20   Ðonne is min willa ðæt ðissa gewriota sien twa gelice: oðer
habben higon mid boecum, oðer mine ærfeweardas heora dei.
Ðonne is ðes londes ðe ic higum selle xvi gioc ærðelondes
7 medwe[1], all on æce ærfe to brucanne ge minne dei, ge æfter
swæ to ationne swæ me mest red 7 liofast sie.

25   Ceolnoð arc' episc' ðiss writo 7 festnię mid Cristes rodetacne.
Alchhere dux ðiss writo 7 ðeafię. Bægmund prb' ab' ðiss writo
7 ðeafię. Hysenoð pr' ðiss writo 7 ðeafię. wigmund. badenoð.
osmund. suiðberht. dyddel. cichus. sigemund. eðelwulf. tile.
cyneberht. eðelred. badanoð.

9TH CENTURY, SURREY

27 (45)

Ælfred[2]. Stowe Ch. 20

871–89

Horsley, Clapham, Chertsey, &c. (Surrey)

Ic Ęlfred *dux* hatu writan 7 cyðan an ðissum gewrite Ęlfrede
regi 7 allum his weotum 7 geweotan, 7 ec swylce minum
megum 7 minum gefeorum, þa męn þe ic mines ęrfes 7 mines
boclondes seolest onn, ðęt is þonne Werburg min wif 7 uncer
5 *ge*mene[2] b*earn.* þæt is þonne et ęrestan an Sondenstede 7 on
Selesdune xxxii hida, 7 on Westarham xx hida, 7 on Cloppaham xxx hida, 7 on Leangafelda vi hida, 7 on Horsalęge x hida,
7 on Netelamstyde vi hida. Ic Ęlfred *dux* sello Werburge 7
Alhdryðe uncum *ge*menum bearne æfter minum dege þas
10 lond mid cwice ęrfe 7 mid earðe 7 mid allum ðingum ðe to
londum belimpað. 7 twa þusendu swina ic heom sello mid
þem londum, gif hio hio gehaldeð mid þare clęnnisse þe uncer
word*ge*cweodu seondan. 7 hio gebrenge ęt Sancte Petre min

---

[1] *foll. by er.*   [2] *the ge is expressed here and below by a* 7 *with
the direction of the upper stroke reversed.*

twa wergeld, gif ðet Godes willa seo þȩt heo þæt fȩreld age.
Ond ȩfter Werburge dȩge seo Alhðryðe þa lond unbefliten on   15
Sondemstyde 7 on Selesdune 7 on Leangafelda. Ond gif heo
bearn hȩbbe, feo ðȩt bearn to ðȩm londum ȩfter hire; gif heo
bearn nȩbbe, feo ðonne an hire rehtfȩderen sio neste hond to
þem londe ond to ðem ȩrfe, 7 swa hwylc minra fȩdrenmega swa
ðȩt sio þæt hine to ðan *ge*hagige þæt he þa oðoro lond begeotan   20
mȩge 7 wille, þonne gebygcge he þa lond ȩt hire mid halfe
weorðe. Ond swe hwylc mon swa ðȩt sio þȩt ðes londes bruce
ofer minne dȩg on Cloppaham, þanne geselle he CC peninga eghwylce gere to Ceortesege for Ȩlfredes sawle to feormfultume[1].
Ond ic sello Ȩðelwalde minum sunu III hida boclondes: II hida   25
on Huȩtedune, . . . s hides an Gatatune, 7 him sello þerto C
swina; 7 gif se cyning him geunnan wille þȩs folclondes to ðȩm
boclonde, þonne hȩbbe he 7 bruce; gif hit þȩt ne sio, þonne selle
hio him swa hwaðer swa hio wille, swa ðȩt lond an Horsalege,
swe ðȩt an Leangafelda. Ond ic sello Berhtsige minum mege án   30
hide boclondes on Lȩncanfelda, 7 þerto C swina; 7 geselle hio C
swina to Cristes cirican for me 7 fer mine sawle, 7 C to Ceortesege; 7 þone oferȩcan mon gedȩle gind mynsterhamas to Godes
ciricum in Suþregum 7 in Cȩnt, þa hwile þe hio lestan willȩn.
Ond ic sello Sigewulfe minum mege ofer Werburge dȩg þȩt   35
lond an Netelhæmstyde; ond Sigulf geselle of ðem londe C
pȩninga to Cristes cirican. Ond eghwylc þara ȩrfewearda þe
ȩfter him to ðȩm londe foe, þonne ageofen hío þa ilcan elmessan to Cristes cirican for Ȩlfredes sawle, þa hwile þe fulwiht
sio, 7 hít man on ðȩm londe begeotan mȩge. Ond ic sello   40
Eadrede minum mege þet lond on Fearnlege ȩfter Eðelredes
dȩge, gif he hit to him geearnian wile; 7 he geselle of ðem
londe xxx omb[ra][2] cornes ȩghwelce gere to Hrofescestre; ond
sio ðis lond *ge*writen 7 unbefliten ȩfter Eadredes dege in

---

[1] *accent on first* m.   [2] *hole in MS.; part of* a *still visible.*

45 Aelfredes rehtmeodrencynn ða hwile þe fulwihte[1] sio on Angel-
cynnes ealonde. Ðeos foresprec 7 þas gewriotu þe herbeufan
awreotene stondað, ic Ælfred willio 7 wille þæt hio sion
soðfęstlice forðweard getrymed me 7 minum ęrfeweardum.
Gif ðęt ðonne God ællmęhtig geteod habbe, ond me þęt on
50 lęne gelið þęt me gesibbra ęrfeweard forðcymeð wepnedhades
7 acęnned weorðeð, ðanne ann ic ðęm ofer minne dęg alles
mines ęrfes to brucenne swa him leofust sio. And swa hwylc
mon swa ðas god 7 þas geofe 7 þas gewrioto 7 þas word mid
rehte haldan wille ond gelęstan, gehalde hine heofones cyning
55 in þissum life ondwardum, 7 eac swa in þęm towardan life;
ond swa hwylc mon swa hio wonie 7 breoce, gewonie him God
almahtig his weorldare[2] ond eac swa his sawle are *in eona
eonum.*

Her sindon ðæra manna naman awritene ðe ðeosse wísan
60 geweoton sindon. Ic Æðered ar' bisc' mid ðære halgan Cristes
rodetacne ðas word 7 ðas wisan fęstnie 7 write. ælfred *dux.*
beorhtuulf *dux.* beornhelm ab'. earduulf ab'. wærburg. sigfreð
pr'. *beonheah pr'. beagstan pr'. wulfheah. æðelwulf pr'.
earduulf pr'. beornoð diac'. wealdhelm diac'. wine sb' diac'.
65 sæfreð. ceolmund m'. eadmund m'. eadwald m'. siguulf m'.—
þis is Ęlfredes ęrfegewrit.

9TH CENTURY, MERCIAN

28 (47)

Wiglaf[2]. Cott. Aug. ii. 9

836

Hanbury (Worc.) arch.

uuiglaf *rex merciorum. monasterium in* heanbyrg. *in* craeft.
liberabo a difficultate illa quam nos saxonice faestingmenn *dicimus*
—uuiglaf. cyneðryþ *regina.* ceolnoð. cyneferð. raeþhun. eaduulf.

---

[1] *accent on the* w.   [2] *foll. by* 7 eac swa his weorldare, *deleted.*

heaberht. eaduulf. alhstan. beormod. husa. cunda. ceolberht.
cynred. eanmund. uueohtred. beornhelm. sigred. mucoel. 5
tiduulf. aeþelhard. cyneberht. aeþeluulf. alhhelm. humberht.
aelfstan. mucoel. wicga. aldred. aldberht. aelfred. hwithyse.
werenberht. wulfred. wiglaf. eanuulf. alhmund. berhtuulf.
ecghard—Ðes friodom waes bigeten aet Wiglafe cyninge mid
ðaem tuentigum hida aet Iddes-hale end ðaes londes friodom 10
aet Haeccaham mid ðy ten hida londe aet Felda bi Weoduman.
End Mucele esninge ðaet ten hida lond aet Croglea—Ðis is
Heanburge friodom, se waes bigeten mid ðy londe aet Iddes-
hale, 7 aet Heanbyrig ten hida ðaes londes, 7 aet Felda ten
hida on Beansetum. 7 Biscop gesalde Sigrede aldormenn sex 15
hund scillinga on golde, 7 Mucele aldormenn ten hida lond æt
Croglea.

29 (48)

Berhtwulf. Cant. arch. Chart. Ant. C. 1280 (Red Book

No. 9)

844-5

Wotton Underwood (Bucks.)

In nomine Domini ego Berchtwulf cyning sile Forðrede
minu*m* ðegne nigen higida lond in Wudotune in ece erfe him
to hiobbanne 7 to siollanne ðaem ðe hit wille mið eaðmodre
hernisse him to geeornigan ofer his daeg : Cisseðebeorg,
feower treowe hyl, 7 Eanburge mere, Tihhan hyl, 7 ut bi geht 5
tu higida lond in erfe ece. 7 he salde to londceape xxx man-
cessan 7 nigen hund scill' wið ðaem londe hi*m* in ece erfe.

Ic Berhtwulf *rex* ðas mine gesaldnisse trymme 7 faestna in
Cristes rodetacne 7 in his ðaere haligran a[1] 7 in his *wotona
gewitnisse. aerist saeðryð *regina*, cyneferð *episcopus*, alchhun 10

---

[1] *prec. by two unexplained marks.*

episcopus, berchtred *episcopus*, deorlaf *episcopus*, *ceored *epi-scopus*, *wichred *abbas*, aldred *abbas*, mucel *dux*, hunbercht *dux*, burgred *dux*, *aefstan, cyneberht *dux*, sigred *dux*, alberht *dux*, aldred *dux*, mucel *dux*, hunstan *dux*, eadwulf, *beornoð,
15 wulfred, mucel, aldred, wicga, eadgar, baldred, werenberht, eadred, aeðelwulf *presbyter*, heaberht *presbyter*, ecghun, ecg-heard, beornhaeð, aldred.

7 we aec alle bibeodað ðe aet ðisse gewitnisse werun on Cristes noman 7 on his ðaere haligra[n], gif aenig monn ðas
20 ure gewitnisse incerre on owihte, ðaet he aebbe ðaes ael-maehtgan Gode[s unhlis . . 7] his ðaere haligran up in heo-fnum ðaes we him [ge]beodan maege.

LATER MERCIAN

30

Werfrið. Add. Ch. 19,791

904

Worcester arch.

Rixiendum on ecnisse ussum drihtne hælende Criste, se ðe all ðing gemetegað ge on heofenum ge on eorðan, þæs inflæscnisse ðy gere þe *agen wæs DCCCC wintra 7 IIII winter 7 ðy VII gebongere, ic Uuerfrid biscop mid mines arweorðan
5 heorodes geðafuncga 7 leafe on Weogerna-ceastre, sylle Wulfsige minum gerefan wið his holdum mægene 7 eadmodre hernesse anes hides lond on Easttune, swa swa Herred hit hæfde on ðreora monna dæg, 7 all ðæt innlond beligeð án dic utane, 7 þonne ofer ðreora monna dęg agefe monn eft ðaet lond
10 butan elcon wiðercwide inn to Weogerna-ceastre.

7 ðis seondan ðara monna noman ðe ðæt geðafedon 7 mid Cristes rodetacne gefaestnedon. uuerfrið biscop, cynehelm abb*as*, uuerfrið pres*byter*, eadmund pres*byter*, berhtmund

pres*byter*, tidbald pres*byter*, hildefrið pres*byter*, ecfrið pres*byter*,
eaduulf pres*byter*, wiglaf pres*byter*, oslac diacon, cynað diacon,
berhthelm, wigheard, monn, earduulf, uullaf, berhthelm,
heahred, cynelaf, uulfred, cynehelm, uulfric, cenfrið, hwituc,
cynelaf, ceolhelm, uullaf[1], ealhmund, earduulf, uulfgar.—
Uulfsiges londboc.

31

Æþelred. Cott. Ch. viii. 27

901

Much Wenlock (Salop) arch.

æðered æ . . . . . .[2] *opitulante monarchiam merceorum tenentes.*
congregatio wininicensis eclesiae. terram in easthope, *in* peatting-
tune, *in* stantune. *terram quae dicitur* cahinglæg. *in* easthope
et in peatingtune. *kalicem pensans* xxx mancusos. mildburge
abbatissae (gen.). *in civitate* scrobbensis—æðered. æðelfled[3]. 5
wired. cuðulf. [t]idelm. wigburg. æðelswið. wulfgyð. culfre.
cineburg. ælfric. wulfsig. aldred. burgred. wulfsig.—easthop.

32

Oswold. Add. Ch. 19,792

969

Worcester arch.

Ic Oswold bisceop þurh Godes gefe, mid geþafunge 7 leafe
Eadgares, Angulkynincges, 7 Ælfheres, Mercna heretogan,
7 þæs hieredes on Wiogerne-ceastre, landes sumne dæl, þæt
sint . . hida on twuam tunum þe fram cuþum mannum Teot-
tingctun 7 Ælfsiges-tun sint gehatenne sumum cnihte, þæm 5

---

[1] *second* l *from beginning of another letter* (f?).   [2] *hole in MS.;*
æ *no doubt belongs to a form of the name* Æðelfled, *although the* e *re-
maining to the right of the hole is apparently too far away to be the ending
of such a form.*   [3] *large hole in MS. at this point.*

is Osulf nama, for Godes lufan 7 for uncre sibbe mid eallum
þingum to freon þe þærto belimpað his dæg forgeaf, 7 æfter
his dæge twam erfeweardum, þæt beo his bearn, swilc lengest
mote, gief him þæt giefeþe bið. Æfter þara bearna dæge fó
10 Eadleofu to his gebedde hire dæg. Æfter hire dæge becweþe
hire broþrum twam swilc hire leofest sy æfter hieora dæge eft
into þære halgan stowe. Sy hit ælces þinges freoh butan ferd-
fare 7 walgeweorc 7 brygcgeworc. þis wæs *godon ymbe nigon
hund wintra 7 nigon 7 seoxtig þæs þe Drihtnes *gebyrdtide
15 wæs on þy nigoþan geare þæs þe Oswold bisceop to folgaþe
fengc. Sancta Maria 7 sanctus Michahel cum sancto Petro 7
eallum Godes halgum gemiltsien þis healdendum. Gief hwa
buton gewyrhtum hit awendan wille, God adilgie his noman
of lifes bocum, 7 habbe him gemæne wið hine on þam ytemes-
20 tan dæge þysses lifes butan he to rihtere bote gecerre. Her is
seo hondseten Oswoldes bisceopes 7 unna þæs hierdes on
Wiogerna-ceastre—wulfric mæssepreost. eadgar mæssepreost.
æþelstan mæssepreost. wistan mæssepreost. ælfred. wulfhun.
*brihstan. wulfgar. cynsige. ælfstan. eadwine. ælfgar. eadward.
25 tuna. ufic. wulfheah. leofwine. wulfnoð.—Teotintun. Eadgar
cyng.

33

Oswold. Add. Ch. 19,794

984

Worcester arch.

ego osuuold. æþelredi *regis anglorum ác* ælfrice *ducis merciorum. ministro meo qui* cynelm *nuncupatur.* æt caldinccotan.
ecclesiae in weogerne-ceastre. þonne is þæs londes þridde half
hid þe oswold arcebisceop selð cynelme his þegne to bóclonde
5 swa he hit him ær hæfde to-forlæten to lænlonde ægþær ge
on earðlonde ge on *homlonde—óswold. wynsige. æþelstan.

ælfsige. eadgar. wistan. eadward. æþelsige. wulfward. æþric.
godingc. leofstan. wulfhún. cyneþegn. wulfgar. leofwine. ufuc.
ælfnoð. aþelwold. wulfnoð—þis syndon þa londgemæru into
caldingccotan. þæt is ærest on ruhwællan. of ruhwællan 7long 10
sices on þone weg. of þæm wege anbutan þone garan eft on
þone weg. of þæm wege a be þæm heafodlonde. þæt eft in þæt
oþer heafodlond ane hwile. þænne in þa furh. þæt andlong fyrh
anbutan þæt heafodlond. þæt swa on cyneburge londgemære.
þæt andlong gemæres on þæt heafodlond. of þæm heafodlonde 15
eft on þone weg. of þæm wege on hlydan. andlong hlydan on
þone heafodweg. of þæm wege on þone hyll. of þæm hylle on
þa díc æt crawan-þorne. of þære díc on cærent. þæt andlong
cærent on þa mylendíc. of þære díc on þa dene. þæt andlong
dene on þone grenan weg. of þæm wege on þa furh. of þære 20
fyrh a be þæm heafdan to breoduninga gemære to þære fyrh
þæs bisceops átlondes. þæt andlong fyrh to þæm heafdon.
of þæm heafdon to þæm heafodlonde. swa anbutan þæt
heafodlond. þæt innan þa furh. þæt andlong fyrh on suðbróc.
þæt andlong broces. þæt eft in rugan wællan. 25

34

Æþelstan. Cott. Ch. viii. 37

c. 1010–23

Worcester arch.

Her swutelað on ðissum gewrite . . . Æþelstan bisceop
gebohte æt Leofrice æt Blace-wellan fif hide landes æt Intebyr-
gan be Æþelredes cynges leafe 7 be Ælfeges arcebisceopes
gewitnesse 7 be Wulfstanes arcebisceopes 7 be ealra þæra
witena þe ða on Engla-lande lifes wæron mid ten pundan 5
reades goldes 7 hwites seolfres unforboden 7 unbesacan to
geofene 7 to syllanne ær dæge 7 æfter dæge sibban oððe

fremdan þær him leofost wære. 7 se cyng het þone arcebisceop
Wulfstan þærto boc settan. 7 Æþelstane bisceope boc 7 land
10 betæcan unnendere heortan. þa æfter þysan manegum gearum
soc Wulfstan 7 his sunu Wulfric on sum þæt land. þa ferde se
bisceop to sciregemote to Wigeran-ceastre, 7 draf þær his
spræce. þa sealde Leofwine ealdor[m]an 7 Hacu[n] 7 Leofric
7 eal seo scir his land clæne, þa he hit unforbodan 7 unbesacan
15 bohte, 7 settan dæg to þæt man to ðam lande scolde faran. 7
þa ilcan þe him ær landgemære læddon hit e . . . an 7 cwædan
gif ða landgemære ealswa wæron swa man heo on fruman
lædde þæt se bisceop þæt land ful riht ahte. þa com se bisceop
þærto 7 se þe him land sealde 7 þa þe him ær [to wit]nesse
20 wæron. 7 com Wulfstan 7 his sunu 7 þa þe hyra geferan wæron.
7 heo ealle þa þa landgemære geridan ealswa heo man on
fruman þam bisceope lædde. 7 heo ealle cwædan þe . . . wæron
þæt se bisceop ful riht þæt land ahte, þa se þær geanwyrde
wæs þe him land sealde. Spæcon ða Leofrices freond 7 Wulf-
25 stanes freond þæt hit betere wære þæt heora seht togæ . . .
de þonne hy ænige . . ce hym betweonan heoldan. Worhtan þa
hyra seht. þæt wæs þ[æ]t Leofric sealde Wulfstane 7 his suna
an pund, 7 twegra þegna að, 7 wære him sylf þridde, þæt he
[þ]am ilcan wolde beon gehealden, gif seo spæc to Leofrice
30 eode swa swa heo þa wæs to Wulfstane gegan. þis wæs ure
ealra seht. Wulfstan 7 his sunu sealdon þa þæt land clæne
Leofrice. 7 Leofric 7 [W]u[lfs]tan 7 Wulfric þam bisceope
clæne land 7 unbesacan ær dæge 7 æfter to gyfanne þær him
leofost wære. Her swutelað seo gewitnes 7 se borh þe þær æt
35 wæron. þæt wæs ærest se bisceop 7 Le[ofric], 7 Wulfstan, 7
Brihtwine, 7 Cynsig, 7 Wynstan, 7 Ægelwig munuc, 7 Ælwine
mæssepreost, 7 Ælmær mæssepreost, 7 Wulfric mæssepreost,
7 Cyneword æt Pebbe-wurðy, 7 Ælewig . . . . . n ham, 7 Eadwig
his mæg, 7 Wulfri[c] æt Cloddes-heale, 7 Sæword æt Uptuny,
40 7 Wulfric æt Bynning-tune, 7 Wulfsig madding, 7 mænig god

cniht toeacan þysan. Nu syndan þissa gewrita þreo: an on
Wigerna-ceastre æt sancta Marian, þær þæt land to herð; 7
oðer on Hereforda æt sancte Æþelbrihte; 7 þridde a mid þam
þe þæt land on hande stande. God ælmihtig þone gehealde
þe þis wille rihtlice healdan. 7 gif ænig man þonn[e] seo þe þis 45
awendan wille, God ælmihtig 7 sancta Maria 7 ealle his leofan
halgan þæne aniðerige ægþær ge her on life ge þær he længast
wunian sceal, buton he hit þe deoppor ær gebete swa bisceop
him tæce.—Huntebergan. Hute (?) beargas.

35

Wulfstan. Add. Ch. 19,795

1003-23

Worcester arch.

ego wulfstan. *in loco qui vocatur* pyriae. *cuidam matronae
cujus vocabulum est* wulgyuu. wiogornensi *ecclesiae* (dat.)—
ðis syndan þære halfre hide londgemæru up æt þære pirian.
þæt is ærest forn ongean þære cyrcan. ollung þære hegreawe
on æglardes mersc. ollung þære hegreawe inne þa strete. 5
ollung þære strete. þæt upp on þæne hyl. of þam hylle dun
in þæt dæll. þæt ollung þæs dæles. þæt up on þone hyll, be-
henon lipperd, ofer midne graf. þæt in þone midlestan holan
weg. þæt innan þa hegreawe. ollung þa hegreawe. innan þone
readan weg. ollung þæs readan weges. þæt innan þa hecce. 10
ollung þa hecce. þæt innan þa hecce forn *igean þære cyrcan.
7 þæt land þærto þe æþelnoþ ahte up æt tan ofran, 7 þæne
hagan þe eadwerd ahte, 7 þæne mædæcer þe þærto hyrð—
wulfstan. eadric. wulfwine. æþelric. ælfgar. þurferð. wulfwarð.
leofric. æþelwine. eadric. byrhtwine. leofric. 15

36

Ælfweard. Add. Ch. 19,796

1016–23

Evesham (Worc.) arch.

Ðis syndon þa foreword þe Ælfwerd abb' 7 se hired on
Eoues-haṃme worhtan wið Æðelmær, þa ða hi hiṃ þæt land
sealdon æt Norðtune wið III pundon þreora manna dæg.
þæt syndon III hida to inware 7 oðer healf to utware, swa swa
5 he hit gebohte þa ða hit weste læg æt Hacune 7 æt Leofrice 7
æt ealre scire. þæt is þæt we hit unnon hiṃ on Godes est, 7
on sancta Marian 7 on þæs halgan weres s[ancte E]gwines, þe
hit into þaṃ mynstre beget. 7 gange ægðer ge cyricsceat ge
teoðunge into þaṃ halgan mynstre swa he mycele þearfe ah
10 þæt hi don; 7 toll 7 team sy agifen into þaṃ mynstre, butan
he hit geearnian mæge to þaṃ ðe þænne ah mynstres geweald.
7 æfter þreora manna dæge gange þæt land in mid I men 7 mid
VI oxan 7 mid XX sceapuṃ 7 mid XX æceruṃ gesawenes cornes.
7 þyssa gewrita synd III: an lið on Wigra-cestre æt sancta
15 Marian mynstre, 7 oðer lið on Eofes-haṃme, 7 þridde hæfð
Æðelmer. Se þe þis gehealde, gehealde hine God, 7 se ðe hit
awende oððe gelytlige, gelytlige God his mede on þaṃ to-
wearduṃ life, butan he hit ær his ende þe deoppor gebete. 7
þis wæs gedon be þyssa witena gewytnessæ þe herwið nyðan
20 awritene standað. þæt is ærest Ælfgeofu seo hlæfdie þe þæs
mynstres walt, 7 Wulfstan arcebiscop, 7 Leofsige biscop, 7
Byrhtwold biscop, 7 Ælfsige abb', 7 Ælfwerd abb', 7 Leofsige
abb', 7 Afa abb', 7 Hacun eorl, 7 Eglaf eorl, 7 Leofwine ealdor-
man, 7 Leofric, 7 Eadwine, 7 Byrhtteg munuc, 7 Byrhtwine,
25 7 Ælfsige m'[1].

---

[1] the last name written much smaller than the others, at the side.

37

Brihtheah. Add. Ch. 19,797

1033-8

Worcester arch.

In nomine domini ic Byrhteh b*iscop* mid Godes geðeahte 7
þæs arwyrðan hiredes on Wigerna-ceastre, 7 on ealra þæra
ðegena gewitnysse into Glæawe-ceastre-scire ic cyþe þæt ic
gean Wulmære minum cnihte twegra hida landes in Easttune
for his godra *gearnunge swa ful 7 swa forð swa he hit hæfde 5
under Leofsige b*iscope* 7 under me. Sydþan hæbbe he 7 wel
bruce þreora manna dæg to rihtere geyrsumnysse into ðære
halgan stowe to Wigerna-ceastre, butan he hit forwyrce. Ðæs
is to gewitnysse se hired on Wigra-ceastre 7 on Glæawe-ceastre
7 on Eofes-hom 7 on Prescoran.   10

38

Leofing. Add. Ch. 19,798

1038

Worcester arch.

ego lyfingus *episcopus. in loco qui* tapenhalan *vocitatur.*
appellamine meo earcytel *utenti nomine. ecclesiae in* uuéogerna-
ceastrae—ðis synd þa landgemæro into tápenhalan. þæt
is ærest of brada-forda east in ða hégreawe. æfter þære
héghreawe þæt cymð innan ða éaldan díc. æfter þære dic þæt 5
to ðam hólan wege. ofer þone weg westriht to þære ealdan dic.
æfter þære dic [t]o þære bradan stræt. of þære bradan stræt
be þam gráfe innan ða port stræt. æfter stráéte innan dílla-
meres díc. of þære díce ende innan þa wǽllan. of þære wæll[a]n
in þa sándihte stræt. æfter stræte norð on bísceopes scírlett. 10
ofer b*isceopes* scírlett in línáceran-wege þam ínnmæstan. of

línáceran innan ðone hége. æfter þam hege on bróccholes weg. of brócchóles wége innan þone croft. of þam crofte be þam gearde innan léofesunes cróft. of þam crofte innan sálewearpan.
15 æfter sálewearpan in oterburnan. æfter óterburnan þæt cymð eft in salewearpan. 7 twégen hagan binnan porte—lyfingus. ælfweardus. æþelstanus. leofric. ælfstan. odda. eadwine. earni. earnwi. leofric. æþelwine. wistan. þurkel. eatstan. wilstan. wulstan. berhtmær. berhtwine. wulfward. eadwig.—earkyteles
20 bóc to tapan-halan. harold *senior*.

39

Leofing. Add. Ch. 19,799

1042

Worcester arch.

In ures drihtnes naman hælendes Cristes ic Leofinc bisceop mid þafunge 7 leafe Hearðacnutes cynges 7 þæs arwurþan hiredes æt Wigorna-ceastre ge iunges ge ealdes gebocige sumne dæl landes minan holdan 7 getreowan þegene, þam is Ægelric
5 nama, 11 hida æt *Eadmunddes-cótan hæbbe he 7 wel bruce for his eadmodre gehersumnysse 7 for his licwurðan sceatte. þæt is þæt he hit hæbbe 7 well bruce his dæg. 7 æfter his dæge twam erfewardum þan ðe him leofest sy, 7 him betst to geearnian wylle. 7 he hit hæbbe to freon ælces þinges butan
10 wallgeweorce 7 brygcgeweorce 7 ferdsocne. God ælmihtig þone gehealde þe þas ure sylena 7 ure gerædnyssa healdan wylle on ælce healfe. Gif ænig þonne sy *uppahofen 7 inblawen on þa oferhyda þære geættredan deofles lare, 7 wylle þas ure sylena gewemman oððe gewonian on ænigum þingum, wite
15 he hine amansumadne mid Annaníam 7 Saphíram on ece forwyrd butan he hit her ǽr wurðlice gebete Gode 7 mannum. Ðis wæs gedon þy geare þe wæs agan fram Cristes *gebyrtide

an þusend wintra 7 twa 7 XLII wintra. Ðis is seo gewitnes: þæt
is Hearþacnut cyng, 7 Ælfgeofu his modor; 7 Lyfing b*isceop*, 7
eall se hired on Wigra-ceastre; 7 Ælfward b*isceop*, 7 se hired on 20
Eofes-homme; 7 Godwine abbod, 7 se hired on Wincelcumbe;
7 Leofric eorl, 7 ealle þa þegenas on Wigra-ceastre-scire ge
Englisce ge Denisce.—To þa*m* II hidan æt Eadmundes-cotan.

40

Ealdred. Add. Ch. 19,800

1053–6

Worcester arch.

ego ealdredus *episcopus cum licentia venerandae familiae in*
uuigorna *civitate dabo viro nomine* balwine. *vico qui vocatur*
westtun. *familiae sancte mariae restituatur*—ealdred. wulfward. berhtwald. mannig. harold. odda. raulf. æglwine. wulfwig. wilstan. wulfstan. edwig. ælfstan. þurkyll. godric. leofwine. 5
wulfwig. godwine. berhtric. tosti. ælfstan. mannig. ælfnoð.
leofwine. godwine. earkyll. eadmær. ealdred. ælfric. æglric.—
twegra hida géanboc 7 anre gerde æt westtune þe ealdred
gebocade baldwine his stiwarde þreora manna dæg.

41

Ealdred. Add. Ch. 19,801

1058

Worcester arch.

ego ealdredus *episcopus*. norðtun. *meo ministro qui nuncupatur*
dodda—Ðis is ðære twegra hida boc 7 anre gyrde æt norðtune, 7 ða feower æceras ðærto of ðære styfycunge into ðam
twam hidan, 7 ða mæde 7 ðone graf ðe þærto mid rihte to-ligeð,
7 ða ðrý æceras mæde on afan-hamme þe s*ancte* oswold geaf 5

bercstane into ðam lande. 7 ðiss synd þa landgemæro into ðam
grafe. ærost of ðære dune andlang þære rode oð hit cymð
beneoðan stancnolle þanon on gerihte to cwennhofoton. of
cwennhofoton be norðon þam mere þanon on gerihte eft up
10 on ða dune—eaduueard *rex*. ealdredus. ægelwig. godric.
eadmund. wulfstan. wulfwig. wylstan. ælfstan. godric. godric.
godwine. brihtric. ægelric. godric. ceolmær. atser. æstan.
eadric. brihtwine. norðman. arngeat.—to norðtune. eadwardi
junioris.

42

Wulfgeat. Harley Ch. 83. A. 2

Worcester arch.

Ðis is Wulfgates gecwide æt Dunnintune. *þæt* is *þonne þæt*
he geann ærest Gode his sawelscættas: *þæt* is I hid æt Tærdebicgan; 7 I pund penega; 7 VI 7 twentig freotmonna for his
sawle; 7 into Wigera-cæstre an bryþen mealtes, healf of
5 Dunnintune, healf of Cylles-hale; 7 into s*anct*e Æþelbrihte
healfes pundes weorð; 7 into s*anct*e Guðlace healfes pundes
weorð; 7 into Leomynstre IIII aldhryðra; 7 into Bro*m*gearde
I hryder; oðer into Cliftune; 7 into Heantune IIII hryðra; 7
to Pencric II hryðra; 7 into Tweongan II hryðra. 7 he geann
10 forgifnesse ælcan þara þe wið hine agylt hæbbe for his sawle
þearfe. 7 he geann anes geares gafol his monnu*m* to gyfe, swa
heo þa are brucon swa heo þa ælmessan gelæstan þa ðer to
londe foð. 7 he geann his hlaforde II hors, 7 II sweord, 7 IIII
scyldas, 7 IIII spera, 7 X mæran mid X coltan. 7 he bit his
15 hlaford for Godes lufan *þæt* he beo his wifes freond 7 his
dohter. 7 he ann his wife þæs landes æt Cylles-hale, 7 æt
Eowniglade, 7 æt Hrodene þa hwile hire dæg beo. 7 ofer hire
dæg ga *þæt* land eft in min cynn þa ðær nehste syn. 7 Wulfgyfe
minre doht*er þæt* land æt Dunnintune, swa hit stont, 7 æt

þornbyrig þæt land þe wæs mid hire moder golde geboht æt 20
Leofnoðe. 7 Wulfgyfe suna mire dohter þæt land æt Ingewyrðe.
7 Wilflede minre dohter þa oðre hide æt Tærdebicgan. 7
Ælfilde mire magan þa hide beneoþan wuda eall swa wit on
wedd gesealdon. 7 gif ic lengc beo þonne heo, þonne hæbbe
ic þæt land æt Wrottes-lea. 7 ealle þa ðe to mire ahte fon gylde 25
Brune xx *mancses goldes. 7 ic geann him vi mæran mid vi
coltan to þance. 7 þa hors þa þe þær to hlafe beon mine wife [7]
minre dohtran eallum gelice fela 7 þeo wellinc æt þære wíc
into Dunnintune. 7 Æþelsige leof cyð þis mine hlaforde 7 ealle
mine freondum.—Wulfgeates cwide.   30

43

Fulder. Harley Ch. 83. A. 3

Worcester arch.

Her swutelað on ymb þa foreward þe wæron geworhte
betwux þam hirede on Wihgera-ceastre 7 Fuldre. þæt is þæt
he hæbbe þæt land æt Ludintune iii gear for þam ðreom
pundum þe he lænde 7 þone bryce þe on þam lande beo iii
gear. 7 binnon þrym gearum agife þæt land þam hirede mid 5
swa myclum swa se hired him on hand sette: þæt synd xii
þeowe men, 7 ii gesylhðe oxan, 7 i hund sceapa, 7 half hundred
foðra cornes. And se ðe þas foreward tobreke, ne gewurðe hit
him næfre forgifen, ac beo he fordemed into helle wite, 7 þær
mid deofle wunige oð to domes dæge.—Ludintun.   10

44

(a) Æþelflæd. (b) Ælfflæd. Harley Ch. 43. c. 4

(a) 962–91. (b) 1000–2

Bury arch.

(a) þis is Æþelflæde cwyde. þæt is ærest þæt ic gean minum

hlaforde þes landes æt Lamburnan, 7 þæs æt Ceolsige 7 æt
Readingan; 7 feower beagas on twam hund mancys goldes,
7 IIII pellas, 7 IIII cuppan, 7 IIII bleda, 7 IIII hors. 7 ic bidde
5 minne leouan hlaford for Godes lufun þæt min cwyde standan
mote. 7 ic nan oðer nebbe geworht on Godes gewitnesse. 7 ic
gean þæs landes æt Domarhame into Glestingabyrig for Æd-
mundes cinges sawle, 7 for Æadgares cinges, 7 for mire sawle.
7 ic gean þes landes æt Hamme into Cristes-cyrcan æt Cant-
10 warebyrig for Eadmundæs cinges sawle, 7 for mire sawle.
7 ic gean þes landes æt Wudaham¹ Bæorhtnoðe æaldormen 7
mire swustær hyre dæg. 7 ofer² hire deg into sancta Marian
cyrcan æt Byorcingan. 7 ic gean þes landes æt Hedham
Bæorhtnoðæ ealdormen 7 mire swuster hæora dæg. 7 æfter
15 hæora³ dæge into Paulusbyrig æt Lundænæ to bisceophamæ.
7 ic gean þæs landæs æt Dictunæ into Ylig to sanctæ Æþæl-
ðryð 7 to hire geswustran. 7 ic gean þara twegra landa æt
Cohhan-feldæa⁴ 7 æt Cæorles-weorþe Bæorhtnoðæ æaldormen
7 miræ swuster hire dæg, 7 ofer hire dæg into sanctæ Ead-
20 mundes stowe to Byderices-wyrðe. 7 ic gean þæs landes æt
Fingringa-hó Bæorhtnoðe æaldermen 7 mire swuster hiræ deg,
7 ofer hire dæg into sanctæ Pætres cyrcan æt Myres-igæ. 7 ic
gæan þæs landes æt Polstede Bæorhtnoðe æaldormæn 7 mire
swuster hire deg, 7 ofor hira dæg into Stocy. 7 ic gæan þæs
25 landæs æt *Hwifersce into Stocy ofer minnæ deg. 7 ic gæan
Bæorhtnoðæ æaldermen 7 mire swuster þæs landes æt Stræt-
forda hire dæg, 7 ofer hire dæg ic his gæan into Stocy. 7 ic
willæ þæt Lauan-ham ga into Stoce ofær þes æaldermannes
dæg 7 mire swuster. 7 ic gean þæs landes æt Byliges-dynæ into
30 Stocy ofer þæs æaldermanes dæg 7 mire swuster. 7 ic gean
þara landa æt Peltan-dune⁵ 7 et Myres-ige 7 æt Grenstede into

---

¹ *from* wudeham, *first* a *above* e.　　² *from* ofor, e *above second* o.
³ *prec. by* er.　　⁴ e *from another letter* (l?).　　⁵ *from* peltendune,
a *above second* e.

Stocy ofer minnæ dæg 7 ofer Bæorhtnoðes æaldormannæs 7
ofær mire swuster. 7 ic gean þes landes æt Ylmesæton Beorht-
noðe æaldormen 7 mire swuster hira dæg, 7 ofær hira dæg ic his
gæan Æadmundæ. 7 ic an þæræ aræ hide æt þorpæ into Hed- 35
læge for mire sawle 7 for mira eldrena ofer . . . . 7 ic gean
ðæra x hida æt Wicforda Sibrihte minum mægæ ofer minne
dæg. 7 ic gean Ægwinæ minum geræfan þara VII hida æt
Hedham ofer *miminne deg swa hit on æalddagum gestod.
7 ic gæan Brihtwolde minum cnihtæ þara twegra hida on 40
Dunninclande ofer minnæ dæg. 7 ic an Alfwolde minum
preoste twægra hida on Dunninglande ofer minne dæg. 7 ic
gean Æþælmære minum præoste twægra hida on Dunning-
landæ *ofæ minne dæg. 7 ic gæan Ælfgæate minum megæ
twegra hida on Dunninglande ofar minnæ dæg. 7 ic gæan ðæs 45
landæs æt Wæaldinga-fælda Crawa mira magan ouær minnæ
dæg. 7 ic wille þæt man frigæ hæalue mine men on elcum tune
for mine sawlæ; 7 þæt man dele æal healf þæt yrue þæt ic
hæbbæ on ælcum tune for mire sawle.

(b) Ælflæd gæswytelaþ on þis gewrite hu hæo wile habban 50
gefadad hiræ æhta for Gode 7 for worldæ. Ærest þæt ic an
minum hlaforde þara VIII landa æfter minum dege. þæt is erest
æt Douorcortæ, 7 æt Fulan-pettæ, 7 æt Æles-forda, 7 æt Stan-
wægun, 7 æt Byrætune, 7 æt Læxa-dyne, 7 æt Ylmesætun, 7
æt Bucys-healæ; 7 twægra bæha on twera punda gewihte; 55
7 twa sopcuppan; 7 an sæolfran fæt. 7 þæ leof æadmodlice
bidde for Godes luuan, 7 for mines hlafordæs sawle lufan, 7
for minræ swystor sawlæ lufan, þæt þu amundie þa halgan
stowæ et Stocæ þæ mine yldran on restaþ, 7 þa are þæ hi
þiderin *sæadon[1] a to freogon Godæs rihte. þæt is *þonno þæt 60
ic gean æalswa mine yldran his er gæuþan : þæt is þonne þæt land
æt Stoce into þeræ halagan stowæ; 7 æal þæt þæt þær to tunæ

---

[1] *from* sæaden, o *above* e.

gæhyrð; 7 þonæ wuda æt Hæþfælda, þæ min swystar gæuþæ
7 mine yldran. þonne synd þis þa land þæ minæ yldran þærto
65 bæcwædon ofær minre swystor dæg, 7 ofær minne: þæt is
ðonne Stredfordæ, 7 Fresan-tun, 7 Wiswyþe-tun, 7 Lauan-
ham, 7 Bylies-dyne, 7 Polstyde, 7 Wifær-myrsc, 7 Grænstydæ,
7 Peltan-dune, 7 Myræs-egæ, 7 þæt wudæland æt Totham
þæ min fæder geuþæ into Myres-iæ, 7 Colne, 7 Tigan. þonne
70 synd þis þa land þe minæ yldran becwædon into oþrum halgum
stowum: þæt is þonne into Cantwarabyrig to Cristæs-circan
þan hired to brece þes landes æt Illan-lege; 7 into Paules
mynstre into Lundene þes landes æt Hedham to biscophame, 7
þes landes æt Tidwoldingtune þan hirede to brece into Paules
75 mynstre; 7 into Beorcingan þam hirede to brece þes landes æt
Babbingþyrnan. 7 ic gean Ælfþræðe minæs hlauordæs medder
Wuduhamæs æftær minum dæge; 7 æfter hiræ dege gange hit
into sancta Marian stowæ into Beorcingan æalswa hit stænt
mid mæte 7 mid mannum. 7 ic gæan into sancte Æadmunde
80 þara twegra landa Cæorles-weorþæ 7 Cochan-felde þam
hiræde to bre[ce][1] æalswa mine yldran his er geuþan, 7 þæs
landes æt Hnyddinge æftær Crawan degæ miræ magan. 7 ic
gæan into Myres-ie æfter minum degæ ealswa min hlaford 7
min swestar geuþan: þæt is Fingringa-ho, 7 þara six hida
85 þæ þæt mynstær on stent. 7 ic gæan ef[te]r Crawan dege þes
landes æt Wealdinga-felda into Suðbyrig to sanctæ Gregoriæ,
ealswa min swestar hit er foræwyrde. 7 ic gean into Ælig
sanctæ Petre, 7 sanctæ Æþældryþe, 7 sancte Wihtburhe, 7
sanctæ Sexburhe, 7 sancte Æormenhilde, þer mines hlafordes
90 lichoma rest, þara þreo landa þe wit buta geheotan Gode 7
his halga: þæt is æt Retten-dune, þe wes min morgangyfu,
7 æt Sægham, 7 æt Dictune, ealswa min hlaford 7 min swæstar
his er geuþan, 7 þaræ anre hide æt Cæafle, þe min swystar
begeat; 7 þes bæahges gemacan þe man sæalde minum hlaforde

[1] ce *now covered*.

to sawle-scæatte. 7 ic gean Æðelm[æ]re æaldorm*en* þes landes 95
æt Lellinge ofer mine deg mid mete 7 mid mannu*m*, æalswa
hit stent, on þet gerad þ*æt* he beo on minu*m* life min fulla
freod 7 forespreca 7 mira manna, 7 efter minu*m* dege beo
þara halgan stowe 7 þeræ are ful freod 7 forespeca æt Stocæ,
þe mine yldran on restaþ. 7 ic gean þes landes æt Lissingtune 100
Eðelmere mines [hlafordes meg]e mid mete 7 mid mannu*m*,
ealswa hit stent; 7 hine eadmodlice bidde þ*æt* he min fulla
freod 7 mundiend beo on minu*m* dege; 7 eft*er* minu*m* dege
gefelste þ*æt* min cwide 7 mira yldran standan mote—þis
sind þa landmearca to byliges-dyne. of *ða burnan æt humel- 105
cyrre. fra*m* humelcyrr[e] . . . . . . to heregeres heafode. fra*m*
heregeres heafode æft*er* ðam ealdan hege to ðare grene æc.
þon*ne* forð þ*æt* hit cymð to þare stanstræte. of þare stanstræte
7lang scrybbe þ*æt* hit cymð to acan-tune. fra*m* acyn-tune þ*æt*
hit cymð to rigendune. fra*m* rigindune æft to þara burnan. 110
7 þær is landes fif hida. þis sind þa landgemæra to hwifermirsce
7 to polestede. of loppan-dyne¹ to scelfleage. fra*m* leage to
mercyl. 7lang mercyle into sture. 7lang sture to leofmannes
gemære. 7lang leofmannes gæmære to amalburnan. fra*m*
amalburnan to norðfelda. ðon*ne* forð to bindhæcce. fra*m* bind- 115
hæcce to tudan-hæcce². fra*m* tudan-hæcce to giddincgforda.
fra*m* giddingforda to hnutstede. fra*m* *huntstede to hwitincghó.
fra*m* hwitingho to wudemannes tune. fra*m* wudemannes tune
to [cær]es-ige-gæmære. fra*m* cæres-ige-gemære to hædleage-
gemære. fra*m* hædleage-gæmære to hligha*m*-gemære. fra*m* 120
hligha*m*-gemære eft to loppan-dyne. to hwifr.mera landes . . .
. . . .

---

¹ y *from* u.   ² t *above expuncted* d; (*second*) d *from* n.

45

Ælfric. Cott. Aug. ii. 85

1035-40

Bury arch.

Her swytelað on þissum gewrite hu Ælfric bisceop wille his
are betéon þe he under Gode geérnode 7 under Cnute kyncge
his leofue laforde, 7 siþþan hæfð rihtlice gehealdan under
Haralde cyncge. þæt is þonne ærest þæt ic gean þæt land et
5 Wilrincga-werþa into sancte Eadmunde for mira saule 7 for
minas lafordas swa ful 7 swa forð swa he hit me to handa let.
7 ic gean þæt land æt Hunstanes-tune beæstan bróke 7 mid
þan lande et Holme into sancte Eadmunde. 7 ic wille þæt þa
munecas on Byrig sellan syxtig punde for þan lande et Tices-
10 welle 7 et Doccyncge, 7 þæt þerto gehérað. 7 ic gean Leofstane
dæcane þæt land et Grimas-tune swa ful 7 swa forð swa ic
hit ahte[1]. 7 ic gean mine cynelaforde Haralde II marc gol[2].
7 ic gean mire hlefdigen an marc gol[2]. 7 gelæste man Ægelrice
IIII pund mire fatfylre. 7 *sela man mina cnihtas þa mina
15 stiwardas witan xxxx punda; 7 fif pund into Elig; 7 fif pund
into Holm; 7 fif pund Wulfwarde muneke minne mæge; 7 fif
pund Ælffæh[3] min sæmestre[4]. 7 ic wille þæt man sella þæt
land et Walsinga-ham swa man derast mage[5]; 7 gelesta man
þæt feoh[6] swa ic gewissod hæbbe. 7 ic wille þæt man selle þæt
20 land et Fersa-feld swa man derast mæge; 7 recna man iungere[7]
Brun án marc gol; 7 mid þan laue scytte man mina borgas.
7 ic gean :: Ælfwine minan preoste et Walsinga-ham xxx akera
et Egge-meera. 7 Uui prouast habba þone ofaræcan. 7 ic gean
Ædwine muneke þa[8] mylne et Gæysæte þe Ringware ahte.

---

[1] 7 ic gean þæt mylne in margin.   [2] foll. by blank space.
[3] e added above er. after h.   [4] prec. by se, er.   [5] from mege,
a above expuncted first e.   [6] above mid þan feo underlined and er.
[7] from iunga, ere above expuncted a.   [8] þ altered from (or to) ꝥ.

7 ic gean Ælfwig preoste þæt land et Rygedune þe ic bohte to 25
Leofwenne. 7 ic gean þæt myln þe Wulnoð ahte into sancte
Eadmunde. 7 ic gean Sibriht þæt land þe ic gebohte on
Mulan-tune. 7 ic gean þæt fen þe þurlac me sealde into
Ælmham þa preostas to foddan. 7 ic gean into Hoxne þa
preostas an þusend werð fen. 7 ic gean þæt fen þe Ælfric me 30
sealde into Holme. 7 ic gean þon hage binnon Norðwic for
mire saule 7 for ealra þe hit me geuðon into sancte Eadmunde,
7 ic gean þan hage into sancte Petre binnon Lunden. 7 ic gean
iungre Brun þæt healfe þusend fen.

46

Þurcytel. Cott. Aug. ii. 84

Bury arch.

þis sendan þa land þe þurkytel gean Gode 7 sancte Marian
7 sancte Eadmunde. þæt is þæt land æt Cule-forde, þæt his
agen wæs swa hit stænt mid mete 7 mid mannum 7 mid sake
7 mid socne; 7 eal þæt land æt Wride-wellan, 7 þæt land æt
Gyxeweorðe, swa hit stent mid mete 7 mid mannum. 5